Abstracts of the

DEBT BOOKS

of the

PROVINCIAL LAND OFFICE OF MARYLAND

Somerset County

Volume II

Liber 43: 1748
Liber 51: 1755
Liber 45: 1759
Liber 54: 1759 addendum

By

V. L. Skinner, Jr.

CLEARFIELD

Printed for Clearfield Company by
Genealogical Publishing Company
Baltimore, Maryland
2015

ISBN 978-0-8063-5770-6

Introduction

The Provincial Land Office of Maryland was responsible for the dispensing of land from 1634 to 1777. Land was initially acquired by a warrant and was then patented. Information concerning these documents are found in the Warrants and Patents series of the Provincial Land Office located at the Maryland State Archives and are indexed by Peter Wilson Coldham in his five-volume series *Settlers of Maryland*, published by Genealogical Publishing Company.

Land was patented according to the desires of the patentee, and the name given to a patent was not necessarily unique within any particular jurisdiction.

The Lord Proprietor's personal hold on land affairs was much weakened during the royal period from 1689 to 1715. However, it was immediately revived when his proprietary rights were restored in 1715 (Hartsook and Skordas, *Land Office and Prerogative Court Records*). Both the Rent Rolls and the Debt Books date from this restoration period.

The Rent Rolls and the Debt Books are the means by which the Lord Proprietor kept track of the rents due him. Each piece of land granted to a person was subject to a yearly rent according to the terms of the patent.

A Rent Roll consists of entries for each tract of land patented, plus the name of the person for whom it was originally surveyed, the present owner, the acreage, and the rent. Alienations, or subsequent sales and leases of the piece of land, are also included.

A Debt Book consists of a list of persons owning land with the names and rents of each tract that he or she owned, all listed in one place under his or her name.

The Debt Books

The Debt Books are arranged by county, by year, and then by the name of the person paying the rent. There are a total of 54 libers, covering all of the counties. The extant Debt Books for the Western Shore counties are essentially annual, dating from 1753 to 1774. (The Debt Books for 1750 for five Western Shore counties–Anne Arundel, Baltimore, Charles, Prince George's, Frederick–are found in the Calvert Papers, located at the Maryland State Archives.) The extant Debt Books for the Eastern Shore counties are also essentially annual, dating from 1733 to 1775.

Each liber contains information for only one county, but for multiple years. For purposes of identification, each section (i.e., year) of any particular liber is given the denotation of the specific year.

Tracking land ownership over various years is particularly important for intestate estates, land inherited by women, and land that is not specified in a will.

The information in this series is presented in a tabular form:

- liber and folio citation, with any pertinent date.
- name of the person paying the taxes.
- name of the tract of land.
- acreage.

Notes to Reader

The following conventions are used in this book:

1. "The" and "A" at the beginning of any tract name has been omitted.
2. The index contains both tract names and surnames, sorted together.

3. "Crossed out" entries in the original libers have been included, as such.
4. Names have been transcribed as they are written; no attempt has been made to standardize any spelling.
5. Introduction and index pages of the original libers have been omitted.

Abbreviations

AA	Anne Arundel County
ACC	Accomac County
AN	Annamessex Hundred
a/s	alias
BA	Baltimore County
BO	Boquerternorton Hundred
BT	Baltimore Hundred
CE	Cecil County
CH	Charles County
cnp	name continued on next page
c/o	child/children of
CR	Caroline County
CV	Calvert County
DE	Delaware
DO	Dorchester County
FR	Frederick County
h/o	heirs of
KE	Kent County MD
KEDE	Kent County DE
MA	Mattapony Hundred
MO	Monokin/Manokin Hundred
MU	Munny/Monie Hundred
n/a	not available
n/g	not given
NA	Nanticoke Hundred
o/c	overcharged
o/o	orphans of
p.	perches
PA	Pennsylvania
PG	Prince George's County
PO	Pocomoke Hundred
pt	part of
QA	Queen Anne's County
SM	St. Mary's County
SO	Somerset County
s.p.	square poles
SU	Sussex County
s/o	son of
<t>	torn
TA	Talbot County
tbc	to be charged to
unr	unreadable
VA	Virginia
WI	Wicomico Hundred
WO	Worcester County

Contents of this volume

This book is the second of three volumes for Somerset County, an original county formed in 1666. Worcester County is formed from Somerset County in 1742; and land was lost to Sussex County (then PA, now DE) in 1766. The debt books for Somerset County cover the following years: 1733, 1734, 1734-1759 addendum, 1735, 1745, 1748, 1750 , 1755, 1759, 1759 addendum, 1761, 1764, 1768, 1769, 1774. The debt book for 1750 has not been located at this time.

From the Debt Books entries, several interesting facts are evident: (1) Somerset County had a Free School established by 1733; and, (2) Princess Ann and White Haven were established communities by 1735, with numerous lots occupied. The 1734 Debt Book not only cites the hundred that the taxpayer is living in, but it also cites the hundred in which the land is located. The leading landowners were: Rev. Alexander Adams, Madam Mary Hampton, Col. Robert King, Capt. Henry Lowes, James Martin, and William Whittington. Some Somerset County landowners were cited as inhabiting the following jurisdictions: Dorchester County, Worcester County, Annapolis, Kent County on the Delaware, Sussex County, Whorekill, Gloucester County (VA), Accomac County (VA), Northampton County (VA), Virginia, Pennsylvania, Carolina, London, Liverpool, England.

43:1748:1 ...		**Acres**
John Horsey	"Plain Harbour" – belongs to Isaac Horsey who is minded to give up the patent	250
Mathew Horsey	pt. "Coleburne" tbc Isaac Horsey	216
Nathaniell Horsey	pt. "Coleburne" tbc: • Nathaniel Horsey – 216⅓ a. • Samuel Horsey – remainder	250
	pt. "Double Purchase" tbc: • Nathaniell Horsey – 300 a. • John Horsey – 200 a.	500
	"Plain Harbour"	250
Samuell Horsey	pt. "Coleburne"	150
	"Yorkshire Island"	150
	pt. "Prices Conclusion" – denied	100
Capt. Thomas Dixon	"Dixon Choice" tbc: • William Dixon – 275 a. • Thomas Dixon – remainder	550
	"First Choice" tbc William Dixon	200
	"Dixons Lott" tbc: • Thomas Dixon – 600 a. • William Dixon – 450 a.	1200
	"Damm Quarter"	100
	"Prestian" from (N) Pollatt tbc Henry Dorman	220
	"Londons Advertisement" – denied	50
	"Johnsons First Choice" – denied	200
43:1748:2 ...		
h/o Robert Coleburne (VA)	"First Choice" – not yet known who owns	150
	"Harts Contract" – not yet known who owns	50
	"Pomfrett" – not yet known who owns	50
Thomas Williams	"Williamston"	100
	"Venture" from (N) Hearn tbc: • John Williams – 150 a.	200
	"Second Choice"	90
	"South Lott"	200
John Watters (cnp)	pt. "Watters River" tbc: • William Waters – 302½ a. • John Waters – 302½	700
	pt. "Partners Desire" tbc: • Elizabeth Waters – 125 a.	231

	• Alice Roads – 11 a.	
	"Waterton" tbc Solomon Tull	120
	pt. "Shadwell" from (N) Brown – denied	150
Thomas Tull	pt. "Watters River" tbc: • Thomas Tull – 100 a. • William Waters – 50 a.	150
	"Winter Range" – tbc Jos. Tull	150
Richard Watters	pt. "Watters River" tbc Elizabeth Waters	430
	"Flatt Land" tbc Elizabeth Waters	840
	"Friends Kindness" tbc Elizabeth Waters	116
	"Convenience" tbc Elizabeth Waters	80
	"Londons Gift" from (N) Johnson tbc Elizabeth Waters	50
43:1748:3 ...		
John Heath	pt. "Streights" – not found	600
Thomas Williams, Jr.	pt. "Williamstons" tbc Isaac Williams	150
	"Williams Adventure" from (N) Dickenson	100
Thomas Beauchamp	"Contention" tbc: • Isaac Beauchamp – 92½ a. • Edward Hull for John Beauchamp – 92½ a.	225
	"Hogg Yards" – already charged to Edward Beauchamp	95
William Palmer a/s Planner	"Boston Towne" – denied	800
	"Cheap Price" – included in "Cheap Price" below	500
	"Williams Conquest" tbc: • Isaac Williams – 50 a. • Thomas Williams – remainder	300
	"Cheap Price" tbc Thomas Williams (146 a. per patent)	725
	"Boston Towne" tbc: • Benjamin Langford – ½ • John Long – remainder	500
widow Conner in R. P. Conner	pt. "Warepoint" tbc John Conner	50
	pt. "Condogue" tbc William Conner	50
	pt. "Irish Grove" – not found	22½
	"Conners Grove" – not found	200
	"Fathers Care" – already charged to John Conner	50
43:1748:4 ...		

John Owton	pt. "Ware Point"	50
	pt. "Cowdogue"	50
	"Webly" tbc: • John Owton – 130 a. • John Conner – 20 a.	150
	pt. "Merchants Treasure" tbc Samson Wheatly	102
	pt. "Simpton" tbc: • William Bishop – 380 a. • William Selby – 100 a. • Abraham Owton – 50 a.	530
	"Discovery" tbc: • Peater Carsley – 50 a. • John Owton – remainder	225
	"Outons Addition"	150
	pt. "Merchants Treasure" from (N) Conner – denied	70
George Wilson	pt. "Dixons Lott"	150
	"St. Giles" tbc Ebenezar Cottman	200
	"Willsons Folly" – denied	50
	"Hogg Ridge" tbc John Wilson	100
Edward Stockdell for his wife	"Boyces Bancks" tbc: • Jane Lysther – 100 a. • Edward Stockdale – remainder	300
Alice Hall	"Halls Choice" tbc Charles & Richard Hall	300
	"Halls Adventure" tbc Charles & Richard Hall	250
	"Halls Humock" tbc Charles & Richard Hall	100
	"Halls Pasture" tbc Charles & Richard Hall	100
43:1748:5 ...		
widow of Forbury Rugg	"Planners Adventure" tbc David Addams	100
	"Little Worth" tbc David Addams	50
Stephen Horsey, Jr.	"Wattkins Point" tbc Stephen Horsy	150
Benjamin Summers	"Emesex" tbc: • George Summers – ½ of 167 a. • John Summers – ½ of 167 a.	216
	"Muskitts Creek" tbc: • George Summers – ½ • John Summers – ½	200
John Roach (cnp)	"Make Peace" tbc Charles Roach	150
	"Exchange" tbc: • Henry Cullins – 150 a. • Charles Roach – 50 a.	200

	"Buldridge" tbc Henry Smith	200
	"Summerfield" tbc Alice Roach	500
	"Roaches Priviledge" – denied	57
	"Vale of Misery" tbc Alice Roach	88
	pt. "Partners Desire" tbc Alice Roach	144
	"Mead Land" tbc: • John Roach – 32 a. • Charles Roach – 32 a.	64
	"Long Acre" tbc: • John Shockly – 175 a. • Benjamin Foulks – 120 a. • Alice Roach – remainder	548
	"Mullins Fields" tbc Alice Roach	50
	"Lott" tbc John Roach	36
43:1748:6 ...		
John Cullens	"Johnsons Lott" tbc Jacob Cullens for 145 a.	50
	"Gravely Hill" – denied	50
	"Winter Pasture" from (N) Blake – denied	50
	"Point Neck" tbc Jacob Cullens	25
John Long	pt. "Bostons Adventure" tbc: • Samuel Long, Sr. – 62½ a. • Coleburn Long – 62½ a. • Samuell Long – 62½ a. • Jeffery Long – 62½ a.	250
	"Longs Prevention" – divide as above in the above proportions	69
	"Longs Purchase" – divide as above in the above proportions	123
	"Longs Lott" – denied by the above	200
Helena Minchell relict of Henry	pt. "Bostons Adventure" tbc Daniel Long	150
	"Hap Hazard" – not found	100
William Cattlin (cnp)	"Harford Broad Oak" tbc: • John Williams – 100 a. • William Catlin – remainder	400
	"Bramford" tbc: • William Cattlin – 36 a. • rest taken by elder surveys	100
	"Meadow" tbc: • William Cattlin – 50 a. • Jos. Tull – remainder	76

	"Cattlins Lott" – denied	300
Thomas Walston	pt. "Desert" tbc Benjamin Sharp	246
	"Desert" – denied	523
43:1748:7 ...		
John Tull	pt. "Desert" called "Tulls Purchase" tbc Jos. Tull	154
	pt. "Costons Trouble" – denied	150
	pt. "Chelsey" tbc William Moore	100
	pt. "Fairham" – denied	50
	"Smiths Choice" tbc John Tull	100
	"Titchfield" – denied	150
	pt. "Suffolk" – deneid	200
	pt. "Winses Range" from (N) Tull tbc Joshua Tull	150
	pt. "Meadow" from (N) Cattline tbc Jos. Tull	24
	pt. "Harrisons Adventure" from (N) Harris – denied	25
	pt. "Newington Green" from (N) Howard tbc John Tull	250
Lazarus Mattux	"Mattus Hope" tbc William Miles	100
	"Bozemans Choice" – denied	300
	"Cakis Choice" tbc Thomas Maddox	300
	"Contention" tbc: • Lazarus Maddox – ½ • Daniell Maddox – ½	100
	"Mattux Adventure" tbc Daniel Maddox	150
	"Mattux Inclosure" tbc Lazarus Maddox	250
	"Whitefield" from (N) Walker tbc: • William Maddox – ½ • Alexander Maddox – ½	700
	"Mattux Inclosure" tbc Daniel Maddox	100
James Curtis	"Salisbury" tbc John Traihairn	200
	pt. "Armstrongs Lott" tbc Charles Curtis	250
	"Adventure" tbc Solomon Long	200
	"Horse Humock" tbc Solomon Long	100
	"Curtis Lott" tbc Charles Curtis	75
	"Sampire" tbc Charles Curtis	80
	"Cow Quarter" tbc Charles Curtis	50
43:1748:8 ...		

Samuell Handy	"Armstrongs Purchase"	200
	"Armstrongs Lott"	50
	"Teags Down" & "Last Choice" tbc: • John Waters – 16 a.	20
	"Black Ridge"	16
	"Londons Adventure"	16
	"Bear Ridge" – denied	200
	"Jericho"	100
	"New Invention" tbc Ebenezar Handy	425
	"Handys Choice"	175
	"Stephens Meadow"	188
	"Last Choice" – denied	10
	"Stake Ridge" from (N) Williams	15
	"Rum Ridge" from (N) Watts tbc Ebenezar Handy	300
	pt. "Suffolk" from (N) Keith tbc William Handy	446
	"Armstrongs Purchase"	120
William Scott	"Ryland" – no found	150
	"Scotts Folly" tbc Joshua Atkinson	50
	"Jones Caution" from (N) Lane – not found	200
	"Scottlands Addition" – not found	65
Robert Hopkins, Sr.	"Joness Island" tbc George Hopkins	100
	"Hartford" from (N) Samuells tbc Robert Hopkins	200
	"Cagers Joy" from (N) Messex – denied	50
43:1748:9 **...**		
John Kirk	"Kirks Purchase" tbc John Gunby	200
	"Recovery" tbc: • Samuell Riggen – 100 a. • John Kellum – 40 a.	200
	"Dickensons Folly" tbc: • John Kellum – 100 a. • Littleton Townsend – 100 a.	200
	"Galloway" tbc Littleton Townsend	150
	"Woover Marsh" tbc Littleton Townsend	150
	"Puzle" tbc Littleton Townsend	170
	"Joanes Hole" tbc Littleton Townsend	230
Hannah Stockley	"Hills Holly" tbc David Bird	150

Cornelius Ward	"Long Island" contains "Long Acre" (225 a.) tbc" • Samuell Ward – 100 a. • Steaphen Ward, Jr. – 100 a. • Cornelius Ward – 100 a. • Stephen Ward, Sr. – 100 a. • Jos. Ward – 100 a.	525
	"Little Ash" for child of (N) Dehorty tbc John Dougherty	100
	"Chesnutt Ridge" tbc Francis Lord	100
	"Cork" tbc: • Stephen Ward, Sr. – 100 a. • Cornelius Ward – 50 a. • Samuell Ward – 300 a. • Stephen Ward, Jr. – 25 a. • John Riggen – 25 a.	500
	"White Oak Swamp" tbc Samuell Ward	150
Thomas Everender	"Hopkins Destiny" – not found	50
	"Johnston" for h/o George Johnston – not found	300
	"Londons Advertisement" for h/o George Johnston – not found	50
	"Discovery" for William Cheesman – not found	50
43:1748:10 ...		
Stephen Horsey	pt. "Moore Worth" tbc: • Anthony Bell – 108 a. • Steaphen Horsy – 24 a.	132
	"Cow Quarter" tbc: • John Davis – 45 a. • Stephen Horsy – remainder	150
	pt. "Double Purchase" tbc: • Burr Outerbridge – 200 a. • Stephen Horsy – 540 a.	740
	pt. "Horsey Downe"	82
	pt. "Toneys Vineyard" tbc: • Benjamin Mitchell – ½ • Stephen Horsy – remainder	216
	"Welephusant" – denied	600
	"Horseys Fancey"	150
	"No Name" – denied	500
Anthony Bell (cnp)	pt. "Mooreworth"	68
	pt. "Horseys Denn" – denied	62
	"None Such" – denied	50

	pt. "Horsey Down" for you & St. Horsey tbc Stephen Horsey	150
	"Bells Purchase"	100
	"Discovery"	50
Robert Dukes	"Bear Neck" tbc: • Thomas Ward – 3 a.	236
Charles Cottingham	"Boston" – contains: • "Charles Gift" from (N) Cottingham – 30 a.	300
	"Vulcans Vineyard"	42
43:1748:11 ...		
Richard Barnes	pt. "Stand Reads Abby" tbc John Sterling	25
	"Barnett" tbc John Sterling	35
John Sterling	pt. "Stand Reads Abby"	25
	"Sterlings Choice"	50
	"Hap Hazard" from (N) Collins	70
Mary Price (widow)	"Prices Vineyard" tbc Thomas Ward	200
	"Mocke Meadow" tbc Thomas Ward	300
	"Agreement" tbc Thomas Ward	100
George Heigh	pt. "Cheesemans Chance" tbc Charles Cottingham	40
	"Mates Enjoyment" from (N) Evans, etc. tbc Thomas Prior	100
Joseph Evans	pt. "Cheesemans Chance" tbc John Colhone	60
43:1748:12 ...		
h/o Thomas Shellitor	"Long Town" tbc John Roach	150
John Gunby	"Middle Ridge"	200
	"Meadow"	100
Thomas Davis	"Hopewell" – 50 a. in patent; tbc John Davis	100
	"Enlargement" – denied	100
	"Hopeworths Pasture" – tbc John Davis	48
	"Daviss Inlett" tbc John Davis	50
	"Kirkminster" tbc John Davis	225
	"Davis Choice" – denied	425
Alexander Maddux (cnp)	"Daniells Denn" tbc Thomas Maddox (AN)	100
	pt. "Irish Grove" tbc Thomas Maddox (AN)	227
	pt. "New Town" tbc Lazarus Maddox	225
	"Lynsey Green" from (N) Parker tbc Thomas	100

	Maddox (AN)	
Randell Revell	pt. "Double Purchase"	160
43:1748:13 ...		
Thomas Mitchell	pt. "Double Purchase" tbc Thomas Mitchell (MO)	250
	"St. Martins Rige" from (N) Shirly tbc Thomas Mitchell (BO)	200
	"Fathers Purchase" – denied	60
Mary King	pt. "Double Purchase" tbc Robert King as "Kings Land" (300 a.)	250
	pt. "Hoggs Downe" – denied	200
	"Wansbrough" – denied	100
	"Hogg Ridge" tbc: • William Heath – 100 a. • Robert Wilson – 50 a.	200
William Foxen	"Double Purchase" tbc Robert King as "Downs Lott"	200
Randell Mitchell	"Adams Garden" tbc Thomas Addams	100
Andrew Thompson	"Welcome" – contains: • pt. "Double Purchase" – 125 a. • pt. "Welcome" from (N) Poole – 95 a.	245
43:1748:14 ...		
Abell Wright	pt. "Double Purchase" – owner not found	120
William Bannister	pt. "Double Purchase" tbc: • Thomas Mitchell – 60 a. • Thomas Bannister – remainder	340
	"Double Purchase" – denied	150
James Furnice	pt. "Double Purchase" tbc h/o William Furnace	245
	"Furnices Choice" – denied	300
	pt. "Pooles Hope" tbc h/o William Furnace	100
	pt. "Amity" tbc: • h/o William Furnace – 100 a. • William Turpin, Jr. – 200 a. • Solomon King – 70 a.	504
	"Faire Spring" tbc h/o William Furnace	300
	pt. "Brothers Agreement" is part of "Amity" tbc James Furnace	200
Capt. John West	pt. "Double Purchase" tbc: • William Bozman – 500 a. • Anthony West – 150 a.	1191

Samuell Tomlinson	"Manloves Lott" tbc: • Archibald White as "Tulley Brisk" – 118 a. • Samuell Tomlinson – remainder	300
	"Venture"	100
43:1748:15 ...		
William Brittingham	"Martins Hope" – not found	100
	"Cherry Hinton" – not found	150
	"Line Lott" – not found	15
	"Crowley" tbc John Brittingham	700
	"Parkers Peace" – not found	70
	"Frustration" – not found	40
	"Troublesome" – not found	130
	pt. "Poplar Ridge" from (N) King	100
	"Beckford" from (N) Bishop	300
	"Aarons Lott" from (N) Bishop	50
Thomas Adams	"Adams Green"	50
	"Adams Garden" tbc Thomas White	100
	"Kings Lott"	300
	"Adams Purchase"	100
	"Turkey Trapp"	200
Jeffory Long	"Holtwell" tbc Samuell Long	100
John Carter, Jr.	"Brickleshoe" – denied	200
	"Long Ridge" – denied	250
John Taylor	pt. "Pimfrett" tbc Ann Taylor	66
	pt. "Pitchcroft" – denied by Ann Taylor	<n/g>
	"Taylors Choice" – denied by Ann Taylor	<n/g>
	"Hartington" – denied by Ann Taylor	200
	"Sand Ridge" – denied by Ann Taylor	100
	"Taylors Choice" – denied by Ann Taylor	200
	pt. "First Choice" – from (N) Cattlin denied by Ann Taylor	70
43:1748:16 ...		
Michaell Holland	pt. "Pimfrett"	50
William Coleburne (cnp)	pt. "Pimfrett"	200
	"Pomfrett" (more) contains: • "Adkins Fancy" – 200 a.	534

	pt. "Drown Cow"	250
	pt. "Ferry Brigg"	100
Ann Coleburne (widow)	pt. "Double Purchase" tbc William Eskridge	250
	pt. "Pomfrett" tbc: • William Colburn – 534 a. • Solomon Colburn – remainder	1034
	"Ferry Bridge" tbc: • William Colburn – ½ • Solomon Colburn – ½	200
	"Drowne Cow" tbc Solomon Colburn	200
	"Drown Cow" (more) tbc Solomon Colburn	50
Vestry of Coventry Parish	pt. "Mitchells Lott" from (N) Mitchell tbc James Robertson	130
John Moore	pt. "Mitchells Lott" tbc Thomas Moore	150
	pt. "Pharsalia" from you & William tbc John Moore (NA)	100
	"Moores Second Choice" tbc John Moore s/o John	50
43:1748:17 ...		
John White	pt. "Mitchells Lott" tbc John White (AN)	100
	"Damm Quarter" tbc John White (MU)	150
	"Oxford" tbc John White (MU)	100
	pt. "Hogg Quarter" tbc: • James Quaturmus – 175 a.	350
	"Outlett" tbc Francis White	100
	"Scottland" from (N) Scott – denied	300
Amos Cook	"Bay Bush Hall" – Rodger Booth & Robert Dies live on this but have no right to it; is escheatable. Lays on Annomessex	100
Samuell & Nathaniell Horsey	"Unity" – not known	100
Jos. Gray	"Rest" – not yet found	150
	"Chance" – not yet found	100
Levin Denwood	"Hackland" – included in "Addition" tbc Betty Gale	1100
	"Denwoods Denn" tbc: • Thomas Denwood – ½ • George Denwood – ½	150
	"Storidge" tbc Betty Gale	300
43:1748:18 ...		

Samuell Covington	pt. "Mannings Resolution" tbc Thomas Covington (MU)	150
	"Covingtons Choice" tbc Thomas Covington (WI)	300
	"Covingtons Folly" – twice charged	70
	"Covingtons Folly" tbc Thomas Covington (MU)	70
Daniell Jones	pt. "Mannings Resolution"	400
William Jones	pt. "Mannings Resolution" tbc James Jones	250
	"Coxs Mistake" tbc James Jones	200
George Downes	pt. "Chance" – denied	150
Thomas Dashield	pt. "Mitchells Choyce" tbc Thomas Dashiell	250
	pt. "Chance" – denied	150
	pt. "Lott" tbc Thomas Dashiell, Jr.	108
	"Becknam" tbc Henry Dashiell	150
	"Shiels Folly" tbc Charles Dashiell	650
	"Summersett" for you & John Jones tbc Vestry of Somerset Parish	50
	pt. "Chance" from (N) Langford tbc William Wright	100
	"Head of Tyaskin Creek" from (N) Body tbc Henry Dashiell	100
	"Batchelors Chance" from (N) Worthington tbc John Jones (NA)	300
43:1748:19 ...		
John White & Richard Wallace	"Friends Choice" tbc: • John White (MU) – ½ • Richard Wallace – ½	270
	"Father & Sonns Desire" tbc: • John White (MU) – ½ • Richard Wallace – ½	85
Ephraim Pollock	"Golden Quarter" tbc: • John Laws – 75 a. • Joy Hobbs – 53 a.	150
	"Clomnell" tbc David Polok	100
	"Long Delay" tbc: • Joy Hobbs – 53 a. • John Laws – 137 a.	274
	"Locust Humock" from (N) Kent tbc Charles Polok	75
William Carney	"Carneys Order" – not found	100

Ann Roberts (widow)	"Davids Destiney" tbc: • Francis White – 100 a. (of this & "Elliotts Choice") • Edward Roberts – 350 a. (of this & "Elliotts Choice")	350
	"Elliotts Choice" tbc: • Lewis Jones – 100 a. • Francis White – 100 a. (of this & "Davids Destiney") • Edward Roberts – 350 a. (of this & Davids Destiney")	200
	"Downs" tbc Lewis Jones	100
	"Roberts Recovery" – denied	100
	"Jeshimon" tbc Edward Roberts	150
	"New Found Land" – denied	125
	"Edwards Lott" tbc Edward Roberts	220
John Jones	pt. "Jones Choice" tbc Robert Jones	350
	"Worcester" – denied	100
	pt. "Golden Quarter" from (N) Polk tbc George Jones (MU)	120
	pt. "Long Delay" from (N) Polk tbc George Jones (MU)	
	pt. "Beverly" tbc Richard Phillips (NA)	50
43:1748:20 ...		
William Turpin	pt. "Jones Choice" tbc William Jones (MU)	175
	"Colebrook" for h/o George Jones tbc William Macclammy	550
	pt. "Amity" tbc William Turpin, Jr.	200
	pt. "Barnabys Lott" tbc: • Barnaby Williss – 22 a. • William Turpin, Sr. – remainder	32
	"Wallis's Chance" – denied	93
	"Little Worth"	6
Robert Jones	pt. "Jones Choice" tbc Thomas Dashiell, Sr.	175
	"Accompson" – not found	150
James Polk	"Contention" tbc David Polok	100
	"Salem" – from (N) Layfield held by Henry & James Polk; not in the county	800
Jos. Austin (cnp)	"Coxs Lott" – from (N) Conner tbc Matthias Gale	100
	"Keep Poor Hall" – from (N) Rawly tbc Robert	100

	Austin	
John Hobbs	pt. "Wathfield" tbc Robert Austin	75
43:1748:21 ...		
Henry Hayman	"Shapleighs Neglect" – not known	50
	"Haymans Hill" – not known	200
	pt. "Pharsalia" tbc Gertrude Harmonson	300
	"Bugg Shott" – not found	200
	"Twittingham" – not found	200
	"Bugg Shott & Button" – not found	200
Joy Hobbs	"White Oak Swamp" tbc Joy Hobbs, Sr.	100
	"Haymans Chance" tbc Joy Hobbs, Sr.	50
	"Abbington" tbc: • Thomas Hobbs – ⅓ • Marthilias Hobbs – ⅓ • Joy Hobbs, Jr. – ⅓	300
	"Barnys Chance" a/s "Carlisle" tbc: • Thomas Hobbs – ⅓ • Marthilias Hobbs – ⅓ • Joy Hobbs, Jr. – ⅓	300
	pt. "Chance" from (N) Booth tbc Joy Hobbs, Sr.	100
Thomas Shaw – "Rainsbury", "Marlborough", & "Chance" tbc: • Thomas Wright – 125 a. • William Stoughton – remainder	"Rainsbury"	200
	"Marlborough"	150
	"Masons Adventure" – denied	100
	"Chance"	120
	"Bloyces Hope" tbc Bloyce Wright	150
George Betts	"Marcombs Lott" tbc Francis Wilson	400
	"Betts Purchase" tbc Francis Wilson as "Betts Delight"	100
	"Habb Nabb"	50
	"St. Giles" tbc Francis Wilson	200
	pt. "Westloes Neck" tbc Thomas Benston	300
	"Georges Adventure" tbc Francis Wilson	364
43:1748:22 ...		
Nehemiah Covington (cnp)	"Covingtons Vineyard" tbc John Leatherbury	300
	"White Marsh" – not found	100
	"Collins Adventure" tbc Robert King	500
	"Suffolk" a/s "Sasafrax Neck" – not found	150

	"Snow Hill" – not found	200
Phillip Covington	"Sweetwood" tbc Elinor Covington	300
	"Second Choice" tbc Elinor Covington	200
	"Sowerwood" tbc Elinor Covington	170
	"Henrys Enjoyment" tbc Elinor Covington	50
	"Amity" tbc Elinor Covington	50
	"Covingtons Meadow" tbc: • Daniel Jones – 295 a. • Elinor Covington – remainder	460
	"Covingtons Comfort" tbc Elinor Covington	180
	"Coving" a/s "Sasafrax Neck" tbc Elinor Covington	206
	"Covingtons Adventure" tbc Elinor Covington	100
	"Timber Grove" tbc Elinor Covington	150
Bloyce Wright	"Success" tbc William Stoughton	300
	"Bloyces Hope" tbc: • Thomas Wright – 25 a. • William Stoughton – remainder	150
	"Penny Wise" tbc William Stoughton	50
	"Penny Wise" tbc William Stoughton	45
James Langrell for o/o James Nicholson	"Worst is Past" tbc Thomas Wright	50
William Waller	"Wallers Adventure" tbc John Waller	300
	"Friends Advice" tbc John Waller	45
	"Success"	100
43:1748:23 ...		
John Painter	"Ignoble Quarter" – not yet found	100
	"Panthers Denn" tbc Robert Laws (200 a.)	100
	"Hanslop" tbc Alice Saucer	50
	"Littleworth" tbc Robert Laws	50
Thomas Carey	"Careys Adventure" tbc Thomas Cary	300
	pt. "Washford" tbc Thomas Cary	75
George Hutchens	pt. "Lunn's Improvement" tbc Lewis Jones	200
	pt. "Belian"	288
	"Manloves Grove" a/s "First Choice"	250
	"Laytons Conveniency" tbc Lewis Jones	140
	"First Choice"	250

Mrs. Mary Woolford	pt. "Lunns Improvement" tbc Samuell Wilson	50
	"Lunns Increase" tbc Samuell Wilson	150
	"Woolfords Chance" tbc: • William Jones (Goose Creek) – 36½ • George Bozman, Jr. – remainder	300
	"Chance"	300
	"Woolfords Venture" tbc John Woolford	50
Benjamin Saucer	"Sawcers Folly" tbc Alice Saucer	100
	"Addition" tbc Alice Saucer	50
	"Sawcers Lott" tbc Alice Saucer	50
43:1748:24 ...		
Charles Williams	"Roberts Lott" – in dispute	100
	pt. "First Choice" tbc James Coldwell	250
	"Charles Adventure" tbc John Williams (MU)	140
Ephraime Willson (cnp)	"Silbury" tbc: • David Wilson – ½ • Samuell Wilson – ½	200
	pt. "Davis Choice" for self & Peter Dent tbc James Lindoe	120
	"Davis Conquest" tbc Samuell Wilson (250 a.)	300
	pt. "Gulletts Advisement" tbc William Turpin, Jr.	50
	"Husbands Love" contains: • "Davis Choice" – 100 a.	100
	"Maidstone" tbc David Wilson	70
	pt. "Durham House" – denied	1300
	pt. "Glascoe" tbc Samuell Wilson	75
	"Davis Lott" tbc Samuell Wilson	300
	"Killglam" tbc: • David Wilson – ½ • Samuell Wilson – ½	1000
	"Willsons Discovery" tbc: • David Wilson – ½ • Samuell Wilson – ½	100
	pt. "Davis Choice" from (N) Davis tbc Samuell Wilson	25
	"Double Purchase" from (N) Lane tbc David Wilson	80
	pt. "Banners Lott" from (N) Murry tbc David Wilson	140

	"Security" tbc: • David Wilson – ½ • Samuell Wilson – ½	300
	"Mount Ephraim" tbc Samuell Wilson	375
	pt. "Double Purchase" – denied	165
	"Glasgowe" from (N) Londow tbc Samuell Wilson	75
widow of Robert Pollock	"Forlorne Hope" a/s "Pollocks Lott" tbc Jos. Polk	100
	"Polks Lott"	50
	"Polks Folly" tbc Jos. Polk	100
Fra. Cradon for o/o (N) Pelky	"Locust Hummocks" tbc Thomas Roe	50
	"Windsors Prevention" tbc Thomas Roe	60
	"Purgatory" tbc Thomas Roe	160
43:1748:25 ...		
Samuell Jones	"Jones Adventure" tbc Lewis Jones	50
	"Jones Meadow" tbc Lewis Jones	300
Capt. Nicholas Evans	"Nice Island" tbc: • Mary Evans – 88 a. • George Dashiell, Jr. – 300 a. • Alexander Lackey – remainder	1000
	"Jones Hole" tbc Daniel Coadry	250
	pt. "Sunken Ground" tbc Day Scott	250
	pt. "Might Have Had More" for h/o Thomas Willin	200
	"Troy" tbc Alexander Lackey	50
	pt. "Cassoway"	550
	"Foxhall" tbc Alexander Lackey	50
	"Ignoble Quarter" tbc John Evans (WI, 200 a.)	550
James Spence	pt. "Dispence" tbc Levin Gale	250
	"Spences Choice" tbc Purnall Johnston	250
	"Hereafter" – not found	100
	"Fatters Quarter" – not found	14
John Spence	pt. "Dispence" tbc Levin Gale	250
Thomas Walker (cnp)	"Last Purchase" contains: • "Dispence" a/s "Woodbridge" – 242 a. • "Addition" – 100 a.	618
	"Everhamp" tbc Alexander Addams & called "Glasgow"	500
	"Suffolk" tbc Alexander Addams & called "Brimilaw"	200

	pt. "Cassoway" – denied	550
	"Woodfield" tbc: • Ralph Low – 100 a. • Richard Wallace – 150 a.	350
	"Cassoway"	1100
	"Last Purchase"	618
43:1748:26 **...**		
Richard Stevens	"Kellums Folly Resurveyed" tbc: • Jonathan Bounds – 300 a. • John Steavens – 213 a. • William Kibble – 198 a. • Richard Steavens – 73 a.	900
	"Stephens Conquest" tbc Phenix Hall	300
	"Goddards Folly" tbc John Parsons (100 a.)	800
John Renshaw	"Crendly" tbc: • Thomas Rencher – ½ • Underwood Rencher – ½	350
	"Chance" – denied	200
Isaac Noble	"Tinsen" tbc William Sulavane	100
	"Winterbourne"	100
	"Canterbury" tbc Richard Mitchell	50
	"Friggs Adventure" from (N) Friggs tbc Susannah Noble (100 a.)	150
c/o Col. Charles Scarborough (VA)	"Bennerfield" tbc: • Temperance Scarbrough – 700 a. • Thomas Selby – 300 a.	2620
George Goddart	"Wallys Chance" tbc Alexander Addams	300
	pt. "Crambourne" tbc Alexander Addams	250
	"Poor Quarter" from (N) Wilson tbc James Fullerton	150
	"Goddarts Lott"	100
Benjamin Nesham for c/o Benjamin Cottman	"Taunton Dean" tbc • Benjamin Cotman – 186 a. • William Cotman – remainder	230
	"Cottmans Point" tbc Benjamin Cotman	50
	"Wrengton" for (N) Cottman tbc William Shurman	200
	pt. "Rich Swamp" from (N) McClester	50
43:1748:27 **...**		

Capt. Charles Ballard	"Hazard" tbc Charles Ballard	400
	"Nutters Purchase" tbc Henry Ballard	300
	"Turky Ridge" tbc Henry Ballard	100
	"Friends Assistance" tbc Henry Ballard	200
	pt. "Wrights Choice" from (N) Wright tbc John Everton	107½
	"Eason" from (N) Wright tbc John Everton	
	pt. "Wrights Venture" from (N) Wright tbc John Everton	
Robert Dashiell	"Johnsons Lott" tbc Matthias Dashiell	300
	"Greenwich" – not found	50
	pt. "Andersons Invention" tbc Charles Hall	100
	"Reedy" tbc Sarah King & Jos. Wails	350
	"Gordons Delight" from (N) Gordon tbc Matthias Dashiell	100
John Winder a/s Windsor	"Kiketan Choice" tbc Thomas Winder	300
	"Whittys Latter Invention" tbc Thomas Winder	200
	"Deptford" tbc Thomas Winder	110
	"Limehouse" – not known	40
	pt. "Pembertons Good Will" – not known	350
	"Coxs Performance" tbc Henry Winsor (250 a.)	1000
Richard Phillips	"Horseys Baylywick"	100
	pt. "Little Belean"	100
	"Phillips Addition" tbc: • Richard Phillips – ½ • Isaac Mitchell – ½	127⅛
James Carroll	"No Name" – not yet known	200
	"Westerne Fields" – not yet known	1400
43:1748:28 ...		
Christopher Piper	"Barbers Rest" tbc: • Christopher Piper – ½ • Robert Hardy – ½	300
	"Barbers Addition"	50
	"Walkertee" from (N) Piper – denied	240
James Hardy	"Orphants Lott" from (N) Cooper tbc Joseph Hardy (155 a.)	500
Richard Nicholson	"Vulcans Vineyard"	300
	"Nicholsons Lott"	100

John Avery	"Averys Pollicy" – not yet found	300
	pt. "Averys Choice" – not yet found	150
o/o Daniell Hast a/s Hull (VA)	"Daniells Adventure" – not yet found	300
	"Holdfast" – not yet found	400
Thomas Carney, Jr.	"Carneys Delight" – not yet found	300
43:1748:29 ...		
James Macmorice	"Whittys Latter Invention"	100
	"Whittys Invention"	300
	"Pasturage" for self & (N) Winwright	200
	"Pasturage" for self & (N) Winwright tbc Cannon Winwright	200
	"Batchelors Adventure" from (N) Masters – denied	150
	"Iron Hill" tbc William Calloway	180
Jos. Venables	pt. "What You Please" tbc Benjamin Venables	250
	"Mitchells Lott" included in "Dear Lott"	30
	"Blackwell" tbc Benjamin Venables	25
	"Supply" tbc Benjamin Venables	25
John Goslin	pt. "What You Please"	50
	"Goslins Lott" tbc: • Benjamin Venables – ½ • John Goslin – remainder	100
Alexander Carlisle	"Hopewell" tbc John Macclesther for (N) Carlisle (orphan)	300
	"Green Hill" tbc Thomas Humphris	50
	"Addition"	100
	"Friends Advice"	30
	"Force Putt" tbc John Macclesther for o/o (N) Carlisle	50
Thomas Humphrys	"Keens Lott"	300
	pt. "Belean" from (N) Hutchinson	3½
43:1748:30 ...		
Benjamin Wales (cnp)	"Tosetor" tbc Jos. Wailes	150
	"Fortune" tbc Jos. Wailes	100
	"Might Ahad More" tbc Jos. Wailes	50
	pt. "Andersons Invention" – denied	100
	"Josephs Lott" – twice charged	70
	"Josephs Lott" tbc Jos. Wails	70

	"Good Luck" – denied	180
	"Golds Delight" from (N) Gold tbc John Keater (50 a.)	450
	"Beaver Damm" tbc Abraham Ingram (80 a.)	180
John Smith	"Cow Quarter" tbc John Smith (BT)	350
	"Islington" tbc John Smith (BT)	200
	"Coards Lott" from (N) Coard tbc John Smith (BT)	430
	"Moris Purchase" from (N) Moris tbc: • William Evans – 150 a. • John Smith – 150 a. • Isaiah Bredall – 100 a.	500
	"Cumberland" from (N) Moris	200
	"Smiths Chance"	100
Richard Chambers	"High Meadow" tbc Thomas Brereton	250
	"Cockmore" tbc: • Richard Brereton – 100 a. • David Vance – 100 a.	200
	"Manloves Venture"	100
	"Vulcans Forge"	100
	"Rowly Ridge"	100
	"James Choice" tbc George Tull (DO)	150
	"Friends Kindness"	100
Abraham Cauthry	"Long Acre"	200
43:1748:31 ...		
John Cauthery	pt. "High Suffolk" from (N) Heath tbc John Cauthery (30 a.)	70
	pt. "Come by Chance" from (N) Heath	70
John Shiles	"Hogg Quarter" tbc Thomas Willin	50
	"Hickory Ridge" tbc Thomas Willin	50
	pt. "Whittys Contrivance" tbc Thomas Willin	14
	"Shiles Meadow" tbc Thomas Willin	60
Edward Rutlidge for o/o Thomas Paswater	"Castle Haven" tbc: • Alexander Fullerton – 160 a. • John Reddish – 40 a.	200
	"Morris Lott" for self	100
Thomas Cox (cnp)	"Coxes Choice" – not found yet	150
	"Wilton" tbc: • Jeremiah Wright – 180 a. • Ebenezar Handy – 150 a.	550

	"Aldermanbury" tbc Jeremiah Wright	172
	"Alderbury" tbc: • Lewis Disharoone – 300 a. • Ebenezar Handy – 150 a.	550
	"Plimpton"	450
	"Salt Ash"	480
	"Alderbury"	550
	"Coxs Folly" tbc John Steavens	117
	"Planters Salt Ash" tbc: • Levin Disharoone – 200 a. • Catherine Carr – 100 a.	463
Alice Worthington	"Second Purchase" tbc Alice Ellis	250
	"Lotts Daughter" from (N) Brown tbc Alice Ellis	30
43:1748:32 ...		
Graves Jarrett	"Hoggs Downe" tbc Graves Boarman	55
William Elgate	"Hachilah" tbc Thomas Bird	150
	"No Name" called "Averys Pollicy" (436 a.) contains: • "Monsly" – 354 a.	480
	"Elgates Lott" tbc: • Thomas Bird – ½ • Catherin Hitch – ½	100
	"Jeshimon" tbc Catherine Hitch	150
	"Elgates Purchase" – denied	70
	"Mitchells Lott" a/s "Dear Lott" tbc Benjamin Venables	96
William Brereton	"Mile End"	25
	"Island Marsh" sold to John Frizell	50
	"Middle Neck" – never patented	300
	pt. "Smiths Adventure"	67
Pascoe Bartlett	pt. "Little Macseley" tbc Thomas Bartlett	100
	"Cherveley" tbc Thomas Bartlett	100
Thomas Lucas	pt. "Little Macsely" tbc William Venables	200
	"Lucas Choice" tbc John Timmonds	200
43:1748:33 ...		
Mary Day	pt. "Sunken Ground" tbc Nicholas Evans	250
John Parsons	"Second Choice" tbc Robert Harris (170 a.)	300
	"Beans Quarter" tbc Robert Harris	100

Robert Crouch	"White Chappell" tbc Sarah Baley	100
	"Bedlam Green" tbc Jervice Jenkins	100
	"Sand Downe" tbc John Davis	300
	"White Chapple Green" tbc Ann Crouch	100
	"Crouches Desart" tbc James Collet	100
	"White Chapple"	200
	"Crouches Desire"	100
	pt. "Do Better" from (N) Gills tbc John Reddish for Robert Crouch (orphan)	150
	pt. "Fair Meadow" from (N) Sheha	48
John Caldwell	"Maidenhead" tbc John Coldwell	300
	"Bally Buggan" – denied	200
	"Cowlett" tbc John Coldwell	380
	"Caldwells Chance" tbc John Coldwell	27
	"Baily Began" tbc John Coldwell	190
	"Purchase" tbc John Coldwell	134
	"Westuxlier" from (N) Pepper – denied; is part of "Paramores Double Purchase"	500
	"Caldwells Chance" from (N) Caldwell – denied	300
	"Bare Swamp" – holds but 13⅓ a.	48
	"Poplar Neck" tbc Thomas Coldwell	100
43:1748:34 ...		
Richard Crockett	pt. "Might Have Had More" tbc: • Robert Crockett – ⅓ • John <no surname given> – ⅓ • Richard Crockett – ⅓	200
	"Sidney" tbc Robert Crockett	50
	"Adventure" – third as above	70
	"Point Marsh" – third as above	9
	"Finish Hall" from (N) Crockett	<n/g>
Benjamin Cottman for h/o (N) Robinson (cnp)	pt. "Robinsons Lott" tbc: • William Robertson – ½ • John Robertson – ½	295
	"Birks" for your self – denied	150
	"Cow Pasture" tbc: • William Robertson – ½ • John Robertson – ½	50
	"Surmans Land" from (N) Surman tbc William	30

	Cotman pt. of "Tinson"	
	"First Choice" from (N) Johnson tbc James Coldwell	100
Thomas Sherman	pt. "Taunton Dean" tbc William Cotman	70
	pt. "Macches Hope"	135
	pt. "Rich Swamp"	
John Davis	pt. "Little Belean" – not yet known the owner	525
	"Sallop" – not yet known the owner	100
	"Battlefield" – not yet known the owner	50
	pt. "Marsh Grown" – not yet known the owner	66⅔
John Pearce	pt. "Little Belean" tbc: • William Venables – ½ • John Venables – ½	400
43:1748:35 ...		
Robert Freeman	pt. "Little Belean" tbc Thomas Colliar	75
Adam Heath	"High Suffolk" tbc: • Elgate Hitch – 241 a. • John Price – 90 a. • William Hitch – 405 a. • Solomon Hitch – 305 a. • Samuell Hitch – 212 a. • John Hitch – 94 a.	1297
	"Come by Chance" tbc Elgate Hitch	173
	"Fortune"	50
	"North Wales" from (N) Russell & (N) Boyer tbc Timothy Atkinson (200 a.)	500
John Booth	pt. "Chance"	200
	"Herman" tbc Marthilias Hobbs	350
o/o William Rodalphus (VA)	pt. "Chance"	200
William Alexander, Jr.	"Trouble" tbc William Alexander	250
	"Dasentry" – only 150 a. in patent & tbc William Alexander	300
	"Rapha" tbc Rencher Roberts	200
	pt. "Monmouth" from (N) Raymond tbc William Alexander	100
43:1748:36 ...		
John Johnson, Jr.	"Angela"	44
John Wood	"Woods Land"	150

William Wright & widow of Solomon Wright tbc: • John Everton – 20 a. of "Wrights Choice", "Eason", & "Wrights Venture"	"Wrights Choice" tbc William Nelson	100
	"Eason" tbc William Nelson	50
	"Venture" tbc Thomas Dashiell, Jr.	50
	"Woofs Quarter" tbc Samuell Fluellin	50
	"Wrights Venture" tbc William Nelson	105
Phillip Ascue	"Timerous Ridge" tbc: • Thomas Pullet – 100 a. • William Polk – 100 a. • Jos. Stanford – 50 a.	250
	"Turky Hall" – not yet known	116
	"Addition" – not yet known	50
	"Horse Baley Neck" – not yet known	150
John Richardson	"Would Have Had More" – denied	50
Phillip Carter	"Whettstone" tbc: • Christopher Piper – 200 a. • John Records, Jr. – 100 a. • John Records, Sr. – 50 a.	350
43:1748:37 ...		
Thomas Colebrook	"Harrington" tbc Thomas Holbrook	200
Peter Sherman	pt. "Crambourne"	100
William Alexander, Sr.	"Hogg Quarter" tbc Moses Alexander	100
	pt. "Monmouth" from (N) Jones tbc William Alexander	100
Nicholas Toadwine	"Gurnsey" tbc Henry Toadvine	150
	"Jersey" tbc Henry Toadvine	100
Richard Wallace	pt. "Camp"	150
	"Friends Acceptance"	95
	"Meadow"	50
James Smith	pt. "Camp" tbc Moses Smith	150
	"Wakefield" tbc John Smith (VA)	300
	"Addition" tbc John Smith (VA)	200
43:1748:38 ...		
Samuell Layfield (cnp)	"Desart" tbc Jos. Schofield	200
	pt. "Convenience" tbc Catherine Layfield	150
	pt. "Hogg Quarter" – denied	850
	"Lebborne" – denied"	500
	"Merrill Hall" tbc Catherine Layfield	200

	"Tonn" – denied	200
	"Creedwill" tbc Catherine Layfield	500
	"Cow Pasture" – taken by elder survey	500
	"Fruitfull Plains" tbc Catherine Layfield	540
	"Hogg Quarter" tbc Catherine Layfield (400 a.)	800
	"Great Gostrean" – denied	500
William Winder (VA)	"Pembertons Good Will" – not known	500
Cornelius Anderson	"Bilboe"	50
	"Come by Chance" tbc Jonathan Baley	100
Ann Brereton	pt. "Samuells Adventure" – not known	367
Peter Pressly (VA)	pt. "Samuells Adventure" – not known	500
43:1748:39 ...		
William Harris	pt. "Lott" tbc: • Richard Harris – 200 a. • Edward Fowler – 100 a. • William Harris, Sr. – ½ of remainder • William Harris, Jr. – ½ of remainder	892
widow of John O'Rhines	pt. "Tonys Vineyard" – not yet found	84
Thomas Ralph, Sr.	"Contention" tbc George Dashiell, Sr.	95
	"Trulock Grange" from (N) Bougher tbc Thomas Ralph & includes: • "Ralphs Purchase" from (N) Collins – 100 a.	88
	pt. "Good Success" from (N) Bougher tbc Thomas Ralph	50
Richard Carey	"Crays Advance" – not found	50
h/o Capt. Henry Smith	"Coxs Advice" tbc Alexander Ergoe	200
	"Davis Choice" – not found	150
	"Assacomoco" – not found	500
	pt. "Lloyds Grove" – not found	250
	"Smiths Hope" – not found	902
	"Oak Hall" – not found	200
	"Moonfields" – not found	500
	"Williams Hope" tbc John Dennis, Jr. (100 a.)	502
John Croutch	"Hogg Neck" tbc: • Thomas Vincent – ½ • John Crouch – ½	200
43:1748:40 ...		

William Whittington, Jr.	pt. "Pharsalia" – denied	400
	"Fairefield" – denied	900
	"Durham House" from (N) Jarman tbc William Whittington	900
	"Bishops Purchase" from (N) Bishop tbc William Whittington	200
Capt. James Dashield for widow of Sampson Walters (New England)	"Supplye" tbc Peater Boaden	375
	"Merchants Right" for your wife tbc James Dashiell	300
	"Long Hill" – charged below	300
	"Meeches Desarts" tbc James Dashiell	200
	"Bentley" for (N) Walters tbc Peter Boaden	150
	"Batchelors Adventure" for (N) Walters tbc Peter Boaden	100
	"Wolfe Trap Neck" for yourself tbc James Dashiell	50
	"Jeshimon" for (N) Walters tbc Peter Boaden	150
	"Faire Ridge" for (N) Walters tbc Joseph Dashiell	100
	"Covent Garden" for (N) Walters tbc Peater Boaden	100
	"Supply" for (N) Walters – twice charged	750
	"Anything" for yourself tbc John Richardson	137
	"Long Hill" tbc Matthais Dashiell	300
	"Woolfe Trapp Ridge" tbc James Dashiell	50
	"Stricts Folly" ½ for self & tbc James Dashiell	650
John Christopher	"Monsham"	100
	"Hearn Quarter" – denied	150
	pt. "White Chapple Green" from (N) Crouch	50
Alexander Browne	"Thornton" tbc Thomas Brown	600
	"Thorns Intention" tbc Thomas Brown	50
	"Jeshimon" tbc Thomas Brown	50
	"Desart" tbc Robert & William Layfield	100
	pt. "Glasgoe" tbc David Wilson	150
	"Hachila" tbc Thomas Brown	100
	"Meadow" tbc Thomas Brown	80
	"No Name" – denied	350
	"Chance" tbc Robert & William Layfield	23
43:1748:41 ...		

Arthur Denwood	"Brownstone" tbc George Denwood	300
	"First Choice" tbc: • George Denwood – 94 a. • Thomas Denwood – remainder	210
	"Nutters Delight" tbc Thomas Denwood	150
	"Wetherlys Chance" tbc Thomas Denwood	150
	"Denwoods Inclusion" tbc George Denwood	21
	"Unexpected" – twice charged	40
	"Stone Ridge" tbc Levin Denwood	300
	"Unexpected" tbc John Waters for Levin Denwood (orphan)	40
John Bozeman	"Bozmans Addition" tbc John Bozman (200 a.)	250
Luke Vallentine	pt. "More & Case" – not found	600
John Henderson	pt. "Barnabys Lott" – denied	46
	"Hap Hazard" tbc Benjamin Henderson	70
	"Chesnutt Ridge"	100
	"Double Purchase" – denied	1100
	"Henderson Conveniency" tbc John Henderson (120 a.)	100
James Willis	pt. "Barnabys Lott"	22
43:1748:42 ...		
Mary Magraugh (widow)	"Owens Choice" tbc: • Henry Newman – 17 a. • William Magrah – remainder	300
	"Owens Improvement" tbc John Magrah	150
	"Owens Delight" tbc John Magrah	100
	"Middle" tbc John Magrah	100
	"Wolfs Denn" tbc Henry Ballard for Richard Magrah (orphan)	120
	"Addition" tbc James Laws	100
Nicholas Fountaine	"Fountains Lott" tbc: • Nicholas Fountain, Sr. – ½ • Nicholas Fountain, Jr. – ½	300
	"Normandy" tbc: • Nicholas Fountain, Sr. – ½ • Nicholas Fountain, Jr. – ½	50
	"New Rumney" tbc Nicholas Fountain, Sr.	150
	pt. "Poyk" tbc William Turpin, Jr.	10
	"Nova Francia" tbc Nicholas Fountain, Sr.	100

Henry Derman	pt. "Shipways Choice" tbc: • Mathew Dorman – 22 a. • John Finch – remainder	150
John Lokey	"Hard Luck" from (N) Christopher tbc Abraham Heath & is pt. "Hearn Quarter"	100
Mathew Dorman	"Nelsons Choice"	300
	"Ellards Choice" tbc Michaell Dorman	200
	"Dormans Purchase"	150
43:1748:43 ...		
John Fisher	pt. "Davis's Choice" tbc Bartholomew Fisher	330
William Davis	"Bennins Lott" tbc David Wilson	340
	"Marish Ground" – denied	33½
	"Sligo" from (N) Willson tbc: • William Davis – 320 a. • Richard Goslin – 100 a. • Samuell Boarman – 80 a.	500
Peter Dent for o/o C. King	"Glanvills Lott" tbc Capell King	550
	"Oxhead" tbc William Turpin, Jr. for Planner King (orphan)	300
	"Gulletts Advisement" for o/o Thomas Williams tbc William Turpin, Jr. for Planner King (orphan)	50
	"Beckford" for self tbc David Brown	500
Peter Elsey	"St. Peters Neck" tbc: • Lewis Rigsby – 650 a. • William Stoughton – 100 a.	750
	"Chance" tbc William Stoughton	50
Col. Arnold Elsey	"Almodington" – resurveyed as below	1000
	"Almodington" tbc: • John Elzey – 900 a. • Jervice Ballard – 300 a.	1200
John Browne	"South Petherton" tbc David Brown	300
	"Brownes Chance" – denied	55
	"Green Hill" from (N) Trewitt – denied	100
43:1748:44 ...		
Mary Fountaine	"Winders Purchase" – resurveyed & is 160 a. tbc Nicholas Fountain, Sr.	200
John Gray (cnp)	"Killmunam" tbc William Gray	150
	"Derry" tbc William Gray	77
	"Patricks Folly" tbc Margaret Smith	118

	pt. "Smith Resolve" from (N) Smith	100
	"Come by Chance" from (N) Newgent	150
	"Goldsmiths Delight" from (N) Goldsmith	100
George Febus	"Nicholsons Adventure" tbc George Phebus	150
Gideon Tilghman	pt. "Pooles Hope" tbc: • Joseph Tilghman – 50 a. • <unr> – 60 a. • Rose Tilghman – 90 a.	200
	"Tilghmans Adventure" tbc Samuell Collins	50
	"Gideons Luck"	50
	"Tilghmans Care" tbc: • Gideon Tilghman – 44 a. • Lazarus Maddox (PO) – 44 a. • remainder taken by elder survey	138
William Pollock	"Smiths Resolves" tbc William Polk	250
	"Long Delay" – denied	274
Samuell Worthington	"Manloves Discovery" tbc Alice Ellis	250
	pt. "Gethseman" – not known	300
43:1748:45 ...		
Robert Cutherwood for o/o Thomas Jones	"Bridges Lottery" tbc: • Samuell Wilson – 600 a. • William Jones (MO) – 500 a.	1100
	"Friendshipp" tbc Thomas Jones (Liverpoole)	500
	"Little Bolton" tbc Thomas Jones (Liverpoole)	850
	"Flatt Capp" tbc Thomas Jones (Liverpoole)	50
	"Apes Hole" tbc John Sterling	200
	"Mistake" tbc Thomas Jones (Liverpoole)	400
Fra. Garden for o/o Thomas Row	"Graves End" tbc Thomas Roe	300
	"North Foreland" tbc Thomas Laws	300
	"Spring Island" tbc John Tunstall	50
Thomas Everton	"Smiths Recovery" – not known	100
John King (cnp)	"Chance" tbc Whittington King	90
	"Webly" tbc Whittington King	250
	"Conny Warren" tbc Whittington King	125
	"Kings Choice" – denied by his son	300
	"Hazard I" tbc Whittington King	160
	"Benjamins Advice" tbc Whittington King	50
	"Hawtree Point" from (N) Highway tbc	100

	Whittington King	
Dennum O'Lannum tbc: • William Bowler – 58 a. • William Collins – 58 a. • Alexander Chain – remainder	"Kings Chance"	100
	"Domine"	50
43:1748:46 ...		
Thomas Laws	"Greenwich"	50
Michaell Gray	pt. "Poyk" tbc William Turpin, Sr.	60
	"Grays Improvement"	140
Richard Plunkett	"Hockley" tbc George Benston	50
Alice Miles	"Trouble" tbc William Miles	50
William Docam	pt. "Harpers Discovery"	100
	pt. "Harpers Increase"	50
John Turpin	"Tottness" – denied	250
	pt. "Grays Improvement"	10
43:1748:47 ...		
James Johnson	"Longvile"	50
William Smith	"Corporalls Ridge" tbc Robert Smith	50
	"Stevenson" – denied by his heirs	150
	"Bringingham" – denied by his heirs	500
	"Cherryton" tbc: • Robert Mills – 400 a. • John Mills – 100 a.	500
	"Barking" – denied	300
	"Addition" tbc Magdalane Smith	74
	~~"Huckleberry <unr>" tbc:~~ ~~• Magdalene Smith – 100 a.~~ ~~• Robert Smith – 50 a.~~	~~150~~
Magdelen Polke	"Richens Addition"	100
William Fassick & John King	pt. "Cramell" tbc William Faucett	500
Charles Gray	"Flint" tbc William Turpin, Sr.	50
John Knox	pt. "Ilchester" tbc: • Margarett Stutt – ½ • James Strawbridge – remainder	150
43:1748:48 ...		

Margarett Goldsmith	pt. "Illchester" tbc John Gray as "Goldsmiths Delight"	100
	"Golden Quarter" tbc John Owens	150
William Knox	pt. "Illchester" tbc James Strawbridge	150
James Strawbridge	pt. "Illchester"	509
	"Bluff Hummocks" tbc John Tunstall	100
	"Dudly" from (N) Dayly tbc John Phillips	50
	"Rowly Hill" from (N) Dayly tbc John Phillips	100
	"Ridge"	60
	"Addition"	82
Samuell Miles	"White Oak" tbc: • Henry Miles – ½ • Samuell Miles – ½	250
	"Foscutt" tbc Henry Miles	50
	"Boddam" from (N) Sangster – denied	400
	"Kill Glass" from (N) Ironmonger – denied	200
William Gullett	"Gulletts Hope"	50
John Ervin	"Saltkirk" tbc Francis Wilson	50
	"Cow Quarter" tbc Francis Wilson	100
	"Cow Quarter" from (N) English tbc Francis Wilson	60
43:1748:49 ...		
Upsher King	"Kings Choice" tbc: • David Wilson – ⅔ • William Turpin, Jr. – ⅓	100
Robert Willson	"Crolliers Folly"	100
	"Willsons Finding"	68
	"Conclusion"	138
	"Norwich" from (N) Shanks	100
h/o Edward Sedbury	"Turky Cock Hill"	120
James Conner	"Coleraine"	200
	"Stooping Pine"	50
William Polk (cnp)	"Harthbury" – denied; tbc: • Magdalane Smith – 100 a. • Robert Smith – 50 a.	150
	"Moarun"	100
	"Dungall"	100
	"Racnax"	100

	"Rosborough" from (N) Vance	210
	"Smiths Hope" from (N) Owens	100
	"Williams Adventure" from (N) Owens	60
	"Rich Land"	200
43:1748:50 ...		
Benjamin King	"Cannady Island" tbc Capell King	50
	"Winter Harbour" tbc Capell King	80
	"London" from (N) Walston tbc Capell King	100
John Mears	"Durham"	150
h/o Bernard Ward	"Kendall"	40
Arthur Smith	"Flodders"	50
Henry Elliott	"Wassawomack"	250
German Gillett	"Owen Glandore" tbc Thomas Evans	300
	"Cold Harbour"	250
43:1748:51 ...		
Edward Stevens	pt. "Blakes Hope" tbc: • William Steavens – 200 a. • Brough Broughton – remainder	233¾
	"Wooten Underidge" from (N) Colv. (?) tbc: • Samuell Dormant – 50 a. • Isaac Whealer – 50 a. • Jane Burnett – 50 a.	150
Archibald Smith for h/o (N) Tripshaw	pt. "Suffolk"	75
	pt. "Suffolk" [!]	75
	"Dear Quarter" from (N) Odeir	<n/g>
William Stevens	pt. "Blakes Hope" tbc: • Thomas Howard – 200 a. • Brough Broughton – remainder	233½
	"Meantmore"	400
	"Fair Meadow"	500
	"Hilliards Choice"	300
	"Stevens Inheritance" from (N) Collier tbc Jos. Husk	120
John Stevens	pt. "Blakes Hope" tbc Brough Broughton	33½
	"Security" – denied	35
	"Cox Craft" tbc John Steavens	50
William Merrill (cnp)	"Arrococo"	250
	"Adventure" tbc Esau Merrill	100

	"Merrill Adventure" tbc: • Esau Merrill – 45 a. • John Merrill – remainder	95
	"Front of Locust Hummock" – denied	75
43:1748:52 ...		
Ralph Wilbourne	"Prices Grove" tbc Caleb Milburne (338 a.)	400
James Jolly	"Cobham"	100
William Matthews	"Edwin" tbc William Mathews & contains • "Hillyards Adventure" – 100 a.	350
	"Worthless" – not found	110
	"Meadow" tbc William Mathews	30
	"Ellis Lott" from (N) Ellis tbc Samuell Mathews	50
	"Meadow" – twice charged	50
	"Mathews Delight" from (N) Ward tbc Samuell Mathews	50
John Ellis	"Barsheba" – denied	100
	"Bethsada" – denied	100
	"Adventure"	70
John Lawrance	"Lawrences" – not found	200
43:1748:53 ...		
Thomas Waughop (SM)	"Piney Point" tbc James Lindoe	800
Teague Reggan, Jr.	pt. "Golden Lyon" tbc Joshua Coldwell	200
	"Ambrosia" from (N) Regan – is pt. "Golden Lyon"	200
John Reggen	pt. "Golden Lyon" tbc h/o Teague Riggan, Sr.	200
John Andrews	pt. "Golden Lyon" tbc Jos. Coldwell	100
Teage Reggen, Sr.	pt. "Golden Lyon" tbc h/o Teague Riggan, Sr.	100
	"Seamans Choice" – denied	150
	"Hilliards Discovery" tbc John Riggan	150
	"Midle Plantation" from (N) Harper tbc Teage Riggan, Jr.	175
Thomas Carroll	pt. "Strand" – not known	300
43:1748:54 ...		
Walter Lane	pt. "Strand" a/s "Lanes Lott" tbc Francis Allen	125
	"Cork" tbc Francis Allen	100
Thomas Layfield	pt. "Strand" tbc Sarah Stewart	112
James Atkinson (cnp)	pt. "Strand" tbc Samuell Atkinson	100
	"Poor Hall" tbc:	350

	• John Pain – 250 a. • William Ellis – 100 a.	
John Macknett	pt. “Strand” tbc Sarah Stewart	88
Mary Gaines	“Lannum Discovery” – not known	300
Domack Dennis	pt. “Smiths Folly” – not known	500
	“Adventure” from (N) Layfield – not known	100
	“Dennis Purchase” from (N) Dennis – not known	140
43:1748:55 ...		
John Dennis	pt. “Smiths Folly” – denied	300
	pt. “Cambrook” – denied	100
	“<unr> Ridge” tbc William Lane	150
	“Parkers Choice” from (N) Mill tbc John Dennis, Sr.	250
	pt. “Rochester” from (N) Devarax tbc John Sturgais	140
Thomas Newbold	“Acquintica”	200
	“Acquintica”	300
	“Friendship”	100
	“Content”	77
William Powell	“Greenfield” tbc: • John Powell – 181 a. • Richard Brooks – 19 a. called “Hickory Ridge” • Richard Brooks – 70 a. called “Gum Neck”	300
	“Powels Addition”	50
	“Gift” from (N) Henry tbc Martin Kennett	200
	“Daughters Recovery” from (N) Stannett tbc William Holland	200
Pearce Bray	pt. “Pimmo”	70
	pt. “Pimmo” from Thomas Jones tbc John Hall	200
	“Clonnell”	40
	“Cork”	200
John Waltham (PA)	pt. “Pimmo”	30
43:1748:56 ...		

Samuell Collins	"Hamm"	50
	pt. "Dales Adventure"	200
	"Late Discovery" tbc: • Collins Addams – 100 a. called "Snow Hill" • John Evans – 150 a. • John Milburn – 50 a.	600
	"Handys Meadows" tbc Thomas Evans	50
	"Collins Addition"	223
Steven White	pt. "Rehobath" tbc William White	600
	"Caldicutt" tbc William White	500
	pt. "Buckangham" tbc John White	400
	"Springfield" from (N) Whittington tbc John White	480
	"Fair Meadow" from (N) Whittington tbc John White	438
Col. Francis Jenkins	pt. "Rehobath" tbc Mary Hampton	400
	"Spring Hill" tbc Mary Hampton	1000
	"Otilbury" tbc John Leatherbury	400
	"Jeshimon" tbc Mary Hampton	150
	"Midlesex" tbc Adam Spence	150
widow Taylor	"Dublin" tbc Robert Taylor	100
Henry Hudson, Sr.	"Hudsons Fortune"	100
	"Poplar Ridge" tbc William Brittingham	100
	"Meant More" tbc William Davis	441
	"Hudsons Purchase"	100
43:1748:57 ...		
Henry Peisley	"Thornbury" – not known	1000
Peter Caersly	"Irish Grove" tbc Peater Kersley	150
Edward Dykes tbc equally between John Kellum & Kirk Gunby	"Hignolls Choice"	150
	"Back Lodge"	150
Maj. John Cornish	pt. "Hignolls Choice" tbc Mary Hampton by name of "Whitely"	150
Robert Worth	pt. "Crambrook" – not known	100
Madam Carter (London)	"Kent" – not known	1500
43:1748:58 ...		

Sampson Wheatly	pt. "Irish Grove"	100
	"Greenfield"	62
John Perkins	pt. "New Towne"	225
William White	"Kings Norton" – denied	100
	pt. "Hogg Quarter" – denied	350
	"Entrance"	400
	pt. "Buckingham" tbc John White	400
John Manlove	"Manloves Improvement" – not known	300
Samuell Young	"Coventry" – not found	300
George Tull	pt. "Colemans Adventure"	500
	pt. "Beckles"	200
	"Chance"	50
43:1748:59 ...		
Richard Tull, Sr.	"Peach & Pine" tbc: • Solomon Tull – ½ • William Wharton – remainder	100
Thomas Wood	"Elgate" from (N) Wright tbc John Coape	150
Jeremiah Maurice	"Affrica" tbc Francis Allen	300
widow Sharrett	"Exchange" – supposed to be pt. "Daughters Recovery" in account of William Holland	100
	"Middle" tbc William Holland	100
Walter Taylor for o/o (N) Henderson	"Landing Purchased" – denied	130
	"Acton" for self – denied	300
	"Barron Lott" – denied	53
	"Timber Lott" a/s "Taylors Lott" – denied	150
	"Taylors Choice" – denied	600
	"Williams Hope" – from (N) Coldwell; denied	40
	"Taylors Lott"	100
43:1748:60 ...		
Honner Small (widow)	"Hendersons Second Choice" – not known	70
	"Small Lott" – not known	75
	"Small Lott" – not known	50
John Mills for o/o David Jones	"Trump Cappsfield" tbc John Mills (250 a.)	229
	pt. "Kingsland" from (N) Bayly tbc John Mills	200
Nicholas Hudson	"Hudsons Folly" tbc Jacob Addams	200

Jacob Adams	"More Clach" tbc: • John Henderson – 325 a. • John Small – 175 a.	500
Henry Bishop	pt. "Snow Hill" – not found	150
Thomas Peterkin for Robert Bishop	pt. "Snow Hill" – not known	50
43:1748:61 ...		
widow Quillin	"New Years Gift" – not known	100
Michaell Clifton	"Morris Hope" tbc Robert Boyard (44 a.)	250
Alexander Tounsend	"Coventry" tbc Charles Tounsend	200
John Houlstone	"Scotts Folly" – denied	100
	"Scotts Lott" a/s "Folly"	100
	"Addition"	75
	"Langton" from (N) Thorowgood	150
Barnard Rumsey	"Second Purchase" – not known	250
William Quinton	"Lodge" tbc Philip Quinton	200
43:1748:62 ...		
George Laws	pt. "Goodwill" – not known	200
John Broughton	"Little Action" tbc Brough Broughton as pt. "Blakes Hope"	100
	"Welsh Folly" tbc: • John Melton – 150 a. • Baly Fisher – 100 a. • Charles Richards – 50 a.	300
	pt. "Taylors Lott" – from (N) Taylor; not known	200
Fran. Benstone	"Benstons Lott" tbc Joseph Benston	100
Rowland Bivian	pt. "Milton" tbc Rowland Bevans	50
	"Warwick" tbc: • Rowland Bevans – 100 a. • Thomas Bevans – 300 a.	400
Thomas Peale	pt. "Milton" tbc Thomas Peal (110 a.)	250
	"Coventry" tbc: • Thomas Peal – 200 a. • John Andrews – 200 a.	450
Dorman Dennahoe	"Smiths Chance" tbc Dorman Donohoe	150
	"Denahoes Second Choice" tbc Teague Donohoe	175
	"Unlookt for" tbc Dorman Donohoe	50
43:1748:63 ...		
widow Pitt	pt. "No Name" tbc John Pitts	200

Robert Blades	pt. "No Name"	200
	"Broughtons Choice" from (N) Houston	<n/g>
Thomas Quillen	"Chance" tbc David Hudson	100
Robert Houlstone	"Second Choice" – not found	100
	"Kechatan Choice" – from (N) Atkinson; not found	150
Morgan Thomas	"Gads Hill" – not found	300
Siland. Chapman	pt. "Kingsland" – not found	100
43:1748:64 ...		
Isaac Piper	"Foolks Choice" tbc: • Archibald Grear – 100 a. • Isaac Piper – 150 a.	250
	"Convey" – from (N) Kemp tbc Joseph Steavenson	250
John Paradice for Phillip Parker (VA)	pt. "Foolks Choice" – not found	250
Adrian Marshall	pt. "Sewards Purchase" tbc Isaac Boston	200
	"Boston Green" tbc Isaac Boston	25
	"Longs Lott" from (N) Long tbc George Marshall	100
Esaw Boston	pt. "Sewards Purchase" tbc: • Betty Boston – 100 a. as "Bostons Purchase" • Esaw Boston – 100 a.	200
John Timmons	"Carters Lott" – denied	100
Richard Wharton for o/o Hum. Reed	"Hard Shift" tbc William Vannetson	150
	pt. "Convenience" tbc Ann Brasier	200
43:1748:65 ...		
Richard Leaster	"Porsimon Point" tbc Robert Boyard	50
Peter Benton	pt. "Bear Point" tbc: • Isaac Costin – 200 a. • John Tull – 125 a. • Cumfort Benton – 25 a.	350
	pt. "Costons Trouble" tbc: • Steaphen Costin – 200 a. • Cumfort Benton – 100 a.	300
	pt. "Taunton" tbc: • Cumfort Benton – 100 a. • Thomas Pirkins – 100 a.	300
	pt. "Emetts Discovery" – taken by elder survey	100
	"Bears Hole" tbc Cumfort Benton	50
	"Sapling Ridge" tbc Cumfort Benton	50

William Tounsend	pt. "Bear Point" tbc: • John Harris – 75 a. • Cumfort Benton – 75 a.	150
John Tounsend	"Towsends Discovery" tbc John Townsend, Jr.	100
	"Riggin Content" – from (N) Riggin tbc John Hails	100
	"Northfield" – from (N) White tbc: • John Pope – 250 a. • Little Tounsend – remainder	500
	"Belks Speedwell" tbc John Tounsend, Jr.	100
	"Addition" tbc John Tounsend, Jr.	50
Peter Dickenson	pt. "Dickensons Hope" tbc Charles Dickenson	40
	"Green Park" tbc Charles Dickenson	200
43:1748:66 ...		
John Keith	pt. "Suffolk" tbc Elizabeth Handy	464
John Harrison	"Harrisons Venture" tbc Caleb Harris (50 a.)	200
	"Midleton" tbc Caleb Harris	125
	"Nodd"	100
Stephen & William White, John Watts, Lawrence Ridgely, & William Mathews	pt. "Convenience" – not known	200
John Watts (VA)	pt. "Convenience" tbc: • Robert King – ½ • Mary Hampton – ½	150
	"Accompsick Island" tbc William Watts	250
	"Timber Island" tbc William Watts	725
	pt. "Newport Bagnell" tbc William Watts (350 a.)	375
	"Watts Convenience" tbc William Watts	600
	pt. "Carmell" tbc Peater Colliar	500
	"No Name" – not known	90
	pt. "Newport Pagnell" – not known	350
	"Sarahs Neck" – from (N) Caldwell; not known	250
	"Partners Choice" – from (N) Hill; not known	250
	"Farloworth" – from (N) Woodcroft; not known	217
	"Smithfield" – from (N) Woodcroft; not known	153
Edward Howard	pt. "Convenience" – not known	100
43:1748:67 ...		
Phillip Fitts Gerrald	pt. "Smiths Recovery" – not known; denied	150
John Pollock	pt. "Smiths Recovery" – not known	150

John Tunstall	pt. "Smith Recovery"	310
	"Long Meadow"	248
	"Double Purchase" – from (N) Rousby	250
	"Beverly Moyety" – from (N) West	250
	"Whelers Desire" – from (N) Wheeler	100
Roger O'Keen	"Old Town" – not known	100
Edward Harper	"Morrises Advisement" – denied	150
	"Heard Quarter" – from (N) Christopher	50
	pt. "Middleton" – from (N) Harris	50
widow Harper	"Norfolk" tbc h/o John Harper	500
	"Midle Plantation" – denied	150
43:1748:68 ...		
Fran. Thoregood	"Hogg Quarter" tbc Robert Nairn	500
	pt. "Buckingham" – not known	350
	pt. "Unity" – not known	325
John Evans (VA)	pt. "Pitchcroft" – not known	100
	"Little Monmouth" – taken by elder survey	100
	pt. "Mount Pleasant"	325
	"Chance" tbc John Evans (WI)	150
	"Pitchcroft" a/s pt. "Smiths Island" tbc: • John Evans (<unr>) – 300 a. • Thomas Tyler – 200 a.	700
	pt. "Black Ridge" – from (N) Glass; not known	150
	pt. "Spence Lott" – from (N) Spence	100
	"Evans Purchase" – from (N) Shiles; taken by elder survey	60
Madam Susanna Littleton (VA)	"Jersey" – not known	500
	pt. "Pharsalia" tbc: • Edward Miflin – 311 a. • remainder taken by VA line	800
Charles Townsend for John Powell	"Winter Quarter" tbc Thomas Coffin	200
Timothy Pead	"Lays" – not known	150
	"Wise Ridge" – not known	150
43:1748:69 ...		
Moses Fenton	"Woodhall" tbc Margaret Fenton	200
	"Naswood Hill" – denied	200

John Lane	"Old Head" – not known	100
	"Friends Discovery" a/s "Kindness" – not known	500
	"Lanes Addition" – not known	150
Dockett Beauchamp	pt. "Ledburn" tbc Edward Beauchamp	100
	pt. "Contention" – from (N) Beauchamp	15
Edward Beauchamp	pt. "Ledbourne"	100
	"Hog Yard" from (N) Beauchamp	95
	"First Choice" from (N) Beauchamp	<n/g>
	"Johnsons Lott" from (N) King	<n/g>
	"Loss & Gain"	100
John Clark for John Walthum	"Georges Marsh" tbc Robert Nairn	50
	"Tearse" tbc: • Robert Nairn – ½ • James Nairn – ½	300
	"Miserable Quarter" tbc Race Clark (300 a.)	400
	"Clarks Marsh" – not known	50
	"Folly" tbc Richard Hudson, Jr.	100
43:1748:70 ...		
William Handy	pt. "Midlesex" tbc Elizabeth Handy	200
Thomas Cole	"Whitby" tbc Cornelius Dickenson	150
William Warwick	pt. "Harpers Discovery" tbc Arthur Warwick	100
	pt. "Harpers Purchase" tbc Arthur Warwick	50
William Bradshaw	pt. "Cowly" – not known	100
	"Bradshaws Purchase" tbc: • Ann Bradshaw – 150 a. • Macajah Brittingham – 50 a.	200
Edm. & Charles Dickenson	pt. "Limbrick" – denied	17
	"Addition to Limbrick" tbc Edm. Dickenson	25
William Williamson	pt. "Truebridge" tbc James Feddeman (200 a.)	400
43:1748:71 ...		
Jeremiah Carey	pt. "Truebridge" tbc John Webb	50
Richard Webb	pt. "Truebridge" tbc John Webb	250
	pt. "Smiths Choice" tbc John Tull	100
William Twyford (ACC)	"Hiccory Levell" – not known	40
	"Cow Quarter" – not known	5
William Noble (cnp)	"Tossiter" tbc Samuell Dormant	150
	"Timber Grove" – not known	150

	"Cherry Garden" tbc David Dredden, Jr.	86
Francis Outwell	"Bashaw" tbc Francis Otwell	200
Solomon Long	"Amity"	150
43:1748:72 ...		
Thomas Wallis	pt. "Golden Quarter" – from (N) Vigerous tbc Thomas Wallace	150
	pt. "Riple" – from (N) Vigerous tbc Thomas Wallace	
	more of the above tbc Thomas Wallace	110
	"Wallaces Chance" tbc Thomas Wallace	95
Peter Waples	"Come by Chance" tbc Edm. Dickenson	100
	"Colechester" tbc Ambros Riggen	169
John Laws	pt. "Lloyds Grove" tbc Charles Ramsey	250
John Brittingham	pt. "Stanleys" tbc John as "Williams Desire"	500
	"Williams Desire" from (N) Brittingham should be "Crowley" tbc: • Peater Dickenson – 150 a. • William Brittingham – 100 a. • John Brittingham – 250 a.	500
Thomas Murphy	pt. "Millbranch" – not known	200
o/o William Major	pt. "Mill Branch" – not known	200
43:1748:73 ...		
John Gillett	"New Macher" tbc John Gillet	200
	"Gillys Addition" tbc Ezekiell Gillis (lives near Annapolis)	100
	"Salem" – from (N) Howard tbc Samuell Gillet	350
Lodowick Fleming	"Venture" tbc John Fleming	300
	"Killglass" tbc John Lay	300
Joseph Ward	"Paxon Hill" tbc Jos. Ward	100
John Powell	"Shoemakers Meadows" – not yet known	109
	"Little Derry" – not yet known	200
	"Providence" – not yet known	200
Robert Mitchell	pt. "Good Success"	150
	pt. "Midlesex" from (N) Langford tbc Robert Mitchell (180 a.)	250
William Nelson	pt. "Castle Hill" tbc William Nelson (125 a.)	85
43:1748:74 ...		

Robert Lamberton	"Bengill" – not known	100
	"Recovery" tbc Jos. Scofield	33
James Weatherly (cnp)	"Ackworths Choice" – not known	100
	"Ackworths Folly" tbc William Weatherly	165
	"Wetherlys Purchase" – not known	100
	"Oak Hall" tbc Joseph Gillis	200
	"Manloves Adventure" tbc Joseph Gillis	50
	"Acworths Contrivance" tbc: • James Weatherly – 50 a. • John Weatherly (orphan) – remainder with Moses Alexander	127
	"Fathers Delight" – not known	100
	pt. "Wetherlys Adventure" tbc Ebenezar Cotman	200
	"Marsh Hook" tbc h/o William Piper	100
	"Wetherlys Ridge" tbc William Weatherly	200
	"Snakey Island" tbc: • William Weatherly – ½ • James – 25 a. • John Weatherly (orphan) – remainder with (N) Alexander	100
	"Once Againe" tbc h/o William Piper	100
	"Wetherlys Chance" – not known	250
	pt. "Whetherlys Contrivance" tbc Daniell Rhodes	150
	"Crane Ridge" – given up many years ago	550
	"Discovery" tbc Solomon Hitch (80 a.)	160
	"Addition" tbc: • James Weatherly – 200 a. • William Weatherly – 128 a. • John Weatherly (orphan) – 122 a.	450
	"Prevention" tbc: • James Weatherly – 70 a. • William Weatherly – 20 a.	90
	"Willsons Discovery" tbc: • William Inglish – 250 a. • James Quaturmus – 150 a. • Robert Islingworth – 100 a.	500
	"Quiakeson Neck" – denied	500
	"Quiakeson Neck" – denied [!]	500
	"Willsons Discovery" – twice charged	500
	"Chance" tbc Jos. Gillis	300

	"Wetherlys Conveniency" – denied	200
	"Quiakeson Neck" – denied	500
Richard Whitemarsh	"Whitemarshes Chance" – not known	<n/g>
43:1748:75 ...		
James Givean	pt. "White Marsh Delight" – not known	150
	"Lyons Lott" – not known	100
	"Giveans Last Choice" – not known	200
	"Dunn Givean" – not known	200
	"Agnes Lowe" tbc James Coldwell (50 a.)	100
	pt. "White Marsh Delight" – not known [!]	150
	"Commons" – not known	250
	"Largee" tbc James Coldwell (150 a.)	600
	"Shantavanah" tbc John Givean	200
Robert Givean	pt. "Whitemarshes Delight" tbc Robert Givans	150
	"Green Meadow" – denied	150
	"Giveans Lott" – denied	150
	"Addition" tbc Robert Givans	100
	pt. "Whitemarshes Delight" – denied	150
	pt. "Beginning" – from (N) Harrington tbc Robert Givans	7
	"Little Neck" – denied	50
	"Cyprus Swamp" tbc Robert Givans	342
	"Inclosed" tbc Robert Givans	437
	"Denn Pasture" tbc Robert Givans	100
Christopher Nutter (cnp)	pt. "Nutters Adventure"	100
	pt. "Dormans Delight" tbc: • Huett & Mathew Nutter – 100 a. • William Nutter – 50 a.	150
	pt. "Nutters Adventure"	275
	pt. "Morris's Lott"	50
	pt. "Sheilds Choice" tbc Mathew Nutter	110
	pt. "No Name" – denied	25
	"Nutters Rest" – denied	450
	"Marsh Hook" – for o/o (N) Piper; denied	100
	"Rich Ridge" – denied	239
	"Marsh Ground" tbc William Nutter	100
	"Delight" tbc:	388

	• William Nutter – ½ • Christopher Nutter – ½	
	"Middle Tract" – denied	100
43:1748:76 ...		
Mathew Nutter	pt. "Nutters Adventure" tbc: • Christopher Nutter – 50 a. • Huett – 25 a. • Mathew Nutter – 25 a.	100
	pt. "Dormans Delight" tbc: • Mathew Nutter with 180 a. of "Dormans Delight" & "Shiles Choice" • Huett Nutter with 290 a. of "Dormans Delight" & "Shiles Choice"	150
	pt. "Nutters Adventure"	275
	pt. "Morris Lott" tbc William Nutter (50 a.)	50
	pt. "Sheilds Choice" tbc: • Mathew Nutter with 180 a. of "Dormans Delight" & "Shiles Choice" • Huett Nutter with 290 a. of "Dormans Delight" & "Shiles Choice"	110
	pt. "No Name" – not known	25
John Bond	<n/g>	<n/g>
Thomas Ralph	pt. "Truelock Grange" a/s "Ralphs Purchase" (f. 39)	100
	"Ralphs Venture"	100
John Bougher	pt. "Ross" tbc: • William Nutter – ½ • Christopher Nutter – ½	25
James Russell	"Truelock Grange"	75
	pt. "Ross" tbc: • William Nutter – ½ • Christopher Nutter – ½	25
	pt. "Good Success"	50
William Giles, Jr.	"Salop" tbc William Giles	250
	"Parramours First Choice" tbc William Giles	300
	"Turky Cock Hill" tbc John Moore	150
	"Giles Lott" tbc William Giles	450
43:1748:77 ...		
Charles Nutter for o/o (N) Piper (cnp)	"Salisbury Plaines" tbc h/o William Piper	200
	pt. "Whetherlys Purchase" tbc James Hardy	200

	"Wilton" tbc h/o William Piper	100
	"Tosswandock" – denied by h/o (N) Piper	130
	pt. "Ottawattaquaquo" – denied by h/o (N) Piper	800
James Traine	pt. "Wetherlys Purchase" tbc James Train	225
	"Jermons Lott" – from James Heath; denied	200
	"Pasturidge" tbc James Train	60
	"Addition" tbc James Train	30
	pt. "Slipe" – from (N) Wetherly tbc James Train (25 a.)	30
	"Compleate" tbc James Train	25
	"Long Tree Island" tbc James Train	374
William Bennett	pt. "Mount Hope" tbc: • Robert Colliar – 45 a. • Elias Venatson – 65 a. • Archibald Ritchie – 40 a.	75
Thomas Larramore	pt. "Mount Hope" tbc Archibald Ritchie	30
	pt. "Ticknell" tbc John Laramore	50
	pt. "Turnstile" tbc: • Archibald Ritchie – 10 a. • Elias Venatson – 65 a.	150
	"Mount Hope" – from (N) Bennett tbc: • Elias Venatson – 65 a. • Archibald Ritchie – 10 a.	75
Richard Ackworth	"Ackworths Delight" tbc Daniell Rhodes	100
	"Hogg Quarter" tbc Charles & Thomas Ackworth	200
	"Manloves Delight" – denied	100
	"Sonns Choice" – denied	50
	"Peckingoe Ridge" tbc Daniell Rhodes	250
	"Marish Point" tbc Charles & Thomas Ackworth	200
	"Ackworths Delight" tbc Charles & Thomas Ackworth	500
	"Cypress" tbc George Scott	18
	"Hackorths Choice" tbc Charles & Thomas Ackworth	100
43:1748:78 ...		
Michaell Williams	"Farmingham" – not known	300
William Green (cnp)	"Partners Choice" tbc Samuell Melson	250
	"Which You Please" tbc: • John Boyce – 225 a.	250

	• John Hufington – 25 a.	
	"Green Land" – not known	2500
Capt. John McClester	"Woodgate Dock"	100
	"Sweetwood Hall"	400
	"Point Marsh"	200
	"Adventure" from (N) Adams	100
	"Adams Choice" from (N) Adams	180
Daniell Magginnis	pt. "Chelsey" tbc Jane Magginnis	100
Stephen Tully	pt. "Chelsey"	150
Richard Samuell	"Ware" tbc: • Ann Samuell – 125 a. • John Hopkins – 140 a. as "Hopkins Gift" • John Phipps – remainder	300
	"Samuells Lott" tbc Stephen Hopkins	200
43:1748:79 ...		
William Wallace	"Middlesex" tbc John Wallace	300
	"Tarkill Humock" tbc John Wallace	30
	"Addition" tbc John Wallace	180
Robert Collier	pt. "Shadwell"	50
	"Dudley" – denied	20
	"Late Discovery" – denied	50
	pt. "Mount Hope" – from (N) Larramore tbc Thomas Colliar	45
	"Colliers Enlargement" tbc Thomas Colliar	90
Sidney Browne	"Lotts Daughter" – from (N) Harris tbc Robert Austin for o/o (N) Fouler	100
	"Sidny Brown Lott" – from (N) Harris; not known	97
Jonathan Jackson	"Abergaving"	100
	"Small Lott"	100
	"Venture" in DO tbc h/o Robert Polk	300
	"Warwick" – from (N) James tbc: • William Richardson – 100 a. • Jonathan Jackson – remainder	200
	"Warrington" – from (N) Jones	50
widow of John Ailworth	"St. Albans" – not known	60
Roger Nicholson	"Illingworths Hope" tbc: • Jane Nicholson – 100 a. • Jacob Messex – 50 a.	150

43:1748:80 ...		
William Wenright	pt. "Doughtys Lott" – not known	50
	"Cannon Shott" tbc Cannon Winright (100 a.)	300
	"Woolhope" tbc Cannon Winright	75
Peter Doughty	pt. "Daughters Lott" tbc Robert Colliar	100
	pt. "Cannons Choice" tbc Thomas Laramore	100
	"Paris" tbc: • Robert Colliar – 100 a. • Sambo Game – 50 a.	150
	pt. "Turn Stile" tbc: • Robert Colliar – 50 a. • Robert Henderson – 100 a.	150
	"St. Jermans" – not known	50
	"Bettys Enlargement" tbc Lewis Beard, Jr. & Sr.	100
	"Doughtys Priviledge" – not found	50
	"Force Putt" tbc John Larimore	50
Thomas Lawrance	pt. "Cannons Choice" tbc Thomas Larimore	182
Oliver Smith for (N) Webb	"Monmouth" – not found	40
Edward Bennett	"Ægypt"	118
James Collier	pt. "Duolly" tbc Thomas Benston for h/o James Colliar	80
	"Colliers Good Success" tbc Thomas Benston for h/o James Colliar	320
43:1748:81 ...		
widow of John Marrett	"Lyons Denn" – not found	200
	"Ferry Hall" – not found	100
Samuell Flewelyn	pt. "Ticknell" tbc Samuell Fluellin	50
	"Prickle Cockshott" tbc Samuell Fluellin	75
	"Milk More" tbc Samuell Fluellin	50
	"Clear of Cannon Shott" tbc Samuell Fluellin	50
	"Flewlynes Purchase" tbc Samuell Fluellin	50
	"Coopers Mistake" tbc John Laramore	100
	pt. "Cannons Lott" – from (N) Quaturmus tbc Samuell Flewellin	50
	"Security" tbc Samuell Flewellin	50
	"Chance" tbc Samuell Flewellin	25

Lewis Beard tbc: • Lewis Beard, Jr. – 130 a. of "Fishermans Quarter" & "Bettys Enlargement" • Lewis Beard, Sr. – remainder	"Fishermans Quarter"	150
	"Calloways Addition" from (N) Killaman	50
	pt. "Recovery" from (N) Larramore	5
	"Bettys Enlargement" – taken up by this father	100
John Cheesman	"Lyons Folly" tbc John Cheasman	150
	"Coopers Hall" – denied	200
James West	"Greens Recantation"	200
43:1748:82 ...		
Capt. Thomas Winder (VA)	pt. "Westloves Neck" tbc Thomas Benston	233
James Jones	"Might Ahad More" tbc John Shiles	200
William Langsdone	"Woodstock"	200
John Kemp	"Gethesemane" – not known	300
Thomas Willson	"Darby" tbc John Wilson	350
	"Darby" – denied	200
	"Radburne" tbc John Wilson	140
	"Willsons Lott" tbc: • Benjamin Venatson – 100 a. • Margaret Wilson (who lives with Richard Gravenour) – remainder	200
John Read	"Weston" – not known	200
	"Reeds Folly" tbc Peater Freeny	100
	"Tatmans Folly" tbc Mathew Parramore	50
	"Chance" – not known	20
43:1748:83 ...		
h/o Thomas Chapwell	"Kingstone" – not known	100
James Caldwell	pt. "Manloves Grove" tbc John Moore	250
	"Good Luck" tbc Mitchell & William Dashiell	63
	"Dougate" – from (N) Shahe; not known	200
	pt. "Pharsalia" – from (N) Parramore tbc Mitchell & William Dashiell	350
	"First Choice" – from (N) Layton tbc Charles Williams	250
	"First Choice" – from (N) Cottman tbc James Coldwell	150
h/o John Nutter	pt. "Attawattaquaquo" – not known	400

Julian Messeck	"Nathz" tbc: • Jacob Messeck – ½ • Nehemiah Messeck – ½	100
George Dashield	"Recovery" – contains "Close Fork" (500 a.) tbc: • Robert Dashiell – 333 a. • Joseph Dashiell for Mitchell Dashiell (orphan) – remainder	500
	"Satisfaction" tbc George Dashiell, Sr.	116
	"Bennetts Adventure" – from (N) Scarborough; resurveyed as "Dashiells Lott" (1740 a.) tbc George Dashiell, Sr.	2500
	"Venture Priviledge" tbc Mitchel, William, Robert, & Joseph Dashiell (equally)	250
	"Improvement" tbc Robert Dashiell	40
	"Littleworth" tbc George Dashiell, Jr.	50
	"Summer Pasture" tbc George Dashiell, Sr.	135
43:1748:84 ...		
Thomas Gordan	"Addition" – not known	250
	"Carlisle" – not known	300
Jenkin Morris	"Morris Delight" tbc Benjamin Ricketts & Sarah Lamee	300
John Hamblyn	pt. "Gethsemane" – not known	300
Robert Laws	"Taylors Hill"	200
	"Something Worth" – taken up by John Panter; charge 325 a.	675
John Gladstone	"Glads Tower" – not known	100
	"Gladsteans Delight" – not known	100
	"John Gladsteans Land" – not known	300
James Wyth & Marmaduke Masters	"Batchelors Delight" – not known	250
	"Batchelors Invention" – not known	250
43:1748:85 ...		
William Keen, Sr.	pt. "Partners Choice" tbc Phillip Riccords	100
	"Wash Water" – not known	36
	"Bells First Choice" – for John Bell; not known	200
o/o William Keen, Jr.	pt. "Partners Choice" – not known	200
George Trotter	"Carters Lodge"– not known	350
James Warrington	"Chance" – not known	300

Thomas Farnall	"Bower" tbc John Phipps called "Good Neighbourhood"	200
	"Venture" tbc Thomas Farrell	30
	"Farrells Folly" tbc Thomas Farrell	200
Daniell Gore	pt. "Pharsalia" tbc Ralph Justice	300
43:1748:86 ...		
John Purnell	pt. "Pharsalia" – escheated	200
	"Purnells Lott" tbc John Purnall	550
	pt. "Timber Quarter"	150
	"Purnells Adventure" – denied	200
	"Cold Harbour" tbc: • Charles Veazy – 90 a. • remainder taken by elder survey	325
	"North Timber Quarter" – denied	250
	"Purnalls Lott" – denied	250
	"Mattapanny Marsh" tbc John Purnall	248
	"Piney Island" tbc John Purnall	126
	"Bantry" from (N) Purnall tbc John Purnall (300 a.)	600
	pt. "Gennisor" – from (N) Purnall tbc Isaac Marshall (375 a.)	600
	"Orkny" – from (N) Purnall tbc John Purnall (Synapux)	80
	pt. "Watermillion" – from (N) Purnall; denied	<n/g>
	"Addition" – denied	50
	"Brothers Love" tbc John Purnall	350
	"New Timber Quarter" tbc John Purnall	200
	"Timber Quarter More" tbc John Purnall	50
widow Carroll	pt. "Transilvania" tbc Thomas Odewey	100
Fisher Walton	pt. "Transilvania"	400
Stephen Walton	pt. "Transilvania"	260
Henry Smock	"Batchelors Lott"	200
	"Yorkshire"	100
	"Convenience"	200
43:1748:87 ...		
Thomas Powell (cnp)	"Richardsons Ridge" a/s "Folly" tbc Samuell Powell	150
	"Rumly Marsh"	100

	"New Fairefield" tbc Elisha Purnall	400
	"Caersurthen" tbc Thomas Powell, Jr.	200
	"Slaughter Ridge" tbc Robert Gott	150
	"Slaughter Ridge" – twice charged	150
William Cord	"Musketoe Point" – denied	400
	"Musketoe Point" tbc: • William Cord – 248 a. • remainder taken by elder survey	400
	pt. "Transilvania"	40
Thomas Robins	"Ingeteage" tbc: • Boadwain Robins – 1160 a. • Barbary Harmonson – 150 a. • John Kendall – remainder	1550
Henry Hall	"Headly Hill" tbc Thomas Milburn	300
	pt. "Middleton" – not known	100
Nathaniell Poasey	"Burmudas Hundred" tbc Charles Veazey	100
Afradosie Johnson	"Paggam" tbc Charles Davis	200
	pt. "Timber Quarter"	50
	"Friends Choice" from (N) Ralph	300
43:1748:88 ...		
Phillip Selby	"Bastable"	250
	pt. "Carraganestick"	200
	pt. "Bantry"	200
	"Ceedar Grove"	610
	"Killkenny" from (N) Selby	234
	"Prevention"	70
	"Prevention" – twice charged; denied	70
John Hall	pt. "Midleton"	200
Richard Holland	"Hollands Discovery" tbc Thomas Latchum	200
	"Little" – know nothing of him	20
William Holland	pt. "Batchellors Adventure" tbc John Jones	50
	pt. "Entrance" from (N) Pollins (?)	95
	"Powells Lott" from (N) Powell	100
	"Bacon Quarter" tbc: • Charles Whale – 150 a. • Joseph Gray – 100 a. • Richard Holland – 140 a.	390
Abraham Hill	"Hogg Hill"	100

Rowland Hudson	"Peterson" tbc: • Peater Claywell – 50 a. • Rowland Hodgson – 200 a.	250
43:1748:89 ...		
Jos. Anderson for Col. John Robins (VA)	"Key" – not known	50
Robert Johnson	"Johnsons Hope" tbc David Johnson	300
	"Purgatery" tbc Peater Johnson	600
	"Green Mead" tbc David Johnson	50
	"Friends Denyall" tbc David Johnson	400
	"Morgans Choice" – not known	201
	"Leg More" – for h/o Clement Giles; not known	200
Mathew Scarbrough	"Timber Quarter" tbc John Scarbrough	250
	"Mordike" tbc Phillip Selby (400 a.)	1000
	pt. "Durham House" tbc: • John Scarbrough – 900 a. • Thomas Wise – 300 a.	1000
	"Islington" – denied	109
	pt. "Jones Choice"	150
Samuell Hopkins	"Nunns Green" tbc Samuell Hopkins, Sr.	350
	pt. "Long Island" tbc: • Johnson Hill – 50 a. • John Atkinson – remainder	100
	"Jones Choice" a/s "Nunns Green" – denied	300
h/o Parker Selby	pt. "Caragonastick" tbc Thomas Purnall	150
	pt. "Bantry" tbc Parker Selby (700 a.)	1200
	"Auskaukin" tbc Phillip Selby	70
	pt. "Brothers Love" tbc Parker Selby	150
43:1748:90 ...		
John Aydelott	"Bridgwater" – sold to a man in ACC	200
	"Reads Folly" – should be "Reads Contrivance" tbc Ambrose Willet	100
	"Convenience" tbc: • Ambrose Willet – 200 a. • Peater Claywell – 100 a.	300
	"Cyprus Swamp" tbc John Aydelot	150
John Collins (cnp)	"Speedwell" – not known	300
	"Point Next the Worst" – not known	25

	"Chance" tbc John Collins (BA)	100
Tobias Pepper	"St. Leonards"	200
	"Milbury" tbc William Pepper	200
Peter Wattson	"Falmouth" tbc Luke Watson	200
	"Crowland" – denied	100
William Ainsworth	pt. "Temple Comb" – not known	100
Nathaniell Waile	"Farmers Hall"	150
43:1748:91 ...		
John Pope	"Rome" tbc: • Samuell Pope – 400 a. • John Pope – 100 a.	500
	"Shaftsbury" tbc Samuell Pope	200
	pt. "Long Island" tbc: • John Pope – ¼ • George Pope – ¼ • Samuell Pope – ¼ • Thomas Claywell – ¼	200
	"Midlemore" tbc: • John Pope – ¼ • George Pope – ¼ • Samuell Pope – ¼ • Thomas Claywell – ¼	123
	pt. "Key" from (N) Andrews	50
	"Addition"	35
	"Red Land" tbc: • John Pope – ½ • Archibald Dale – ½	300
Walter Read	"Cart Wheele" tbc: • Walter Read – 100 a. • William Beachboard – 50 a.	150
	"Taunton" – heir is in SU	110
	"Taunton" – not known	100
	"Lanes Caution" tbc Jos. Feddeman called "Old Berry" we suppose	200
Thomas Ackford	"Thornbury" tbc William Turner	400
	"Oldbury" tbc Jos. Feddeman	200
	pt. "Parramores Double Purchase" tbc William Turner	200
John Wheelton	"Vale of Eason" – not yet known	200
Rowland Sheppard	"Peilly" – not yet known	100

43:1748:92 ...		
Capt. John Westland	"Shousberry" – not known	150
	"Motiluck" – not known	200
Nathaniell Hopkins	"Good Hope"	150
	"Stockleys Adventure"	300
	"Jones Choice" – denied	150
	"Stockleys Adventure" – denied	300
Peter Wattson (VA)	"Black Ridge" tbc Peater Watson	150
William Selby (VA)	"John Boqueto Norton Hundred" – from (N) Jenkins tbc William Selby called "Selbys Purchase" (600 a.)	446
	"Partners Choice" – from White & Co.; denied	1750
	pt. "Simpleton" – from (N) Selby tbc John Selby (this & 100 a. more)	520
	pt. "Richardsons Land" – from (N) Richards;denied	163
	"Wattermillion Point"	60
Francis Joyce	"Littleworth" tbc John Pope	100
	"Nothing Worth" tbc John Pope	225
Benjamin Scotchfield	"Unity" – not known	300
	"Smiths First Choice" tbc: • Addam Spence – 233 a. • Jos. Scofield – remainder	700
	"Smiths First Choice" – denied	700
43:1748:93 ...		
Laurance Riely	pt. "Newport Pagnell" tbc Thomas Riley	350
	"Winter Range" tbc Thomas Riley (62¼ a.)	250
William Massey	pt. "Buckingham" tbc William Faucett, Jr.	350
	pt. "Carmell" tbc William Faucett, Jr.	500
	pt. "Unity" tbc William Faucett, Jr.	395
Thomas Thompson	pt. "Mount Ephraim" – not known	650
Charles Richardson	pt. "Mount Ephraim" tbc Charles Richardson & brothers	1150
John Bratton	pt. "Mount Ephraim" tbc: • Samuell Bratton, Jr. – 135 a. • William Nelson – 100 a.	235
	"Penny Street" – from (N) Henderson tbc James Bratton	200

John Ricketts	pt. "No Name" – not known	163
	pt. "Fair Haven" tbc Madam Davis	150
	pt. "Ricketts Chance"	150
	"Cross" – not known	150
43:1748:94 ...		
John Webb	pt. "No Name" – denied	437
Johnson Hill	pt. "Robinsons Inheritance"	500
	"Hills Purchase" – from (N) Johnson; denied	125
	pt. "Robinsons Inheritance" – from (N) Sturgoe	100
John Sturgis	pt. "Robinsons Inheritance"	450
John Porter for Thomas Parramore (VA)	pt. "Parramores Double Purchase" tbc: • Mason Abbot – 100 a. • Thomas Parramore – 450 a.	550
	"Weavers" – for yourself; not known	300
	"Portland" – not known	62
John Sanders for Thomas Parramore (VA)	pt. "Parramours Double Purchase" tbc Thomas Parramore	550
Richard Pepper	pt. "Parramores Double Purchase" tbc Thomas Newton	200
43:1748:95 ...		
John Bishop	pt. "Skipton"	200
	pt. "Reserve" – denied	100
Thomas Selbye	pt. "Skipton" – denied	30
	pt. "Fairefield" – from (N) McClester tbc Thomas Selby (300 a.)	380
John Croper	"Assateague Field" a/s pt. "Wrixham" tbc John Cropper	500
	"Golden Valley" – denied	250
	"Hogg Quarter" tbc: • John Cropper – 100 a. • Ebenezar Cropper – 100 a.	200
Ebenezar Croper	"Assateague Field" a/s pt. "Wrixham" tbc: • Ebenezar Cropper – 500 a. • Wrixam Cropper – 150 a. • William Simpson – 50 a.	700
William Robinson (cnp)	pt. "Cow Quarter" tbc John Robertson	250
	pt. "Fair Haven" tbc Michaell Robertson	150
	pt. "Assawoman" tbc Michaell Robertson	75
	"Salem" tbc William Robertson	250

	"Spring Quarter" – not known	200
	"Robinsons Purchase" tbc Michaell Robertson	150
43:1748:96 ...		
Richard Woodcroft	pt. "Cow Quarter" tbc William Woodcroft	250
	pt. "Dummfrize" tbc William Woodcroft	100
	"Woods Croft" – not known	100
	"Cellor" tbc: • William Woodcroft – 58⅓ a. • Thomas & Richard (N) – remainder	175
	"Farleworth" – not known yet	217
	"Hopewell" tbc William Woodcroft	200
William Ricketts	pt. "Fairhaven" tbc John Ricketts	150
	pt. "Assawoman" – not known	75
	"Medly" tbc William Richards	100
	pt. "Ricketts Chance" tbc Madam Davis	210
Thomas Purnall	"Fairefield" tbc: • John Purnall – 400 a. • Charles Ratclief s/o Elias – 400 a.	800
	"Farnhill" – denied	130
	"Chance" tbc Thomas Purnall	360
	"Fernhill" tbc John Purnall	150
	"Adams Fall" tbc: • Thomas Purnall – 3/7th • Elisha Purnall – 1/7th • John Fullerton (SU) – 1/7th • Mathew Purnall – 1/7th • Walton Purnall – 1/7th	200
Wrixam White	"Endeavour" tbc Jacob White	200
	"Fishing Harbour" tbc Jacob White	400
	"Windsor Forrest" tbc Jacob White	370
	"Arraratt" tbc Jacob White	250
	"Whites Addition" tbc Jacob White	70
	"Happy Entrance" tbc Jacob White	400
43:1748:97 ...		
William Fannell (cnp)	"Burley" tbc: • William Faucett – 200 a. • Thomas Collins – 100 a.	300
	"Goshen" tbc: • William Faucett – 1030 a.	1500

	• Nathaniell Cropper – 200 a. • Charles Ratclief – 170 a. • Richard Holland – 100 a.	
	"Mayfield" tbc William Faucett	500
	"Fishing Harbour" tbc William Faucett	100
	"Addition to Goshen & Mayfield" tbc William Faucett	500
Jerremiah Pointer	pt. "St. Lawrences Neck" tbc Dennis Hudson (400 a.)	700
Argalus Pointer	pt. "St. Lawrences Neck" tbc John Gillet	400
Madam Mary Edger	"Colickmore" tbc James Round	500
	"Bletching Hook" tbc James Round	500
	"Mill Angle" tbc James Round	25
	"Morehuss" tbc Archibald Dale	200
	pt. "North Bennefitt" tbc Thomas Purnall	200
Benjamin Burton	"Dicerss" tbc John Burton	614
	"Burtons Chance" – he took up tbc John Burton	86
43:1748:98 ...		
John Franklin	"Exchange" – not known	400
	"Freemans Contentment" tbc Thomas & John Collins	400
	"Long Acre" tbc Edward Franklyn	125
	"Assoetrage" tbc: • Edward Franklyn – ⅓ • William Fauset, Sr. – ⅓ • h/o (N) Venables – remainder	500
	"Exchange" tbc Edward Franklyn	600
Robert Perrey	"Bengrave" tbc: • Addam Spence – 66⅔ a. • Robert Smith (SU) – remainder	200
Thomas Pointer	"Highfield" tbc: • Elias Pointer – 172 a. called "Brothers Gift" • Thomas Pointer – 356 a.	528
Walter Evans	pt. "Hillyards Discovery" tbc Gamage Evans	75
	"South Petherton" tbc: • William Evans – 215 a. • John Evans – 215 a.	430
William Wouldhave	"Teaxbury" tbc Nehemiah Cropper	400

Peter Cammell	pt. "Golden Quarter" tbc John Cammell	150
	pt. "Niple" tbc John Cammell	
	"Holds More" tbc John Cammell	200
43:1748:99 ...		
John Cavenough	"Winktfield" – not known	200
Hugh Neilson	"Poplar Hill"	200
	"Nelsons Security" or pt. "Partners Choice"	250
John Devorix	pt. "Rochester" – from (N) Godin; should be 356 a.	160
Thomas Morrice	"Lineath" tbc William Morris (100 a.)	149
	"Ado." – for h/o Ri. Hill; not yet known	325
	"Turners Hall" – not yet known	200
	"Bus Morrice" – not yet known	200
Nathaniell Ratcliffe	pt. "Taunton" – not known	300
	pt. "Genzar" – not known	300
	"Howards Desire" tbc Jos. Miller	500
	"Ratcliffe" tbc Jos. Porter	200
	"Scandercen" – not known	150
43:1748:100 ...		
Samuell Sandford (London)	"Coram" – not known	500
Alexander Massey	pt. "Carmell" tbc: • Benjamin Walton – ⅓ • Alexander Mersy – ⅓ • William Mersey – ⅓	500
John Walton	pt. "Neighbourhood" tbc John Waltom	350
	"Walters Addition" – denied	200
	"Adams Purchase" – denied	18
William Walton	pt. "Neighbourhood" tbc William Waltom	700
Aaron Bishop	pt. "Scarboroughs Adventure" tbc Daniell Wharton	250
William Round	"Amee Downe" tbc Edward Round	448
	"Mulberry Grove" tbc Edward Round	
	"Conveniency" tbc James Round	
	"Conveniency" tbc James Round [!]	
	"Fleedbury" tbc John Dennis, Sr.	250
43:1748:101 ...		
Col. William Whittington (cnp)	"Sandy Wharfe" – not known	400
	"Choice" – not known	1200
	"Summer Fields" tbc Edmond Hough	400

	"Baltimores Gift" tbc: • William Whittington – ¼ • Southy Whittington – ¼ • Isaac Morris – ¼ • Edmond Hough – ¼	1000
	"Refused" – not known	325
	"New Haven" tbc: • John Lacatt – ½ • Littleton Whittington (VA) – ½	1034
	"Midlemore" tbc Addam Spence	190
	"Woodmans Folly" tbc David Hazard	150
	"Cadar Neck" tbc: • Daniell Wharton – 265 a. • John Onorton – 127 a.	633
	"Assoteague Beach" tbc George Douglass	1300
	"Aquango" tbc Isaac Morris	760
	pt. "Ann Downe" – from (N) Round; not known	650
	pt. "Mulberry Grove" – from (N) Round;not known	
	pt. "Conveniency" – from (N) Round; not known	
	pt. "Conveniency" – from (N) Round; not known	
	pt. "Diggs Point" – not known	310
Ephraim Heather for h/o Daniell Selby	"Sandy Point" tbc Parker Selby (BO)	200
	pt. "Yorkshire" – for self tbc Parker Selby (BO)	300
	"Mulberry Grove" – not known	169
	"Enlargement" – not known	100
	"Bellinghurst" – from (N) Round; not known	7
David Hudson	"Cropton" tbc Samuel Showell	700
	"Hillyards Mistake"	200
	"Cadds Addition"	234
43:1748:102 ...		
Ebenezar Franklyn for Edward Wallis	pt. "Mount Pleasant" tbc William Waltom	225
Henry Rich for Ri. Hill	"Husbands Forrest" tbc Richard Hill (350 a.)	396
Presgrave Turvill (cnp)	pt. "Riple" – not known	100
	pt. "Winchester" tbc William Hook for George Taylor	400
	pt. "Royall Oak" – not known	223
	"Royall Oak" tbc William Turvill	200

	"Turvilles Lott" – not known	50
Francis Hamblin	pt. "Winchester"	400
Edward Wall	pt. "Genezar" tbc John Purnall	800
Elias Ratcliff	pt. "Genzar" tbc: • John Purnall – 420 a. • William Whale – 105 a.	500
43:1748:103 ...		
Charles Ratcliffe	pt. "Genzar"	500
	½ of "Royall Oak" – denied	275
	"Goshen" – from (N) Burton; denied	70
	"Ratcliefs Quantity"	200
Hugh Tingall	pt. "Hillyards Discovery" tbc Daniel Tingle	75
	pt. "Powells Inclusion" tbc Daniel Tingle	128
	"Scottish Plott" tbc Hugh Tingle (300 a.)	400
	pt. "Dumm Frize" tbc John Tingle	200
	"Parkers Denyall" tbc John Tingle (20 a.)	100
Thomas Mumford	"Vernam Dean" tbc James Mumford	350
	pt. "Cropton" – from (N) Sewell tbc: • Thomas Mumford – 50 a. • Charles Mumford – 50 a.	100
	"Brents Marsh" – from (N) Johnson tbc: • James Mumford – 25 a. • William Mumford – 25 a. • Charles Mumford – 25 a. • Thomas Mumford – 25 a.	100
	"Shewells Addition" – from (N) Shewell tbc William Mumford	170
Henry Scotchfield	pt. "Rehobeth" – from (N) Howard tbc Henry Scofield	200
James Gray	"Friends Gift" tbc Jos. Gray	150
	"Grays Lott" – denied by the heir	250
	"Grays Lott" – denied by the heir	50
	"Annamessex" – denied by the heir	250
43:1748:104 ...		
Cornelius Ennis	"Carrdee" tbc: • Nathaniell Ennis – 200 a. • Mary Ennis – 300	500
	"Farn Hill" – not known	215

Chris. Homerson (Whore Hills)	"Silver Street" tbc Benjamin Tulley	100
	"Friends Assistance" – not known	100
	"Cumberland" – not known	140
	"Baynams Purchase" – not known	100
John Godden	"Bassing" tbc Catherine Purnall (925 a.)	1050
	"Point Look Out" tbc Catherine Purnall	150
	"Rochester" tbc Catherine Purnall (1804 a.)	2150
	"Thomas's Court" – denied	500
	"Upner" tbc William Simpson	250
	"East Gate" tbc Catherine Purnall	500
	"Long Acre" – denied	73
	"Adventure" – denied	600
Margerett Towers	"Supply" tbc Robert Gott	300
	"Towers Addition" tbc Robert Gott	112
	"Towers Pasture" tbc Robert Gott	125
Margery Turvill	pt. "Royall Oak" tbc John Turvill (175 a.)	225
	"Northampton" – for John Turvill tbc: • John Fall – 100 a. • Abraham Fall – 150 a.	250
43:1748:105 ...		
John Macmanis	"Chance" – not known	100
Charles Junis	"Cannadee" tbc William Innis	300
	"Junis's Addition" tbc William Ennis before	100
George Truett	pt. "Mulberry Grove" tbc: • Phillip Truett – 300 a. • George Truett – 300 a.	600
	"Truetts Harbour" tbc: • William Truett – 95 a. • George Truett s/o Phillip – 95 a. • George Truett – 100 a.	300
	"Truetts Purchase" tbc George Mumford	130
	"Hoggsdon" tbc: • Donock Dennis – 200 a. • George Loe – 100 a.	300
	"Long Lott" – from (N) Morris tbc George Truett	80
	pt. "<unr>" – from (N) Morris; denied	151
	"Truetts Goodwill" – denied	100

Henry Hudson	"Jones Adventure" tbc William Davis	250
	"Andover" tbc William Hudson (250 a.)	300
	pt. "Spalding" – not known	131
	"None Such" tbc William Davis	130
Daniell Patrick	"St. Patricks Hill" tbc: • John Bishop – ½ • William Poarter – ½	200
43:1748:106 ...		
William Richardson	"Weymouth" tbc Thomas Wise for o/o (N) Richardson	500
	"Wiltshire" tbc John Richardson	500
	pt. "Warwick" – from (N) Ralph	100
	pt. "Mount Ephraim" – from (N) Cade; denied	350
Thomas Osborne	"Ratcliffs Adventure" – not known	200
o/o Nicholas Cornwell	"Huntington" tbc: • John Burbadge – 137 a. • Vestry of Allhallows Parish – remainder	350
John Truett	"Bossworth" tbc John Donaldson	150
	pt. "Spittlefields" – not known	225
	"Truetts Lott" – not known	30
Martin Kennett	pt. "Eagle Point"	250
William Bulger	pt. "Eagle Point" – not known	100
43:1748:107 ...		
Edmond Cropper	pt. "Eagle Point" tbc Thomas Goddart	150
	"Little Worth"	100
	"Well Beck"	450
	"Tomkins Meadow"	53
	pt. "Neighbourhood" – from (N) Turvill; denied	350
John Boden	pt. "Kelly Hill" – not known	100
John Simpson	pt. "Kelly Hill" – not known	200
George Howard	"Bear Quarter"	160
	pt. "Vines Neck" – from (N) Derickson	230
	"Howards Chance"	80
Martha & Mary Foster (London)	"Herring Quarter" – not known	300
Richard Hadder for h/o Ri. Warren	"Ratcliffs Late Discovery" tbc Nicholas Warren	320
43:1748:108 ...		

Richard Hudson	"Harry Gate"	500
Warren Hadder	"North Fleet"	200
Thomas Proffitt	"Brick Hill Hoe" – not known	200
Jeremiah Tounsend	"South Fleet"	200
	"Desire"	100
	pt. "Brents Marsh" – from (N) Miller	200
	"Hogg Quarter"	100
Joseph Brittingham	"Mount Hope" tbc Elizabeth Brittingham	300
	pt. "Cornhill" tbc Elizabeth Brittingham	200
Samuell Powell for c/o Charles Fassitt	"Holyhead" – not known	100
43:1748:109 ...		
William Browne	"Willsons Mistake" tbc William Brown	200
William Bowen	"Bowens Choice" tbc: • John Purnall – 200 a. • John Bowen – 150 a.	350
	pt. "Sturbridge" – from (N) Cropper tbc Littleton Bowen	100
	"Teagues Addition" – denied	78
John Teage	pt. "Spalding" tbc John Teague	100
Alwin Ross	pt. "Spalding" tbc John Maccauley	100
Thomas Purnell	pt. "Spalding" tbc Thomas Purnall	79
John Patrick	"Pinders Neglect" tbc Thomas Collins for o/o Charles Collins (100 a.)	200
	"Patricks Lott" – not known	100
43:1748:110 ...		
Robert Dyne	"Meadfield" – not known	400
	"Spring Banck" – not known	500
William & Lewis Desharoon	"Nova Francia" – patent returned to John Coldwell long ago	300
David Harris	"Hearts Content" – not known	300
John Lammee	pt. "Mile End" tbc William Yong	150
	"Pasturage" – not known	50
h/o William Lewis (cnp)	"New Scotland" – sold to William Benston, don't know where he is	500
	"Cumberland" tbc John Sturgace for o/o William Laws	150
	"Laws 2nd Choice" tbc John Sturage for o/o	100

	William Laws	
William Cockshall	"Bacon Quarter" – not known	200
43:1748:111 ...		
Richard Russell for o/o Lawrance Young	"New Ireland" – not known	500
John Frizell	"Hungary Quarter" – not known	200
	"Island Marsh" – not known	50
James Knox	"Brothers Agreement" – not known	300
	"Long Expect" – from (N) Turpin; not known	50
Isaac Irenshaw	"Carpenters Enjoyment" tbc Mary Ironshire	150
William Collins	<unr>" – not known	200
	"Spences Lott" – from (N) Spencer; not known	200
William Jarman	pt. "Enlargement" – not known	200
	pt. "Winkfield" – from (N) Reynolds tbc John Purnall	100
43:1748:112 ...		
Simon Foskin	"Basing Stroke" tbc John Foskin	400
John Fancett [!]	"Inch" tbc: • John Steavenson – 350 a. • Franklyn Faucett – 150 a.	500
	"Onortons Lott" tbc Franklyn Faucett	300
Andrew Whittington	"Monmouth" – not known	50
h/o John Hewett	"Conveniency" tbc George Dashiell, Sr.	400
	"Convenience" – not known	13
	"North Wales" tbc Huett Nutter	200
Thomas Houlster	"Liverpoole" – not known	500
Leonard Johnson	"London Derry" tbc Leonard & John Johnston	500
43:1748:113 ...		
John Miller	"Partners Contention"	500
	pt. "Brents Marsh" – denied	100
h/o Alexander Macullagh	"Inch" – not known	200
h/o William Ingle	"Chance" – not known	100
Peter Parker	"Margeretts Rest" – not known	300
Phenix Hall	"Castle Fine" – denied	60
	"Doggsdome Bottom" tbc Elizabeth Hill (150 a.)	200
Peter Kellaway (cnp)	"Cockland" tbc Thomas Waller (50 a.)	246
	"Harrington" – not known	200

	"Little Brittain" – not known	200
	"Colloways Prevention" – not known	100
43:1748:114 ...		
Michaell Goddon	"Rochester" tbc Michaell Goddin	500
	pt. "Huntington" – denied	175
Woney McLaney	pt. "Spittlefields" tbc George Jones	265
Walter Evans	pt. "Powell Inclusion" tbc Gamage Evans	128
	"Neberry" – for h/o (N) Wouldhave; not known	230
	pt. "Cumberland" – for h/o (N) Wouldhave; not known	180
h/o Edward Williams	"Bettys Rest" tbc Mary Irinshire	100
John Holder	pt. "Coxs Fork" tbc Eben Handy	75
	"Chance" – not known	32
John Desharoon	"Friends Good Will" tbc William Haymond	200
	"Come by Chance" tbc John Disharoon	85
	pt. "Averys Choice" – from (N) Clifton tbc John Disharoon	150
	"Frizells Enjoyment" from John Disharoon	150
43:1748:115 ...		
Charles Taylor (VA)	pt. "Winter Pasture"	250
	pt. "Pharsalia" – from (N) Walters tbc John Walker	400
	pt. "Winter Pasture"	22½
John Blake	pt. "Winter Pasture" – not known	100
h/o Edward Green (ENG)	pt. "Winter Pasture" – not known	100
	"Partners Desire" – not known	300
	"Forlorne Hope" tbc George Truett	250
	"Partners Desire" – not known	300
	"Parkers Adventure" – not known	400
Robert Tirer	"Retirement" – not known	200
Richard Ashton	"Gladstrons Choice" – not known	150
Edward Shipham	"Oak Hall" tbc Jos. Jones	200
43:1748:116 ...		
Charles & Phill. Parker (VA)	pt. "Dummfrize" tbc Henry Jerman	323
	pt. "Brotherwood" tbc Henry Jerman	
John Freeman, Sr.	"Unpleasant" tbc Isaiah Bredall	140
	"Teags Content" tbc John Holloway	160

Jonas & Jonathan Woodman	"Palys Folly" – not known	200
Benjamin Aydelott	"Forrest of Dean" tbc Benjamin Aydelot	200
	"Adelotts Ignorance" tbc Benjamin Aydelot	200
	"Fancey" tbc Benjamin Aydelot	100
	"Forrest" tbc Benjamin Aydelot	150
	"Duckhead" tbc Benjamin Aydelot	150
	"Sand Reach" tbc Benjamin Aydelot	110
	"Pleasant Meadow" – included in "Joynt Meadow" tbc John Aydelot	500
	"High Meadow" – included in "Joynt Meadow" tbc John Aydelot	500
	"Good Success" tbc Benjamin Aydelot	300
	"Fairefield" tbc Benjamin Aydelot	442
	"Dead Cyprus Swamp" tbc Benjamin Aydelot	100
	"Great Swamp" tbc Benjamin Aydelot	200
43:1748:117 ...		
Thomas Huggett	"Carpenters Folly" – not known	190
	"Woolfs Denn" – not known	500
John Barron (ye Whore Kills)	pt. "Scarboroughs Adventure" – not known	250
David Hazard	"Midlesex"	500
	"David Lotts"	66
	"Hills Venture"	200
	"Chance" – denied	300
	"Hazard" – denied	200
	"Cornhill" – from (N) Cornwell tbc widow Brittingham	93
	"Cornhills Adventure" – from (N) Cornwell tbc widow Brittingham	50
	"Agreement" – from (N) Hickman	250
	"Vinkerpinns Hall"	100
William Millard	"Dennahoes Choice" – denied by his heir	207
	pt. "Conveniency" – from (N) Osborne; held by Mary Millard (his daughter), not setled	425
John Parsons, Jr.	"Elizabeths Choice" tbc John Leatherbury	200
43:1748:118 ...		
h/o John Rutter a/s Alexander Carlisle	"Tower Hill" – not known	150

h/o William Goldsmith	"Bears Denn" – not known	100
James Townsend	"Porters Discovery" tbc Elizabeth Townsend	232
	pt. "Dennoho's Second Choice" tbc Daniell Townsend	175
	"Freemans Discovery"	500
Charles Wharton	"Piney Heap" tbc Nathaniell Brumball	300
	"Chance" tbc John Dennis, Jr.	15
	"Whartons Folly" tbc Nehemiah King	100
Robert Whattson	"Grove" – denied	200
	"Lanes Chance" tbc Robert Watson	100
Gabarill Walters (VA)	"Refuge" – not known	160
43:1748:119 ...		
William Hall	pt. "North Petherton" tbc John Marsey	250
	"Halls Lott" tbc Jo. Hall	450
	pt. "St. Lawrances Neck"	183
William Stockley	"North Petherton" tbc William Evans	250
	"Great Neck" – from (N) Wallace tbc John Shockley	100
	pt. "Newtown" – of (N) Long tbc John Shockley	175
William Dickson	"Friendship" tbc: • Thomas Robertson – 250 a. • Sturgace Dixon – 250 a.	500
John Peter	"Lozange" – not known	100
William Bound	"Pombridge" – not known	300
Robert Perry	"Pontland Hills" – not known	170
43:1748:120 ...		
Henry Ackworth	"Friends Discovery" – charge this & 100 a. more	200
John Langford	"Chance" – denied	100
	pt. "Whetherlys Adventure"	100
h/o Maj. Peyton (Gloucester Co. VA)	"Cuckolds Delight" – not yet known	500
Abraham Ingram	"Poor Fields" – denied	150
	"Moor Fields" tbc Moses Gordie	130
	"Strife"	200
	"Peasleys Likeing"	100
	"Late at Night"	100
James Wilks	"Hendersons Chance" – not known	90

John Parramore	pt. "Mile End" – not known	75
	"Parramores Double Purchase" – not known	1500
43:1748:121 ...		
John Parker	"Cambridge" – not known	300
	"Wickenoughts Neck" tbc George Parker	400
	"Armenia" tbc Henry Jerman for o/o (N) Parker	400
	"Castle Green" from (N) Henry tbc Phillip & Charles Parker	300
Edward Day	"Days Beginning" tbc John Goddart	295
	"Cosx Discovery" – not known	745
	pt. "Dunkirk" – from (N) Marsh; not known	200
Martin Curtis	"Limsome" – not known	200
Hugh MacNeale	"Promise Land" tbc Absolom Foard	100
George Benstone	"Leather Land" – denied	150
	"Nap Hill" – not patented	100
	"Winter Quarter" – will give up the patent	50
	pt. "Painters Denn" – from (N) Connerly tbc William Stuart	100
	"Woolver" – from (N) Plunkett tbc George Benston	100
	pt. "Kendall" – from (N) Connerly tbc William Stewart	60
43:1748:122 ...		
h/o Thomas Ball	"Called What You Please" – not known	250
William Ailford	"First Lott" – not known	600
Rebecca Price (widow)	"Newberry" tbc: • Solomon Hitch for James Smith (orphan) – 150 a. • Alexander Price (orphan) – 150 a.	300
	"Prices Purchase" – not known	100
h/o Col. David Brown	"No Name" – denied; included in "Hachilah" tbc Thomas Brown	345
William Trayle (ENG)	"Chance" tbc William Lane	200
John Drayden	"Parkers Adventure" tbc Hannah Dreddon	300
	"Castle Fine" – from (N) Stevenson; denied	140
43:1748:123 ...		
Jacob Truett	"Bellfast" tbc: • Nehemiah Truett – 250 a. • George Truett s/o Job – 100 a.	300

George Phebus	"Littleworth"	200
Thomas Pollett	"Prestian" – denied	30
	"Smithfield" – from (N) Gray tbc Thomas Pullett	100
Robert Downes	"Beverly" tbc Robert Downs (NA)	150
	"Mitchells Choice" tbc Robert Downs (MU)	250
John Wheeler	"Troublesome" tbc William Polson	100
Cornelius Johnson	"Rotterdam" – not known	250
43:1748:124 ...		
Robert Caldwell	"Desart" tbc Robert Coldwell	250
	"Anything" tbc John Coldwell	100
	"Come by Chance" – lies in SU	380
Christopher Dasheild	"Downes Choice" – not known	62
Gaberall Cooper	"Bedford" from (N) Whetherly tbc Gabriell Cooper	500
Jeremiah Barenclough	"Peace" – not known	200
James Lammee	"Algate" – not known	150
David Shockley	"Scotch Inland"	300
43:1748:125 ...		
William Joseph	"Friends Endeavour" – not known	2700
James Hogg	"Shewells Addition" tbc: • James Murray – 100 a. • Thomas Forsith – 320 a.	420
William Broadwater	"Gordans Lott"	200
James Nevell	"Nevells Folly" – not known	200
John Perkins	"Winter Harbour"	150
Phill. Hunting for William Phillipson	"What You Will" – not known	200
h/o Chr. Thompson a/s Edmondson (VA)	"Thompsons Purchase" – not known	500
43:1748:126 ...		
George Parker (ACC)	"Walchett" – not known	90
	"No Name" – not known	600
	"Mattapony" – not known	390
	"Wickenoughs" – not known	600
William Ailward	"Aylwards Addition" – not known	100
	"Aylwards First Choice" – not known	425
Francis Heap	"Rotten Quarter" tbc Nathaniell Brumball	100

Thomas Ward for h/o (N) Price	pt. "Prices Conclusion" tbc: • John Riggan – 50 a. • Cornelius Ward – 100 a. • Thomas Ward – 150 a. • Samuell Horsey – 100 a.	200
	"Prices Vineyard" tbc Thomas Ward	200
	"Bear Neck" – from (N) Dukes; not known	10
William Layton	pt. "Laytons Recovery" – not known	200
James Breedy	pt. "Laytons Recovery" – not known	100
	"Wallaces Adventure" – from (N) Smith; notknown	200
43:1748:127 ...		
Richard Horsman	"Chance" tbc Henry Toadvine	140
William Hayman	"Polehamilton" from (N) Luckey tbc James Longer	100
	"Haymans Exchange" – from (N) Crouch tbc Thomas Gillis	100
John Clay	"Clays Adventure" – twice charged but one piece & is sold to Henry Toadvine; not conveyed; the heir not in province; land unsettled	160
	"Clays Adventure"	160
Dennis Driskell	"Kingsaile" tbc Moses Driskell	350
	"Dennis Addition"	100
	"Forked Neck" – from (N) Mclan	400
Thomas Potter	"Mitchells Choice" tbc Henry Potter	180
	"Sunken Ground" from (N) Dukes tbc Henry Potter	100
	"Owens Lott" – from (N) Owens; denied	100
Jos. Stanford	"Long Ridge"	125
	"Pleasure" – from (N) Vance	50
43:1748:128 ...		
Thomas Pryor	"Dixons Kindness"	100
William Curry a/s Thomas Phillips	"Haphazard" – not known	125
	"Midle Neck" tbc Samuell Davis	200
widow of Phillip Conner	"Rambling Point" tbc John Conner	10
Michaell Desharoon	"Brittain" tbc Edward Hilman	100
	pt. "Second Purchase" – from (N) Dasheild tbc Ann Disharoone	300
William Yaulding	pt. "Hounsloe" – not known	50
George Smith	"Bacon Quarter" – from (N) Parsons	200
43:1748:129 ...		

Lambrook Thomas	"Mill Lott" tbc Levin Gale	100
John Kellum	"No Name" – denied	300
	"Wing" tbc: • Jos. Holston for o/o (N) Kellum – 300 a. • John Bevans for o/o (N) Taylor – 300 a.	600
	"Kellums Choice"	300
	"Chance"	50
	"Addition"	100
Stephen Deer	pt. "Emmitts Discovery" – not known	160
Daniell Selby	"Coids Contrivance" tbc Richard Blizard	50
Capt. Edward Powell	"Powells Recovery" tbc William Holland	112
John Tarr	"Sonderdall" tbc: • Michaell Tarr – 175 a. • Samuell Hosier for o/o John Tarr – 175 a.	350
43:1748:130 ...		
Thomas West	"Wests Recovery" tbc George West	432
Timothy Harvey	"Timothys Choice" tbc Timothy Harney	240
Richard Covell	"Coveys Purchase" – not known	100
h/o Richard Hull (VA)	"Holdfast" – not known	400
John Cornwell	"Peterborough" – not known	50
Richard Penneck	"Weavors Portion" tbc George Pennywell	125
43:1748:131 ...		
John Getty	"Gettys Adventure" tbc James Collins	100
	"Maiden Lott" tbc John Gillis	300
	"Rich Ridge" tbc: • Thomas Gillis – 70 a. • George Oliphant – 30 a.	200
Samuell Turner	"Samuells Adventure" – denied	50
	"Turners Choyce"	68
Andrew Spearce	"Donningall" tbc Henry Spear	200
Robert & William Davis	"No Name" tbc: • Robert Davis – 300 a. • William Davis – 300 a.	600
	pt. "Adventure" – from (N) Adelott; supposed to be same as above	600
Andrew Derrickson	"Vines Neck" – not known	270
Peter Boddy	"Cannons Peace" – not known	100
43:1748:132 ...		

Charles Godfrey	"Alexanders Desire"	200
Andrew Dickason	pt. "Bable" – not known	150
Charles Cottingham	"Goshen" tbc Charles Cotingham	100
Owen Moses	"Moses Lott" – not known	100
John Norton	"Nortons Lott" – not known	180
	"Hoggs Northen" tbc John Onorton	180
John Willson	"Batchellors Choice" – not known	100
	"Williams Lott" – not known	50
	"Williams Lott" – not known	38
	"Batchelors Choice" – not known	100
43:1748:133 ...		
John Bivian	"Poyk" tbc John Bevan	100
	"Acquintico Savannah" tbc John Bevan	100
Andrew Bashaw	"Bashaw" – not known	100
Samuell Davis	"Beyond Expectation" tbc John Donaldson	220
	"Davis Neck"	150
David Dryden	"Davids Destincy" tbc David Dredden	100
widow Lowe	"Adventure" – not known	70
Charles Francklyn	"Long Acre" – not known	125
43:1748:134 ...		
John Freeman	"Freemans Lott" – not found	250
Jenkin Price	"Gliniah" – not found	400
	"Prengatessex" – not found	500
James Tolly	"Tollys Delight" – not found	700
Edward Dixon	"Contention" a/s "Dickstone" – not found	300
Mathew Armstrong	"Skippers Plantation" – not found	600
Ambros Crouch	"Crouches Choice" – not found	500
43:1748:135 ...		
Pursivell Read	"James Governour" – not found	200
Henry Sewell	"Wiccomo" – not found	1000
Henry Ellerey	"Ellereys Island" – not found	100
Richard Hacworth	"Hackworths Charety" – not found	600
George Whale	"Whales Island" – not found	150
Col. Edward Carter (VA)	"Revell Grove" – not found	1500
43:1748:136 ...		
William Whitefield	"Whitefield" – not known	300

Raymond Stapleford	"Staplefords Neck" – not found	250
Peter Kersey	"Tounsends Neck" – denied	150
	"Kerseys Industry" tbc Peater Kersey	300
Edward Price	"Prices Hope" – not known	200
Sampson Wheatly, Thomas Mattocks, & Phill. Conner	"Irish Grove" – not known	150
Cornelius Ward	"Bear Point" – not known; denied	200
43:1748:137 ...		
Daniel Curtis	"Curtis Improvement" – not known	150
William Furnis	"Chance" – not known	600
	"Furnis Adventure" – not known	200
John Mervill	"Locust Ridge" a/s "Humock" tbc Charles Polk	50
	"Marvells Chance" tbc Charles Polk	27
William Walters	"A Friends Choice" – not found	600
George Johnson	"A Friends Choice" – not found	1200
Arthur Brisco	"Briscoe Lott" – not found	600
43:1748:138 ...		
Thomas Gillis	"Do Better" – denied	1850
	"Bedlam Green" – from (N) Crouch	50
	"Haymans Exchange" – from (N) Hayman	100
	"Smiths Adventure" – from (N) Presly	500
	"Second Choice" – from (N) Presly	
	"Gillis Meadow"	100
Samuell Jackson	"Danbury" – denied; never patented	300
	"Partner Choice" – from (N) Keen	150
John Walker	"Friendship" – not known	500
Robert Richardson	"Mount Ephraim" tbc: • Thomas Purnell – 400 a. • William Nelson – 100 a. • Magdalane Victor – 100 a.	2000
Richard Robinson	"Robinsons Inheritance" – not found	1050
William Brittain	"Hastford Purchase" – Brittain dead by a fall from a horse; no relation or will	200
43:1748:139 ...		
Mathew Parker (Whore Kill)	"Kingsaile" – not known	150
Richard Lewis	"Stepney" – not found	150
Andrew Kellaway	"Recovery" – not found	288

Ambros Reggan	"Riggans Mine" tbc Peater Dickenson	100
Roger Phillips	pt. "Little Belean" – from (N) Shearman;not known	100
	pt. "Phillips Addition" – from (N) Shearman; not known	12½
Richard Shackly	"Chockleys Purchase" – not found	200
43:1748:140 ...		
Richard Jefferson	"Barren Quarter" – from (N) Wright; not known	25
William Marrutt for John Lyon	"Wales" – not known	50
John Crouch	"Forked Neck" – not known	300
Alexander Thomas	"Happy Enjoyment" – not known	144
William Godden	"Friendship" – not known	500
Robert Waples	"Colichester" tbc Ambros Riggen	150
Robert Pollock	"Bally Hack" tbc Jos. Polk	200
43:1748:141 ...		
John Conner	"Fathers Care"	50
James Truett	"Ryleys Portion"	200
William Bevans	"Bevans Chance" – not known	100
Thomas Roe	"Purgatory" tbc: • Thomas Roe – ½ • Jos. Roe – ½	75
James Poalk	"James Meadow" tbc David Polk	200
	"Green Pasture" tbc: • Edward Roberts – 100 a. • Henry Polk (who is not in the county) – remainder	200
Sylus Chapman	"Sylus's Chance" – not known	200
Abraham Heath	"Spittle" tbc Abraham Heath, Sr.	22
43:1748:142 ...		
William Walton, William Turvill, & Richard Holland	"Bald Beach" tbc: • William Turvill – 100 a. • William Walton – 100 a. • Richard Holland – 100 a.	450
Charles Nicholson	"Green Land" tbc Mathew Hopkins for Mathew Nicholson (orphan)	280
	"Poplar Ridge" tbc Jos. Nichols (80 a.)	160
Jos. McClester	"Beauty" – from (N) Dashield tbc Jos. Macclesther	600
	"McClesters Purchase" – from (N) Round; pt. "Years Land"	100

John Henry	"Henrys Addition" tbc Mary Hampton	50
	"Hopewell" – from (N) Berry tbc John Gibbans	300
	"Buck Land" – from (N) Mills tbc Mary Hampton	800
	"Pharsalia" – from (N) Paramore	100
	"Dickensons Hope" – from (N) Dickenson tbc Mary Hampton	134½
	pt. "Limbrick" from (N) Linsey tbc Mary Hampton	133½
	"Sherburn" – from (N) Hammond; denied	400
	"Friends Assistance" – from (N) Caldwell tbc Mary Hampton	300
	"Marys Lott Necessity" – from (N) Mills tbc Francis Jenkins called "Rehoboth"	<n/g>
	pt. "Highland" from (N) Mirch tbc Mary Hampton	<n/g>
Weacommocomis the Indian Queen, etc.	"Askeckstry" – not known	1000
43:1748:143 ...		
William Waples	"Hobbs Choice"	158
William Burton	"Chance"	340
	"Folly"	163
	"Trouble"	265
	"Hogg Ridge"	100
	"Panther Swamp"	100
	"Crooked Project"	200
	"Confusion"	200
	"Conclusion"	100
	"Marshy Point"	100
	"Rich Island"	150
	"Sneads Purchase"	310
	"Late at Night" – denied	60
	"Piney Neck" – denied	40
Daniell Wharton	"Daniells Luck"	75
Morris Morris	"Good Hope" – not known	100
Thomas Sluggs	"Sluggs Purchase" – not known	100
43:1748:144 ...		
Rev. Mr. Alexander Adams (cnp)	"DalSerfe"	195
	"Barrowfield"	75
	"Eastwood"	234

	<n/g> from John Goddin & uxor – charged in "Wallys Chance"	150
	"Fathers Care" – from (N) Walker	200
	pt. "Wallys Chance"	250
	pt. "Crambourne"	210
	pt. "Windsor"	100
	"Breretons Chance" – from (N) Brereton; denied	300
	pt. "Monmouth" – from (N) Goddard; included in "Wallys Chance"	60
	"Glascow" – from (N) Walker	500
	"Mile End" – from (N) Brereton; does not hold	300
	"Green Brimlaw" – from (N) Walker	200
	"Smiths Adventure" – from (N) Brereton	160
	"Maile" – from (N) Brereton; denied	250
	"Friends Denial"	50
	"Sana"	50
	"Glasgow Swamp"	300
	"Addams Purchase" – he took up	18
	"Smiths Adventure" – from (N) Brereton	140
William Lowe	"Lowes Purchase" – not known	100
Lazarous Kenny	"No Name" – "Oak Hall" should be charged to Richard Reynolds	100
	"Kennys Lott" – not known	200
Mark Kannaday	"Purchase" – not found	56
43:1748:145 ...		
William Pepper	"Luck" – not known	200
	"Folly" – not known	150
	"Safety" – tbc William Burton for o/o (N) Pepper	100
	"Peppers Delight" tbc William Evans	100
	"Peppers Lott" – not known	80
John Pearson	"Good Luck" tbc Robert Harris	40
Jonathan Raymond – not in the county	"Raymonds Chance"	69
	"2nd Choice" – from (N) Spence	15
Simon Kollock	"Good Hope" tbc Ebenezar Jones	150
Mark Webb	"Little Neck" tbc William Webb	100
Benjamin Johnson	"Johnsons Lott" – not known	150
43:1748:146 ...		

Mathew Hosua	"New Dublin" tbc Mathew Hosea	100
Jos. Direckson	"Streights Mouth"	100
	pt. "Bable"	150
William Freeman	"Freemans Choice" – not known	100
John Wharton	"Whartons Adventure" tbc Frances Wharton	150
	"Luck" tbc Frances Wharton	100
Robert King	"Good Luck"	320
	"Piney Island"	10
	"Barbados"	300
	"Johns Towne" – from (N) Johnson; charged in "Conclusion"	300
	"Streights" – from (N) Johnson; charged in "Conclusion"	600
	"Everdines Lott" – from (N) Kennerly; charged in "Conclusion"	500
	"Double Purchase" – from (N) West	214
	"Addition to Collins Adventure" – from (N) Wales	420
	"South Foreland" – from (N) Jarrett	50
	"Double Purchase" – from (N) Wills	79
	"Cross" – from (N) Roe	30
	"Partners Choice" – from (N) Kenney	150
	"Downes Lott" – from (N) Foxen	200
	"Closure" – from (N) Cattlin	66
	"Conclusion"	1500
	"Timber Tract"	280
43:1748:147 ...		
Solomon Tilghman	"Gideons Luck" – not known	100
John Bradford	"Johns Lott"	50
Edward Clarke	"Richard Ridge" tbc Thomas Roberts	50
	pt. "Fenwicks Choice"	350
Phillip Quinton	"Phillips Priviledge"	100
	pt. "Houstons Choice" – from (N) Brittingham	75
	pt. "Houstons Choice" – from (N) Thorowgood tbc: • Phillip Quinton – 25 a. • remainder – denied	75

Robert Martin	"Carlascrak" tbc James Martin	200
	"Ryans Chance" tbc: • James Martin – 200 a. • Mathew Rain – 100 a.	300
	"Desart" tbc James Martin	11
	pt. "Snow Hill" – from (N) Dale tbc James Martin	200
	pt. "Snow Hill" – from (N) Murry tbc James Martin	100
43:1748:147 [!] ...		
James Bouger	"Johns Folly" tbc Francis Bougher	55
Elizabeth Townsend	"Townsends Choice" – denied	60
	"Hoggs Neck" – denied	40
James King	"Poor Choice" – not known	50
Rachell Powell	"Rachells Lott" – not known	33
John Murray	"Exon" – from (N) Glass	250
	"White Oak Swamp" – denied; not patented	40
William Carey	"Williams Chance" tbc Levin Carey	100
	"Mount Pleasant" – from (N) Richards tbc Jonathan & Thomas Carey	150
43:1748:148 ...		
John Coodry	"Coodrys Beginning" – denied	100
Samuell Owen	"Fellowship" – not known	200
William Gray	"Grays Adventure"	110
	"Greens Chance" – from (N) Gray tbc John Sheldon for William Gray (orphan)	125
	"Herring Swamp" tbc William Gray (NA)	50
Daniell McClester	"Oak Grove" tbc Daniell Macclesther – in the West Indies some years	200
	"McClesters Inheritance" – in the West Indies some years	88
James Boucher	"Camp Neck" tbc Frances Bougher	50
Thomas Maddux	"Cow Quarter" tbc Thomas Maddox (AN)	160
	"Ruscommend" – from (N) Conner tbc Thomas Maddox (AN)	100
43:1748:148 [!] ...		
William Dunahoe	"What You Will" tbc William Porter (150 a.)	250
	"Sams Designe" – not known	100
John Fleming (cnp)	"Unity"	20
	"Hogg Harbour" – denied; not patented	80

	"Flemings Purchase" – from (N) Denson	150
James Deale	"Cassell Hill" tbc John Dale	200
Bridget Kirk	"Bridgetts Lott" tbc Littleton Tounsend	100
John Cobb	"Cobbs Purchase" tbc William Cobb	50
Teauge Dennahaw	"Swine Harbour" tbc Teague Donohoe	50
	"Bacon Hill" from (N) Smith tbc Teague Donohoe	200
43:1748:149 ...		
James Chadwick	"Chadwicks Adventure"	50
William Marle	"Marles Privelidge" – not known	70
	"Hoop Rich" – not known	30
Robert Wood	"Temple Hall" – not known	500
John Gilliard	"Kitten" tbc John Gilleland	100
Edward Chapman	"Chapmans Choice" – not known	100
Thomas Jones	"Hogg Pallice" – not known	100
	"Golden Quarter" – not known	50
	"Chance" – not known	150
43:1748:150 ...		
Capt. John Ryder	"Three Brothers" tbc John Rider (DO)	136
	pt. "Stannaways" – from (N) Barclay tbc Alexander Addams	160
	pt. "St. Albans" – from (N) Barclay tbc Alexander Addams	140
Mary Hampton	pt. "Conveniency" – from (N) Dickenson tbc John Henry	134½
	pt. "Dickensons Hope" – from (N) Dickenson	125½
	"Goose Marsh" – from (N) Dickenson	50
	"Cow Marsh" – from (N) Dickenson	50
	pt. "Golds Delight" – from (N) Mathewson	50
	"Sisters Gift" – from (N) King; included in "Buckland"	200
Southy Whittington (cnp)	"Snow Hill Landing"	2
	"Hope Still"	220
	pt. "Emmissex" – from (N) Sommers	84
	"Little Worth" – from (N) Sommers	100
	"Choyce" tbc: • Southy Whittington – 1750 a. • Solomon Tounsend – 200 a.	1950

	"Adventure" tbc Jos. Poarter	150
	"Goshen"	340
Robert Weir	"Increase" – not known	350
John Huffington	pt. "Cambridge" – from (N) Gordon tbc John Hufington	95
	"Huffingtons Adventure" – denied	100
43:1748:151 [!] ...		
James Parramore	"Purchase"	50
	"Wetherlys Purchase" – from (N) Wetherly	300
	"Parramores Folley" – denied	50
Samuell & Robert Owens	"Gosherne" tbc Manuell Manlove guardian to c/o Samuell Owens	100
	"Owens Chance" tbc: • Robert Owens – 50 a. • c/o Samuell Owens – remainder	100
Robert Hasting	"Betty Margery"	50
Ambros Willett	"Willetts Discovery" tbc Moses Watson	50
William Hackman	"Old Castle" tbc William Hickman, Sr.	50
	"New Castle" – from (N) Langerell tbc William Hickman, Jr.	175
	"Fair Meadow" – from (N) McClester tbc William Hickman, Sr.	700
Jacob Messex	"Pasturidge" tbc: • Nehemiah Messex – ½ • Jacob Messex – ½	45
43:1748:152 ...		
John Colloway	"Coley Folly" tbc John Calloway	50
William Bozman	"Agreement" tbc: • Richard Hickman – ½ • David Hazard – ½	500
Alexander Lackey	"Contention"	556
Thomas Waller	"Parish"	100
	"Pleasant Green" tbc Thomas Waller	100
William Owens	"Williams Adventure" tbc William Polk	64
	pt. "Smiths Hope" – from (N) Phillips tbc William Polk	100
	"Owens Venture"	100
	"Owens Security"	140
Mathew Raine	"Green Land"	200

43:1748:153 ...		
Edward Kellum	"Tower Hill"	100
	"Cambridge" – from (N) Hovington	205
Jacob Ingram	"Ingrams Lott" tbc Josephus Potter for Jacob Ingram (orphan)	50
	"Gummhill"	50
	"Jacobs Ridge"	50
John Massey	"Dorseys Quarter"	100
Charles Tindall	"Stones"	50
Samuell Tindall	"Assekitons Neck" tbc John Smith	50
Joseph Timmonds	"Content" – not known	30
43:1748:154 ...		
James Nicholson	"Kings Dale"	100
Robert Nearn	"Nearns Addition" tbc James Nairn	87
	pt. "Neighbourhood" – from (N) Walton; denied	350
Moses Driskell	"Cow Quarter" tbc John Ruark	50
Sarah Davis	"Hopewell" – not known	50
James Perry	"Towne Hill"	100
	"Dunns Improvement"	200
John Wooten	"Chance" tbc John Wootten	50
43:1748:155 ...		
Edward Wooten	"Inclosed" tbc Edward Wootten	100
Joseph Houlstone	"Flatt Lands"	100
	"Hogg Penn Ridge"	40
James Taylor	"Hogg Quarter" tbc John Bivane	50
Isaac Stutt	"Smiths Pollicy" tbc Archibald Stutt	75
John Lynch	"Adventure"	200
Peter Claywell	"Lanes Survey" tbc Peater Claywell	230
	"Reads Conveniency" – from (N) Owens; denied	100
	"New Yarmouth" – from (N) Russell tbc Peater Claywell	200
43:1748:156 ...		
Richard Carey	"Refuge" tbc John Magrah	50
John Muney	"Woolf Pitt Ridge" tbc James Macdaniel	115
Benjamin Easom	"Benjamins Good Success" – not known	16
	"Easoms Chance" – not known	34

Joseph Kennerly	"Discovery" – from (N) Planner tbc Sarah Beauchamp	150
Henry Miles	"Harts Ease" – from (N) Coleburn	400
	pt. "Marsh Ground" – from (N) Bannister	50
	"Miles Choice" – taken by older survey	77
Thomas Billins	pt. "Entrance" – from (N) Stevens tbc Thomas Billings (305 a.)	355
43:1748:157 ...		
John Fowler	pt. "Leadburne" – from (N) Heath; not known	150
Thomas Beauchamp, Jr.	pt. "Contention" – from (N) Beauchamp;not known	50
William Beauchamp	pt. "Hogg Yard" – from (N) Beauchamp; not found	<n/g>
	pt. "First Choice" – from (N) Beauchamp;not found	<n/g>
David Treharne	pt. "Dixons Lott" – from (N) Wilson tbc James Traehairne	100
Joseph Langford	"Vulcans Vineyard" – from (N) Cottingham	86
William Cox	"Waterford" – from (N) Davis	450
	"Anglesey" – from (N) Davis	100
43:1748:158 ...		
John Davis	"Undue"	300
	"Troublesome"	250
	"Cow Quarter" – denied	1150
	"Davis's Choyce" tbc John Davis (WI)	50
Charles, Randall, & William Revell	"Double Purchase" – from (N) Revell tbc: • Randall Revell – 170 a. • Charles Revell – 233 a.	1000
Stephen Odeer	pt. "Amity" – from (N) Furnice tbc Steaphen Odear	196
Patrick Dayley	"Windsor Castle" – from (N) Webb tbc Patrick Daley	200
Nathaniell Brittingham	pt. "Line Lott" – from (N) Brittingham; not known	35
	pt. "Exchange" – from (N) Brittingham; not known	35
Jonas Smith	pt. "Johnsons Lott" – from (N) Johnson	75
	pt. "Johnsons Lott" – from (N) Lynch	75
43:1748:159 ...		
Daniell Long	pt. "Prevention"	10
	pt. "Purchase"	
	"Fathers & Sonns Enjoyment" – taken by elder survey	<n/g>

William Mills	pt. "Suffolk" – from (N) Morris	200
	pt. "Winter Quarter" – from (N) Whittington; denied	100
	"Something Better than Nothing" – from (N) Tripshaw	75
John Twyford	pt. "Fitchfield"	100
	pt. "Fairham"	
	"Prickly Pear Island" – denied	5
	pt. "Fairham" – twice charged; denied	50
	pt. "Fitchfield" – from (N) Bennett; twice charged; denied	50
James Dahaughty	"Long Ridge" – from (N) Sullivan tbc Daniell Hull	135
Francis Land	"Puzzle" – from (N) Ward; not known	150
43:1748:160 ...		
Randall Long	"Hoggs Humock" – from (N) Dukes	208
	"Chance" – he took up	103
Mary Pryor, Jr. & Sr.	pt. "Bear Neck" – from (N) Linsey tbc John White	52
Robert Scott	"Bear Neck" – from (N) Dickenson	52
	"Conveniency" – from (N) Spence tbc Robert Scott (MA)	100
	"Friends Assistance" tbc Robert Scott (MA)	200
David Adams	"Partners Agrement" – from (N) Cottingham tbc David Addams	200
Jonathan Cottingham	"Vulcans Vineyard" – from (N) Cottingham;denied	72
	"Worton" – from (N) Smith	200
43:1748:161 ...		
Thomas Hayward	"Haywards Dear Purchase" tbc Thomas Howard	240
	"Profitt" tbc Thomas Howard	250
	"Houstons Choice" – resurveyed for you & Quinton; includes 75 a. from (N) Quinton tbc: • Thomas Howard – ½ • Phillip Quinton – ½	160
Samuell Moore	pt. "<t> Peace" – from (N) Martin; not known	60
Samuell Mayo	"Neighbours Goodwill" – from (N) Rowland tbc Samuell Mayhew	200
John Phipps	"Good Neighbourhood" – from (N) Kellum	200
Lewis Jones	"Hope"	100

Elizabeth Gray	pt. "Greens Chance" – from (N) Gray tbc James Tounsend	125
43:1748:162 ...		
John Magoe	"Coxes Choice" – from (N) Wooton; not known	300
John Shoars	"Whittys Lott" – from (N) Knox, etc.	50
Thomas Wright	"Long Lott" – from (N) Langrell	50
	<n/g> from (N) Robinson – charged to him elsewhere	100
	<n/g> from (N) Sloughton – charged to him elsewhere	50
Charles Dean	"Gladstones Industry" – from (N) Rawley	170
William Sasser	"Roody" – from (N) Sasser tbc Alice Saucer	200
	"Newport Pagnell" – from (N) Sasser tbc Alice Saucer	50
John Handy	pt. "Belean" – from (N) Hutchinson	317
43:1748:163 ...		
Robert Harris	"Chance" – from (N) Woolford	300
	"Heath Quarter" – from (N) Heath	100
	"Little Worth"	50
Edmund & William Smullen	"Harmsworth" – from (N) Woolford tbc Joseph Riggen	150
Stephen Bayley	"Fatters Quarter" from (N) Booth tbc Robert Knox	186
George Gale	"Hereafter" tbc: • Levin Gale – 200 a. • remainder – denied; no more in patten	700
	"Ralphs Prevention" – from (N) Ralph tbc Levin Gale	9
	"Carys Choice" – from (N) Carey tbc Betty Gale	164
	"Mothers Care" – from (N) Mattux; included in "Addition" & tbc Betty Gale	300
Timothy & Anthony Kennedy	"Midle Neck" – from (N) Walker; dead; 2 orphans, one with Michaell Disharoone, the other with John Disharoone	400
William Sloughton	"Adventure" – from (N) Bozman tbc James Robertson	200
	"Chance" – from (N) Wallis	50
	"Peters Neck" – from (N) Wallis	100
	"Adventures Amendment" tbc James Robertson	37
43:1748:164 ...		

John Cottman	"Nobles Lott" – from (N) Noble tbc Jos. Cotman	73
John Leatherbury	pt. "Tinson" – from (N) Noble tbc: • John Leatherbury – 150 a. • William Sulavine – 50 a.	200
	"Discovery" – from (N) Layton tbc: • Thomas Taylor – 100 a. • Jacob Morris – 200 a.	300
	"Partners Choice" – from (N) Elgate tbc John Moor	150
John Goddart	"Windsor" – from (N) Goddart; denied	150
William Vaughan	pt. "Merches Hope" – from (N) Nesham tbc William Vaughn	115
	pt. "Rich Swamp" – from (N) Nesham tbc William Vaughn	
Margarett Green	"Meays Choice" – from (N) Humphrys tbc Richard Greene	200
Thomas Dellahyde	pt. "Gloucester" – from (N) Richards tbc: • George Baley – 75 a. • Sarah Baley – 75 a.	180
43:1748:165 ...		
Patrick McDowell	pt. "Glocester" – from (N) Muleay; not known	70
John Richards	pt. "Cow Quarter" – from (N) Welburn tbc John Records	150
John Odeer	"Wolf Pitt Ridge" – from (N) Chambers;not known	115
John Cornish	"Ignoble Quarter" – from (N) Shiels tbc Thomas Shiles	300
Solomon Wright	pt. "Mary Lott" – from (N) Ballard	200
John Carr	pt. "Pembertons Good Will" – denied	100
43:1748:166 ...		
Thomas Bashaw	pt. "Hoggs Downe" – from (N) Jarratt tbc Jacob Coadry	170
Giles Bashaw	pt. "Hoggs Downe" – from (N) Jarrett tbc: • Gerard Bashaw – 100 a. • Thomas Goslin – 50 a. • Robert Hardy – 50 a.	225
George Scott	"Sunken Grounds" – from (N) Day tbc Day Scott	149½
Abraham Turner	pt. "Sunken Grounds" – from (N) Round; not known	350
Madam Betty Gale (cnp)	pt. "Robinsons Lott" – from (N) Robinson tbc Levin Gale	30
	"Addition" – from (N) McClester tbc John Gale	713

	<n/g> from (N) Crouch tbc Thomas Cary	300
	"Fathers Bare" tbc Levin Gale	250
Timothy Broomly	"Newberry" from (N) Griffin tbc Christian Broomley	150
	pt. "Teauxbury" – from (N) Griffin tbc Christian Broomley	100
43:1748:167 ...		
Edward Shurman	pt. "Meeches Hope" – from (N) Booth tbc John Collins for Thomas Shurman (orphan)	150
	"Bettys Choice" – from (N) Wood	200
Fran. Lancake	"Come by Chance" – from (N) Heath tbc: • George Langcake – 117 a. • Frances Langcake – remainder	317
	pt. "Suffolk" from (N) Heath tbc George Langcake	83
	"Georges Folly" tbc Frances Langcake	47
John Larramore	pt. "Wolf Quarter" – from (N) Furbush	50
James Adams	"What You Please" – from (N) Askew tbc James Chadwick (50 a.)	150
	"Carlife" from (N) Fittsgarrett tbc James Chadwick	100
George Clifton	"Ascews Choice" – from (N) Ascew; not found	150
Edward North	"Phillips" – from (N) Dunston tbc John North	100
	"Addition" – from (N) Dunston tbc Edward Chambers	50
43:1748:168 ...		
James Dickenson	pt. "Conveniency" – from (N) Layfield	165
John Griffith	"Little" – from (N) Layfield tbc William Booth	160
	"Tonn" – from (N) Layfield; not known	100
William Hearne	"Stains" – from (N) Layfield tbc: • William Hearn – ½ • Thomas Hearn – ½	850
	pt. "Harrisons Adventure" – from (N) Harrison; denied	200
Mary Jenkins	pt. "Conveniency" – from (N) Layfield tbc Mary Hampton	100
Samuell Marchment	pt. "Convenient" – from (N) Jenkins tbc Mary Hampton	100
Robert Mills	"Adventure" – from (N) Brittingham	400
43:1748:169 ...		

Daniell Lingoe	pt. "Pembertons Good Will" – from (N) Stevens; not known	100
	pt. "Plumbton Salt Ash" – not known	100
Richard Harris	pt. "Lott" – from (N) Harris tbc James Durham	200
Arthur Parkes & Thomas Summers	"Pitchcraft" a/s "Smiths Island" tbc: • Arthur Parks – 75 a. • Aaron Fogg – remainder	150
George Sharpe	pt. "Hogg Neck" – from (N) Crouch tbc George Sharp	100
Peter Samuells	"Forked Neck" – from (N) Hopkin tbc Richard Samuells (200 a.)	300
	"Samuells Adventure" tbc Andrew Collins	59
	"Samuells Folly" tbc Peater Samuells	44
Isaac Handy	"Pemberton" – included in "Pemberton" below	900
	"Whittingtons Choice" from (N) Pemberton	300
	"Pemberton"	970
43:1748:170 ...		
William Lane	"Chance" from (N) Whittington	200
Peter Bodine	pt. "Jeshimon" tbc Peater Bodine	150
	pt. "Batchellors Adventure" tbc Peater Bodine	100
	pt. "Bently" tbc Peater Bodine	150
	pt. "Covent Garden" tbc Peater Bodine	100
	pt. "Supply" tbc Peater Bodine	375
Jonathan Noble	"Hachilah" – from (N) Noble tbc David Dredden	200
William Bozman s/o George	<n/g> from William Bozman s/o John tbc William & George Bozman	442
George Bozman	pt. "More & Case It" tbc George Bozman (200 a.)	350
John Bozman, Jr.	pt. "More & Case It" – denied	200
43:1748:171 ...		
William Bozman s/o John	<n/g> from William Bozman s/o George tbc William Bozman	158
James Robertson	<n/g> from William Bozman	420
Edward Wootten	"Houns Ditch" – from (N) Bozman tbc: • Edward Wootten – 300 a. • James Cooper – 117 a.	417
William Henderson	pt. "Barnabys Lott" tbc Solomon Tull	100
Henry Newnam	"Marys Adventure" – from (N) Magraugh	40
	"Newmans Vineyard" – he took up	50

Mary Fountaine	"Newfound Land" tbc Nicholas Fountain, Sr.	20
	"Benson Lott" – from (N) Davis tbc David Wilson	120
	"Fishing Island" – from (N) Lane tbc Nicholas Fountain, Sr.	20
43:1748:172 ...		
John Dorman	"Dormans Chance" – from (N) Dorman	100
John Hailes	"Elliotts Improvement" – from (N) Dorman; denied	200
William Bannister	pt. "Marsh Ground" – from (N) Davis tbc Thomas Bannister	50
William Munrow	"Wood Land" – from (N) King; not known	150
Ralph Milburne	pt. "Dales Adventure" – from (N) Tilghman tbc John, Ralph, & Caleb Milburn	200
	"Desire" tbc John, Ralph, & Caleb Milburn	13
Aaron Tilghmand	"Small Hopes" – from (N) Tilghman tbc Aaron Tilghman	100
John Owens	"Golden Quarter" – from (N) Polk	150
43:1748:173 ...		
Easter Murray	"Friends Choice" tbc Easther Murray	30
Visitors of the Free School	"Smiths Recovery" – from (N) Evans	199
Hugh Macoagin	"Turkey Cock Hills" – from (N) Docum; not known	125
Nathaniell Davis	"Conveniency" – from (N) Macall	100
William Kender	"Gulletts Asshurance" – from (N) Gullett; not known	100
Robert Atkins	"Magdelins Choice" – from (N) Highway	100
Owen Connerly	"Panters Denn" – from (N) Smith; not known	100
43:1748:174 ...		
Esau Merrill	<n/g> from Joshua Merrill	45
Rachell Andrews	pt. "Golden Lyon" – from (N) Rigin; not known	100
Alexander Wordie	"Chuckatuck" from (N) Layfield tbc Robert Gaddes	1000
Francis Allen	pt. "Strand" – from (N) Lane	275
	"Porters Island" – included in "Sarahs Security" tbc Jos. Poarter	50
Donnock Dennis, Jr.	pt. "Smiths Folly" – not found	200
Jacob Waggaman	"Kings Neck" – for William Whittington	400
43:1748:175 ...		
Patrick Connelson	pt. "Pharsalia" – from (N) Caldwell; not known	50
Phillip Gravener	"Bass Legg" – from (N) Jenkins; 150 a. in patent tbc Thomas Gravenour	250

Robert Gibbs	pt. "Hudsons Purchase" – from (N) Wroth tbc Thomas Dashiell, Sr.	100
John Merrill	"Little Towne"	300
William Wheatly	pt. "Greenfield" – not known	62½
William Wood	"Allens Contest"	100
43:1748:176 ...		
William Adams	pt. "Minshalls Adventure" tbc: • Phillip Addams – 200 a. • William Addams – remainder	325
George Adams	pt. "Minshalls Adventure" tbc George Addams	125
Edward Martin	pt. "Snow Hill" from (N) Bishop tbc James Martin	100
	"Dumfrieze" tbc James Martin	200
Hugh Porter	"Clain Fasting" tbc Francis Poarter	100
Mary Gray	"Mount Hope" – from (N) Freeman; not known	100
William Jenkins	pt. "Winter Quarter" – from (N) Mills; not known	200
43:1748:177 ...		
Samuell Brittingham	pt. "Stanlys" – from (N) Holston tbc John Brittingham	250
Samuell Gillett	pt. "Kingsland" – from (N) West tbc Samuell Gillet	200
Abraham Lamberton	pt. "Carters Lott" – from (N) Timmons	100
	"Broad Ridge" – not patented	100
John Bradford	"St. Martins Desart" – from (N) Tounsend	300
James Harris	pt. "Harrisons Adventure" tbc Jeremiah Harris	150
Richard Knight	"Harrisons Adventure" – from (N) Harris tbc Richard Knight (350 a.)	300
43:1748:178 ...		
Samuell Taylor	pt. "Harrisons Adventure" – from (N) Lewis; not known	100
	"Shocklys Purchase" – from (N) Shockley tbc John Maccuddey	200
Christopher Glass	pt. "Partners Choice" – from (N) Hopkins; charged below as "Glass Security"	250
	pt. "Rochester" – from (N) Godin tbc Addam Bell	50
	pt. "Castle Hill" – from (N) Taylor; denied	120
	"Glass Security"	250
Randall Smullen	"Goshen" – from (N) Winn & (N) Baker tbc: • Ambros Rigen – 150 a. • Randall Smullen – 150 a.	300

William Mister	pt. "Pitchcroft" – from (N) Evans	100
Theod. Berry	"Winter Quarter" – from (N) Brittingham tbc Thomas Lambdon	135
Robert Melvin	pt. "Bradshaws Purchase" – from (N) Broughton	50
43:1748:179 ...		
James Burnett	pt. "Wooton Underidge" – from (N) Benstone	50
Mathew Purnall	"Ravenstone" – from (N) Hammond	400
	"Shafsbury" – from (N) Hammond	700
	"Shearbourne" – from (N) Hammond	400
Thomas Slinger	"Lansdowne" – from (N) Hammond	200
David Dennis	pt. "Good Success" – from (N) Purnall; not known	150
Nathaniell Ennis	pt. "Killkenny" – from (N) Murphy tbc Richard Manklin	200
Richard Macklin	pt. "Killkenny" – from (N) Ennis; same land as above in Nathaniell Ennis account	200
43:1748:180 ...		
Edmond Hough	pt. "Lock" – from (N) Dane	250
	"Dull Folly" – from (N) Murry	500
	"Addition" – from (N) Murry	85
	"Houghs Purchase"	100
Edward Jones	pt. "Aberdeen" – from (N) Sangster	200
John Templin	pt. "Aberdeen" – from (N) Sangster	100
John Doberly	"Westchester" – from (N) Millian tbc Thomas Doberly	200
Patrick Guttery	pt. "Castle Hill" tbc Patrick Guttry	43½
David & Samuell Acworth	"Acworths Purchase" tbc Samuell Ackworth	300
43:1748:181 ...		
Robert Bowdwick	"Ackworths Folly" – from (N) Ackworth tbc Solomon Hitch (50 a.)	300
William Farrington	"Pasteridge" – from (N) Twilly tbc: • Robert Givans – 7 a. • William Farrington – remainder	50
	"Wetherlys Purchase" – from (N) Twilly	225
	pt. "Slipe"	25
Temperance Traine	pt. "Slipe" – from (N) Wetherly tbc James Train	25
Patrick Donnellson	"Flowerfield" from (N) Givean tbc James Anderson	165
John Huett Nutter (cnp)	pt. "Sheilds Choice" – from (N) Jones; not known	<n/g>
	pt. "Dormans Delight" – from (N) Jones;not known	<n/g>

	pt. "Nutters Adventure" – from (N) Jones; not known	25
	"South Wales" – not known	200
Abraham Taylor	pt. "Wetherlys Contrivance" – from (N) Ackworth	150
	"First Choice"	100
43:1748:182 ...		
Stephen Tully, Jr.	pt. "Fairham" tbc Steaphen Tully	78
	pt. "Ægipt" tbc Steaphen Tully	82
Timothy Roades	"Stevenson" – from (N) Tully tbc Timothy Rhoads	85
George Langerell	pt. "Shadwell" tbc Richard Dunn	100
William Hanglin	pt. "Stannaway" – from (N) Evans tbc Edward Fowle called "Evans Purchase"	140
John Phillips	"Stannaway" – from (N) James; denied	100
Robert Henderson	"Turn Stile" – from (N) Robinson; not known	300
43:1748:183 ...		
Richard Ryder	"Midfield" – from (N) Abbott tbc Heathly Rider	200
	"Westlocks Adventure" tbc Wilson Rider	200
Jane Hasely	"Warrington" – from (N) Givean tbc Thomas Smith	200
Richard Dunn	pt. "Cannons Lott" – from (N) Fluelin; sold to David Evans; Evans is dead, no heirs nor will; not conveyed	50
John Hopkins	"Cannons Lott" – from (N) Johnson tbc John Hopkins, Sr.	100
	"Hopkins Gift" – from (N) Samuells tbc John Hopkins, Jr.	140
	"2 Brothers" – denied	200
Charleton Smith	"Glascow" – from (N) Gordon tbc: • John Collins – 150 a. • John Smith – 150 a.	300
Thomas Mervill	"Gladstones Adventure" – from (N) Elzey tbc Thomas Marvill	150
	"Hardshift" tbc Thomas Marvill	200
43:1748:184 ...		
William Moore	pt. "Partners Choice" tbc Richard Phillips for an orphan (unnamed)	150
Phill. Richards	pt. "Partners Choice" – from (N) Keen; not known	100
William Hurly	"Rumly Marsh" – from (N) Robertson; not known	200
William Veazey	pt. "Burmudas Hundred" – from (N) Veazey; not known	100

Moses Duskey	"Golden Quarter" from (N) Hall tbc Moses Driskell	100
William Adelott	pt. "Batchellors Adventure" – from (N) Holland tbc William Aydelot	150
	"Durdam Downe" tbc William Aydelott	77
	"Little" tbc William Aydelott	30
43:1748:185 ...		
Joseph Morris	pt. "Morgans Choice" – from (N) Johnson tbc Thomas Robertson	50
	pt. "Rochester" – from (N) Johnson tbc Thomas Robertson	200
Comfort Ayres	"Penny Purchase" – from (N) Scarbrough tbc John Ayres	200
Joseph Pope	pt. "Durham House" – from (N) Jarman tbc Thomas Claywell	200
John Atkinson	pt. "Long Island" – from (N) Hopkins	100
	"Coopers Purchase" – from (N) Sturgoe; denied	200
Nehemiah Holland	"Dublin" – from (N) Selby tbc Benjamin Holland	300
Thomas Bayley	pt. "Newport Pagnell" – from (N) Hall; not known	375
43:1748:186 ...		
Nathaniell Crapper	"Providence" – from (N) Hamblin tbc Nathaniell Cropper	125
Mathew Patrick	pt. "Reserve" – from (N) Selby; not known	100
Thomas Preston	pt. "Spring Quarter" – from (N) Robertson tbc William Booth	300
Jacob Kellock	"Happy Entrance" from (N) White tbc Jacob White	400
Sarah Tull	"Hopewell" – from (N) Tull; not known	75
William & Edward Bowen	"Deale" – from Elizabeth Bowen tbc: • Elizabeth Adkins – 200 a. • Samuell Truett – 200 a.	600
43:1748:187 ...		
John Hampton	"South Benfleet" – from (N) Spence tbc Mary Hampton	500
	"Fair Meadow" – from (N) Spence tbc Mary Hampton	334
	"Hogs Norton" from (N) Morris tbc Mary Hampton	200
Vestry of Allhallowes Parish	pt. "Highfield" – from (N) Pointer	72
	pt. "Huntington" – from (N) Johnson	213
William Simpson	pt. "Teauxbury" – from (N) Evans	100
	pt. "Kelly Hill" – from (N) Roberts	100

Henry Alexander	pt. "Golden Quarter" – from (N) Taylor; not known	100
	pt. "Ripple" – from (N) Taylor; not known	
George Taylor	pt. "Golden Quarter" – from (N) Hill; not known	200
	pt. "Ripple" – from (N) Hill; not known	
	"Goodwill" – not known	50
Isaac Brittingham	"Conclusion" from (N) Schofield tbc Richard Tull	146
	"Husbands Forrest" – from (N) Schofield tbc Richard Tull	54
	pt. "Jones Adventure" – from (N) King	250
43:1748:188 ...		
John Onorton	pt. "Cadar Neck" – from executors of (N) Whittington	127
	pt. "Diggs Point" – from (N) Rumsey	165
Charles Collins	"Charles Choice" – from (N) Patrick; not known	100
Isaiah Breedell	"Olivers Portion" – from (N) Madux	150
William Ennis	pt. "Carradie" – from (N) Ennis	100
	"Chance" now called "Ennis Addition"	100
Robert Pointer	"Spalding" from (N) Harminson tbc Robert Lonton	100
	"Fathers Care" – from (N) Harminson; not known	109
John Records	pt. "Fenwicks Choice" tbc John Records, Jr.	150
	pt. "Newington Green" for your self & (N) Tull tbc John Records	250
	"Good Luck" – not known	40
	"Records Delight" – not known	100
43:1748:189 ...		
William Records	pt. "Diggs Point" – not known	150
James Munford	pt. "Mulberry Grove"– from (N) Godden tbc James Mumford	100
William Patten	pt. "Rochester" – from (N) Glass; not known	50
	pt. "Rochester" – from (N) Goddin; not known	150
James Thompson	pt. "Sturbridge" – from (N) Bowen; not known	50
Robert Hall	pt. "Head of St. Laurences Neck"	183
Archibald Deale	pt. "Red Land" – from (N) Davis	150
43:1748:190 ...		
Stanton Addkins	"Woolfs Denn" from (N) Truett tbc Stanton Adkins	100
David Desharoon	"Frizells Enjoyment" – from (N) Bashaw tbc John Disharoon	150

Richard Bretherd	"Contentment" – from (N) Green	150
Robert Hedge & Lodowick Fleming	"Sandowne" – from (N) Fosken tbc Robert Hoddg (250 a.) – John Lay married Lodowick Fleming's widow & has his children with him but will not pay the rent of 250 a. of "Sandowne" which belongs to them.	500
	"Chance" – from (N) Richardson tbc Robert Hoddg	100
	"Chance" – he took up tbc Robert Hoddg	100
Alexander Merriday	"Mathews Adventure" – from (N) Dickerson tbc Alexander Macreddy	135
Devoria Drygoose	pt. "Cornhill" – from (N) Cornwell tbc David Johnson	75
	"Cornhill Addition" – from (N) Cornwell tbc David Johnson	
43:1748:191 ...		
Samuell Tull	pt. "Denwoods Denn" – from (N) Hill	150
Ebenezar Handy	pt. "Coxs Fork" – from (N) Holder	75
	"Holdens Chance"	65
William Olivin	pt. "Coxs Fork" – from (N) Desharoon; not known	150
Skinner Wallop	pt. "Winter Pasture" – from (N) Taylor tbc Charles Taylor	18
John & Dennis Martiall	pt. "Winter Pasture" – from (N) Waggaman; not known	33
Dorothy Parker	pt. "Dumfrize" – from (N) Hurtly; not known	217
	pt. "Brotherhood" – from (N) Hurtly; not known	
43:1748:192 ...		
William Evans	pt. "North Petherton" – from (N) Johnson	250
Robert Taylor	"Friends Assistance" – from (N) Cropper; not known	200
Thomas Smith	pt. "Mile End" – from Edward Wright	75
	pt. "Troublesome" – from (N) Wheeler tbc William Polston	100
Edward Whitty	pt. "Mile End" – from (N) Parramore tbc William Wheatly	75
Paul Whaples	"Piney Point" – from (N) Parker	500
	"Swamp in Fellowship" tbc: • Paul Whaples – 50 a. • John Smith – 50 a. • (N) Bevans – 50 a.	150
	"Abigalls Chance"	200

James Cathell	"George Purchase" – from (N) Benson	100
	"Cathells Venture" – took up by John Haymond	50
43:1748:193 ...		
John Shehan	"Marlborough" – from (N) Wheeler tbc John Shehane	150
James Nobles	"Delaps Choice" – from (N) Porter tbc Nathaniell Mills	100
Abraham Lewin	"Walbrook" – from (N) Evans; not known	260
William Lingoe	"New Holland" – from (N) Curle tbc: • John Kersey – 100 a. • John Perdue – 100 a. • Edward Maglamry – 150 a. • Richard Lingoe – 100 a. • widow Lingoe – 150 a.	600
John Cotton	"Quiett Entrance" from (N) Coldwell tbc John Gray	100
Bryan Suice	"Point Patience" – from (N) Dashield tbc Samuell Hall	143
43:1748:194 ...		
Andrew Scott	"Coldwell Lott" – from (N) Coldwell tbc Richard Wallace, Jr.	200
Thomas Hovington	"Bakers Folly" – from (N) Baker	150
John Robertson	"Inlands Eye" – from (N) Nicholson	300
James Hayman	"Hopewell" tbc James Haymond	350
James Stevenson	"London Derry" – from (N) Spence tbc James Steavenson	200
Charles Cottingham & Randall Long	"Rambling Point" tbc: • Randall Long – ½ • Charles Cottingham – ½	90
43:1748:195 ...		
William Sasser	"Hounslow" – from (N) Soser tbc Alice Saucer	50
	"Woolf Harbour" – from (N) Soser tbc: • Alice Saucer – 50 a. • John Hall (Kent on the Delaware) – remainder	100
John Kerter	pt. "Golds Delight" from (N) Gold tbc John Carter	50
George West	pt. "West Recovery" from (N) West	68
	"Long Acre"	50
John Newbold	"Bashan" – from (N) Muire; denied	300
	"Holly Head" tbc John Newbald	100

David Evans	"Barren Neck" – from (N) Higgens; Evans dead without heirs in MD	100
Boaz Walton	"Goshen" – from (N) Revell tbc Boaz Walstone	100
43:1748:196 ...		
Archibald Still	"Dear Lott" a/s "Dear Quarter" – from (N) Smith tbc Archibald Stutt	160
Joseph Ward	"Come by Chance" – from (N) Davis	100
Stephen Handy	"Williams Hope" a/s pt. "Perth" – from (N) Robertson tbc Thomas Hayward	260
Darby Regan	pt. "Chocklys Purchase" – from (N) Shockly tbc Darby Riggen	200
Thomas Vincent	"Cockland" – from (N) Jefferson	200
Thomas Warrington	"Bevans Choice" – from (N) Bevans tbc Thomas Worthington	100
43:1748:197 ...		
Cæsar Godden	pt. "Hunting Quarter" – from (N) Stockley	100
George Lane	"Golden Mine" – from (N) Stockley tbc James Wonnell	200
Sarah Morris	pt. "Hunting Quarter" – from (N) Brereton tbc William Morris	1001
Hannah Derickson	"Daniells First Choice" – from (N) Wharton; not known	100
Bevan Morris	"Turtle Swamp" – from (N) Wharton	78
Gabariell West	"Good Luck" – from (N) Kenny tbc Richard Reynolds	64
	"Little Neck" – not known	60
43:1748:198 ...		
Rebecca Brittingham	pt. "Exchange" – from (N) Brittingham; not known	115
Richard Newnam & William Powders	"Clarks Lott" – from (N) Clark tbc William Whaley	100
Joseph Jones	"Nine Pin Branch Neck" – from (N) Martin tbc William Swain	100
William Harrison	pt. "Rachells Lott" – from (N) Powell	100
Charles Dashield	"Lodogate Hill" – from (N) Robertson	100
	"Whittys Contrivance"	100
	"Fathers Purchase"	100
	"Mount Alexander"	105
	pt. "Ignoble Quarter"	32
43:1748:199 ...		

Thomas Waller	"What You Please" – from (N) Kellaway tbc William Calloway	50
William Taylor	"Roundpoon" – from (N) Hoffington	100
William Argoe	"Choice" – from (N) Enderwood tbc Alexander Ergoe called "Coxes Advice"	200
Angell Atkinson	"Atkinsons Adventure" – from (N) Atkinson tbc: • James Atkinson – 50 a. • Angelo Atkinson – remainder	200
John Beauchamp	"Well Wisht" – from (N) Beauchamp; not known	100
43:1748:200 ...		
Betty Boston	"Bostons Purchase" – from (N) Boston tbc Hope Taylor	100
Samuell Boarman	pt. "Sligoe" – from (N) Tull; not known	80
Abigall Coleburne	½ "Fathers Care" – from (N) Coleburne; not known	250
Edward Davis	"Davis Change" – from (N) Harmanson & is: • 70 a. of "Cumberland" • 50 a. of "Silver Street"	120
Edmond Evans	"Evans Purchase" – from (N) Berkley; not known	<n/g>
43:1748:201 ...		
Edward Fowler	"Evans Purchase" – from (N) Twyford tbc Robert Austin for o/o (N) Fouler	140
Ezekiall Green	"Ennalls Frolick" – from (N) Ennalls	150
Alexander Hall	"Bellandrett" – from (N) Polk	150
Edward Hull	"Well Wisht" – from (N) Beauchamp; pt. of "Leadburn"	100
Elioner Handy	"Handys Beginning" – from (N) Cox tbc Ebenezar Handy	300
43:1748:202 ...		
William Horsey	"Sarahs Joy" – from Sarah Horsey; pt. "Double Purchase" tbc: • Nathaniell Horsey – 300 a. • John Horsey – 200 a.	500
Stephen & Elizabeth Hopkins	"Bettys Lott" – from (N) Samuells tbc Stephen Hopkins (60 a.)	68
William Health	"Leak" – from (N) King tbc William Heath (50 a.)	150
	"Hogg Ridg" tbc William Heath	50
Giles Jones	½ "Gann" – from (N) Griffith; not known	100
Ebenezar Jones	"Peppers Chance" – from (N) Chollick	150
	"Jones Neck" called "Jones Chance"	96

43:1748:203 ...		
Joan Kellum	"Dickasons Quarter" – from (N) Kirk; not known	100
William Kibble	"Kibbles Assurance" – from (N) Stevens; denied	270
James Kelly	"Landing" – from (N) Henderson; not known	120
James Linsey	"Linseys Purchase" – from (N) Russell; not known	200
	"Linseys No Name" – not known	<n/g>
Fran. Lane – lost at sea	"Dennis Adventure" – from (N) Dennis; not known	100
	"Friends Assistance" – not known	100
43:1748:204 ...		
John Larramore	"Priveledge" – from (N) Furbus; 50 a. in patent	500
Edward McGlammery	"Contrivance" – from (N) Keen; not found	300
John McCarty	"Labelly Castle" – from (N) Glass; not known	100
Thomas Marvell	"Hardship" – from (N) Phillipson	200
Daniell & Alexander Manlove	"Woolfe Harbour" – from (N) King tbc Alexander Munrow	150
43:1748:205 ...		
George McGlammery	"Huggs Purchase" tbc Joseph Murphy	100
Thomas Newton	"Breeding" – from (N) Pepper	200
William Nelson, Jr.	"Castle Lowe" – from (N) Nelson tbc William Nelson	50
Bar. Outoridge	"Mothers Care" & "Brothers Good Will" – from (N) Horsey tbc John Outerbridg	200
John Williamson	"Davis Branch" – from (N) Blades; not known	40
	"Adventure" – from (N) Blades; not known	100
43:1748:206 ...		
Elias Pointer	"Brothers Gift" pt. "Highfield" – from (N) Pointer	172
Ann Phillips	"New England" – from (N) Samuell; not known	16
John Scarbrough	"Scarbroughs Castle" pt. "Durham House" – from (N) Scarbrough	900
John Scott	"New Glascow" – from (N) Dennis	300
	"Dennis Purchase" – from (N) Dennis; charge 500 a.	400
Joseph Tillman	"Tillmans Purchase" – from (N) Williamson; not known	200
43:1748:207 ...		

Benjamin Tull	pt. "Sligoe" – from (N) Davis; denied	80
	"Tulls Purchase" – from (N) Harmonson & is: • 50 a. of "Silver Street" • 70 a. of "Cumberland"	120
Archibald White	"Tully Brisk" – from (N) White	118
Mary & Martha Woolford	<n/g> from Thomas Woolford tbc Samuell Wilson	<n/g>
Randall West	"Brothers Conveniency" – from (N) West; not found	<n/g>
John Breedy	pt. "White Chapple" – not known	<n/g>
43:1748:208 ...		
Samuell Ball	"Conveniency" – from (N) Gattey tbc: • William Duer – 75 a. • Potter Shehe – 50 a.	<n/g>
Edward Clift	"Adventure" from (N) Dukes tbc Thomas Hayward	60
	pt. "Blakes Hope" tbc Edward Clough	200
Richard Drummond – not in the county	<n/g> – from (N) Drummond	700
Richard Kibble	"Fairefield" – from (N) Stevens; denied	165
Samuell Mellson	"Partners Choice" – from (N) Robinson tbc Samuell Melson (250 a.)	150
	"Poplar Ridg" – he took up; tbc Samuell Melson	150
43:1748:209 ...		
Henrietta & Ann Bonluc – no heir	"Prestons Addition" – lies in forrest of Wicomoco	125
Thomas Benson	"Bensons Lott" – denied; tbc Edward North called "Addition"	50
Samuell Derickson	"Vines Neck" tbc: • George Howard – 230 a. • Joshua Robertson who married the widow – remainder	711
Josias Wroughton	"Lazey Hill" – he says 85½ a. in patent & charge Josas Roughton (35½ a.)	35½
John Harvey	"Wattsons Folly"	50
43:1748:210 ...		
Edmond Huggins	"Johnsons Folly" – not known	50
Dingett Gray	"Maiden Choice" tbc Dinget Gray	100
John Williams	"Williams Lott"	200
James & William Weatherly	"Weatherlys Marshes" – not found	136
John Tilghman	"Tilghmans Lott" tbc Rose Tilghman	50

43:1748:211 ...		
Samuell Taylor	"Golden Purchase"	80
Ralph & Charles Tindall	"Poole Thickett" tbc: • Charles Tindall – 50 a. • John Scott (not yet conveyed) – remainder	100
Daniell Sherridon	"Sherridons Desire" – not known	20
John Sherly – not in the county; gone to Carolina	"Smiths Chance"	300
Edward Roberts	"Edwards Lott"	220
43:1748:212 ...		
James Round	"Jacobus Addition"	40
Andrew Collins	"Teauges Folly" tbc Mary Collins	150
Patrick Carsey	"Beaver Damm" tbc Patrick Kersey	50
Joshua Edge	"Good Luck" tbc Joshua Eddge	50
	"Batchellors Folly" tbc Joshua Eddge	50
Job Jarman	"Nine Pinn Neck" tbc Jobe Jarman	50
43:1748:213 ...		
Mathew Givan	"Purchase" – not known	32
Erasmus Harrison	"Lott" – not known	100
Benjamin Houston	"Houstons Lott" tbc James Noble, Jr.	100
Jeremiah Hailes	"Ivey Neck" tbc: • William Robertson – ½ • Hannah Hails – ½	300
John Harris	"Lott" tbc Giddeon Tilghman	100
43:1748:214 ...		
Thomas Darsey	"Littleworth"	100
Walter Darby	"Batchellors Chance"	50
Cornelius Dickenson	"Cornelius Choice"	25
Samuell Mayhew	"Mayhews Lott"	60
William Fassett	"Second Adventure" tbc William Faucett, Sr.	173
	"Pleasant Grove" tbc William Faucett, Sr.	250
	"Meadow" tbc William Faucett, Sr.	100
43:1748:215 ...		
Phillip King	"Kings Luck" tbc William Oliphant	50
Pendall Long	"Come by Chance" – not known	103
John Nicholson	"Johns Folly" – not found	100

Charles Polk	"Charles Purchase" – denied	100
	"Charles Adventure"	50
	"Polks Priveledge"	50
	"Second Purchase"	400
William Planner	"Security" tbc: • Janet Dougherty – 70 a. • Elizabeth Owens – 70 a. • Watt (Negro) – 10 a.	150
43:1748:216 ...		
William Planner	"Security" – see f. 215	150
William Pointer	"Pointers Ignorance" tbc Isaiah Bredall	150
Joseph Weat	"Weats Humour"	100
Sarah King & Jos. Wails	"Sarahs Security" tbc Jos. Poarter	350
Abraham Outon	"Outons Security" pt. "Partners Choice" tbc: • Jonathan Sturgace – 58 a. • Abraham Outon – 192 a.	250
43:1748:217 ...		
Christopher Godfrey	"Godfreys Security" tbc Charles Godfrey	250
Thomas Nairn	"Narons Security" tbc Robert Nairn	250
John & Lewis Desharoon	"Nantwick" – denied; tbc William Venables	300
Francis Willson	"Long Lookt for"	48
	"Habb Nabb"	216
Levin Gale	"Supplye"	365
43:1748:218 ...		
Samuell Griffeth	"Griffiths Choice" – not known	50
Aaron Lyne	"Aarons Folly"	150
	he holds land name not known tbc Aaron Lynn	250
Mathew Young	"Youngs Second Chance" – not known	50
James Winson	"Winsons Choice" tbc James Vincent	125
Henry Toadvine	"Arabia"	200
43:1748:219 ...		
John Tatum	"Tatums Habitation"	40
Thomas Taylor	"Taylors Adventure"	100
John Sharpe	"Midsfield" tbc h/o Isaiah Quaturmus	50
	"Sharps Grove"	100
James Pollock	"White Oak Swamp" tbc David Polok	100
Jos. Parramore	"Ryans Cove" tbc Edward Calloway	50

43:1748:220 ...		
George Oliphant	"Georges Choice" tbc John Magdowell	50
	"Drumany"	50
John Morris	"Morris Second Addition"	87
John Langsdale	"Langsdale Purchase"	100
	"Woodstock"	50
George Langcake	"Francis Solomon" tbc: • George Langcake – ½ • Solomon Wright – ½	100
William Kenny	"Third Choice"	50
43:1748:221 ...		
Stephen Kenny	"Kennys Luck" – not known	50
Patrick Kersey	"Eagles Point"	40
Isaac Ingram	"Horse Head" tbc Mary Ingram	100
	"Sheep" – from (N) Mill tbc Abraham Ingram	50
Francis Haynes	"Hains Grove"	50
James Groome	"Poor Chance" tbc James Groom	100
43:1748:222 ...		
Henry Cimey	"Cimeys Desire"	50
Roger Woolford	"Woolford" tbc John Woolford	900
James Lindowe	"Dispute" – included in "Turners Purchase"	40
Patrick Caldwell	"Good Luck" tbc: • Patrick Coldwell – 36 a. • George Dashiell, Sr. – remainder	100
John McGlarlin	"Macglarlins Chance"	50
43:1748:223 ...		
Thomas Pridix	"Spring Garden" – not known	400
John Outerbridge	"Colbourn" – from (N) Horsey	250
John Anderson	"Friends Discovery" – not known	30
Tunstall Hack	pt. "Pembertons Good Will" – from Peter Hack; denied by John Tunstall guardian to Tunstall Hack	250
Lazarus Windsor	"Woolwidge"	150
43:1748:224 ...		
Jos. Caldwell	"Friends Denyall"	300
	"Kirk Minster"	200
James Wonnell	"Hunting Quarter" – denied	100

John Finch	"Diep" – denied by (N) Finch; tbc Abraham Heath, Sr. (150 a.)	300
	pt. "Shipwayes Choice"	100
William BowLand	"Dublin" tbc: • William Bowland or Bowler – 97 a. • Alexander Chain – remainder	125
Thomas Lambden	pt. "Barren Lott"	57
43:1748:225 ...		
Thomas Langford	pt. "Good Will"	100
David Smith	"Givans Last Choice"	200
William Dashield	"Yeare Land" tbc: • John Collins – 75 a. • Jos. Bounds – 37½ a. • William Dashiell – 37½ a.	150
	"Runsell" tbc William Dashiell	120
Nehemiah Messick	pt. "Illinsworths Hope"	50
Thomas Coffin	pt. "Powells Lott" tbc William Holland	343
43:1748:226 ...		
Roger Taylor	pt. "Temple Comb"	100
Littleton Bowen	pt. "North Benflitt" tbc Thomas Purnall	200
Thomas Goddart	pt. "Eagle Point" – not known	150
Neale McClester	"White Chapple"	300
John Messick	pt. "Rotterdam"	150
43:1748:227 ...		
John Turner	"Turners Choice"	150
John Hoffington, Jr.	"Youngs Purchase"	150
	"Barren Quarter"	250
Ahab Costin	pt. "Harmsworth" tbc Isaac Costin	150
Henry Benston	pt. "Hounds Ditch"	83
James Martin	pt. "Partners Choice"	250
43:1748:228 ...		
Elisha Purnell	pt. "Partners Choice"	250
Alexander Lynch	pt. "Friends Assistance"	300
Thomas Hobbs	"Hobbs Adventure"	100
Robert Ingram	"Night"	50
William Booth	"Nottingham" – not found	12
Arthur Cunningham	"Second Choyce"	80

George Waller	"Wallers Choyce"	100
43:1748:229 ...		
Jos. Adkins	"Chance" tbc Richard Walton	190
Thomas Stevens	"Forrest Chance"	100
William Ralph	"Good Luck at Last" tbc: • William Ralph – 100 a. • Thomas Parramore – 50 a.	150
	"Anything" tbc Ebenezar Collins	50
James Oneale	"Rum Ridge" tbc James Neal	100
Thomas Johnson	"Johnsons Delight" – not found	50
Dennis Morris	"Careys Project"	100
Phil. Wingate	"Hickory Ridge"	50
43:1748:230 ...		
Edward Wright	"Wrights Choyce" – not found	100
Henry & William Benston	"Turtle Ridge" tbc William Benston	50
	"Loot for Henry" tbc Henry Benston	50
George Fisher	"Fishers Fancy"	100
Daniell Davis	"Bottle Ridge"	50
Samuel Neilson	"Poplar Ridge" tbc Samuell Melson	150
John Oneale	"Snow Hill"	100
Thomas Gray	"Grays Purchase" tbc Mary Anderson for Mary Gray (orphan)	100
Adkins Mercey	"Adkins Lott"	100
43:1748:231 ...		
Joseph Miller	"Troy Towne" tbc John Miller	200
Michael Terrey	"Chance" tbc Michall Tarr	60
Daniell Darby	"Long Ridge" – not known	50
Job Sherman	"Jobs Lott"	100
Alexander Draper	"My Fortune"	300
43:1748:232 **<blank>**		

51:1755:1 ...		**Acres**
Smith Horsey	pt. "Coulbourn"	108½
	"Yoarkshire Island"	190
	"Horseys Venture"	40
	pt. "Smiths Island", pt. "Yorkshire Island", pt. "Prices Conclusion", pt. "Pissommon Hemmock" – included in above lands	150
h/o John Horsey	pt. "Double Purchase"	200
Capt. Thomas Williams	"South Lott"	200
	"Williams Adventure" (17 a. taken by elder survey)	83
	pt. "Williams Conquest"	228
	"Cheap Price"	725
	"Double Purchase"	150
	"Winter Harbour" pt. "Dixons Lott"	150
	"Eastern Bounds"	100
	"Chance"	36
	"Security"	150
	"Woodstock"	50
	pt. "Dixons Lott"	50
	"Sunken Ground" pt. "Ackham"	256
	"Last Choice"	344
Thomas Tull	"Boston"	89
	"Goshen"	100
	"Troublesom"	24
51:1755:2 ...		
Capt. John Waters	"Teagues Down"	16
	"Teagues Addition"	78
	"New Rumney"	43
	"Salem"	490
Richard Waters (cnp)	pt. "Waters River"	525
	"Flat Land"	840
	"Friends Kindness"	116
	"Conveniency"	80
	"Londons Gift"	50
	"Partners Desire"	125
	"Security"	53

	"Miles's Choice"	77
	"Schoolhous Ridge" tbc Joshua Hall	98
William Waters	"Waters River"	452½
	"Peach & Pine"	50
	"Wilsons Lott"	20
	"Bear Ridge"	49
Benjamin Langford	pt. "Boston Towne"	180
	"Golloway"	150
	"New Brittain"	50
	"Discovery Inlarged"	64
	pt. "Watkins Point"	33
51:1755:3 ...		
Abraham Outton	"Webly"	130
	"Discovery"	116¾
	"Outtons Addition"	125
	"Wairpoint Inlarged"	134
	"Irish Grove"	27½
	"Discovery"	58⅓
Benjamin Cottman	pt. "Boyces Banks"	32½
George Wilson	"Security"	243
	"Wilsons Folly" – unknown	50
Richard Hall	pt. "Halls Choice"	148
	"Halls Adventure"	249
	"Halls Hammock"	50
	"Halls Pasture"	50
John Wilson	"Hogg Ridge"	100
51:1755:4 ...		
Joshua Tull	"Harrisons Adventure" – owner unknown	50
	"Desart" a/s "Tulls Purchase"	154
	"Winter Range"	200
	"Meadow"	50
	"Hopwell"	37½
	"Addition"	100
Lazarus Maddux	"Lazarous's Lott"	641
John Summers	pt. "Emesex"	108
	"Musketo Creek"	200

Jacob Cullen	"Johnstons Lott"	137
	"Point Next the Worst"	25
	"Haphazard"	6
William Catlin	"Hartford Broad Oak"	290
	"Branford"	44
	"Catlins Venture"	50
	"Catlins Lott"	21
51:1755:5 ...		
William Maddux	"Whitefield"	350
Alexander Maddux	"Whitefield"	350
h/o Charles Curtis	"Armstrongs Lott"	66½
	"Curtis's Lott"	75
Samuel Handy	"Armstrongs Lott" – owners unknown	50
	"Last Choice" – owners unknown	10
	"Bear Ridge" – in dispute	200
	"Londons Adventure"	25
	"Jericho"	100
	"Handys Choice"	175
	"Stephens Meadow"	188
	"Stake Ridge"	10
	"Black Ridge"	16
	"Strugle"	200
	"Small Lott"	8
	"Loss & Gain"	40
David Bird	"Hills Folly"	150
51:1755:6 ...		
Daniel Maddox	"Barnabys Lott"	6
	"Security"	310
Stephen Horsey, Sr.	"Welipcuant" – in dispute; was sold to Stephen Cannon by another name	600
	"No Name" – taken by elder survey	500
	"More Worth"	24
	"Cow Quarter"	105
	"Double Purchase"	401
	"Horseys Fancy"	150
	"Horseys Down"	150

John Cottingham	"Boston"	154
	"Rumling Point"	15
Jessee Lister	"Boyces Banks"	100
	"Addition"	40
Thomas Linsey	"Boston"	8
	"Cheasmans Chance"	40
	"Mumford"	92
51:1755:7 ...		
James Gunby	"Meadow"	100
	"Kirks Purchase"	200
	"Gunbys Venture"	75
Randal Revell	"Double Purchase"	330
Sarah Tompson	"Welcom" pt. "Double Purchase"	51⅓
h/o Thomas Bannester	pt. "Double Purchase"	127
	"Woolf Harbour"	150
	"Bears Chance"	15
	"Low Lands" – surveyed 18 October 1749	100
Isaac Holland for h/o William Furnis	"Fair Spring"	300
	"Pools Hope"	100
51:1755:8 ...		
Seward Tomblinson	"Manloves Lott"	44
	"Venture"	100
	"Linseys Green"	25
Thomas White	"Adams Gardin"	100
	"Littleworth"	53
Isaac Adams	"Adams First Choice"	208
	"Kings Lott"	204
	"Adams Gardin"	42
William Tayler	"Haphazard"	125
James Furnice	"Brothers Agrement" pt. "Amity"	200
	"Sumthing Worth"	44
51:1755:9 ...		
Michael Hollond	"Increase" – taken by elder survey	50
	"Pomfrett"	127
	"Ferry Bridge"	100
William Coalbourn	"Pomfrett"	918

Thomas Moor	"Mitchells Lott" now called "Fathers Gift Securd"	75
John White	"Damquarter"	110
	"Oxford"	100
	"Friends Content"	135
	"Fathers & Sons Desire"	33½
James Covington	"Mannings Resolution"	150
51:1755:10 ...		
Daniel Jones	"Coxes Choice" – taken by elder survey	80
	"Mannings Resolution"	400
	"Jones's Purchase"	127
	pt. "Sweet Wood"	100
Mary Jones	"Mannings Resolution"	250
	"Jenkins Mistaken"	163
Whittey Turpin	"Barnabys Lott"	10
	"Poyk"	60
	"Furniss Choice"	300
	"Good Luck"	22
	"Flint Situate"	50
Capt. John Jones	"Accompson" – land unknown	150
	"Jones's Chance"	331
	"Downs Choice"	62
h/o Thomas Covington	"Covingtons Choice"	150
51:1755:11 ...		
Edward Roberts	"Newfound Land" – taken by elder survey	125
	"Ellits Choice"	50
	"Edwards Lott" & "Jeshimon"	270
	"Green Pasture"	200
	"Polks Meadow"	200
	"Roberts Recovery"	100
	"Davids Distoney"	50
	"Venture Previledge"	100
	"Edwards Chance"	100
Capt. Robert Jones	"Jones's Choice"	350
Whitty Macclemmey	"Colebrook"	350
h/o Absolem Hoobs (cnp)	"White Oak Swamp" – denied, owner not in the county	100

	"Hamans Chance"	50
	"Chance"	100
51:1755:12 ...		
Mary Benston	"Westlocks Neck"	300
h/o John Waller	"Wallers Adventure"	300
	"Friends Advice"	45
	"Locust Ridge"	50
	"Marvells Chance"	27
	"Front of Locust Hammock"	75
	"Wallers Inlett"	64
h/o John Williams	"Roberts's Lott" – land unknown	100
	"Charles' Adventure"	140
Maj. Day Scott	"Cypriss" – taken by elder survey	18
	"Ackham"	392
	"Last Choice"	6
	"Manmoth"	300
h/o Thomas Walker	"Cascoway"	50
	"Last Purchase"	548
51:1755:13 ...		
Purnaell Johnston	"Spences Choice"	125
	"Friends Choice"	115
h/o Mathew Kemp	"Gettisemany"	300
	"Levins Grief" – surveyed 23 May 1751	12
John Polk	"Good Luck"	100
Isaac Mitchell	"Amity"	200
Charles Ballard	"Hazard"	400
	"Covingtons Meadow"	100
51:1755:14 ...		
h/o Thomas Winder	"Lime Hous" – land unknown	40
	"Whitteys Latter Invention"	200
	"Debtford"	100
	"Kickatans Choice"	300
Christopher Piper	"Barbers Rest"	150
	"Barbers Addition"	50
	"What You Please"	58

William Cannon in right of his wife	"Vulcans Vineyard"	161
	"Nicholsons Lott"	
h/o John Hardy	"Orphans Lott"	136⅓
James Mackmurray	"Whitteys Invention"	300
	"Whitteys Latter Invention"	100
51:1755:15 ...		
Benjamin Vennables	"Goslins Lott" – land can't be found in office records	50
	"Mile End"	75
	"Wilsons Lott"	100
	"Mile End"	150
	"Western Fields"	1400
	"Bells First Choice"	200
	"Little Massaley"	200
h/o John Goslin	"Goslins Lott" – land can't be found in office records	50
	pt. "What You Please"	50
Thomas Humphriss	"Keens's Lott"	150
	"Green Hill"	25
Joshua Humphriss	"Keens Lott"	150
	"Green Hill"	25
Nicholas Row	"Purgotory"	37½
51:1755:16 ...		
William Brereton	"Smiths Adventure"	67
	"Breretons Chance"	360
	"Mile End"	250
Daniel Wailes	"Beaverdam" – denied; in possession of PA people	100
	"Good Luck" – land unknown	150
	"Tosator"	150
	"Fortune"	100
	"Might Have Had More"	50
	"Josephs Lott"	58
	"George Priviledge"	50
Thomas Willin (cnp)	"Hogg Quarter"	25
	"Whitteys Contrivance"	50
	"Handys Pasture" pt. "Miles Folly"	175

	"Turnstile"	70
	"Hickory Ridge"	76
	"End of Strife"	5
h/o Graves Boarman	"Ralphs Venture"	100
	"Giles Purchase"	17
	"Good Suckuss"	50
h/o Benjamin Cottman	"Berks" – land unknown	150
	"Coxes Discovery"	100
51:1755:17 ...		
Joshua Caldwell	"Maidenhead"	300
	"Caldwells Chance"	27
	"Balley Buggan"	190
	"Purchase"	134
	"Anything"	100
	"Bear Swamp"	16
Perkins Vennables	"Little Belean"	200
Elgit Hitch	"High Suffolk"	141
	"Comby Chance"	173
Benjamin Cottman	"Tauntin Deane"	114
	"Shurmans Land"	30
Thomas Holbrook	"Harrington"	200
	"Previledge"	106½
	"Last Vacancey"	60
51:1755:18 ...		
Grace Wallis	"Friends Acceptance"	95
	"Father & Sons Desire"	51½
	"Damquarter"	40
Jonathan Baley	"Rich Ridge"	100
	"Baleys Lott"	50
	"Pleasant Green"	50
William Harris	"Lott"	452
h/o John Crouch	"Hogg Neck"	100
John Christopher	"Monsham" – taken by elder survey called "Horseys Baliwick"	100
	"White Chappel Green"	50
51:1755:19 ...		

Thomas Denwood	"Weatherleys Chance"	90
	"Brownstone"	300
	"Denwoods Inclusion"	21
Barnaby Williss	"Barnabys Lott"	44
	"Good Luck"	15
	"Littleworth"	6
h/o John Magraw	"Owens Improvement"	150
	"Owens Delight"	100
	"Middle"	100
	"Refuge"	50
Mary Fountain	"Fountins Lott"	150
	"Normondy"	25
	"Newfound Land"	10
	"Marsh Ground"	55
	"Fishing Island"	10
Massey Fountin	"Fishing Island"	10
	"Marsh Ground"	55
	"Neighbours Agreement"	41
	"Newfound Land"	10
51:1755:20 ...		
Abraham Hath	"Carlisle"	100
	"Chadwicks Adventure"	50
	"Welth"	13
	"End of Strife"	37
Nehemiah Dorman	"Nelsons Choice"	70
	"Dormans Purchase"	150
	"Shipways Choice"	22½
	"Dormans Priviledge"	30
	"Dormans Addition"	104
	1 lot in Princess Ann Town – No. 14	<n/g>
Mathelias Hobbs	"Abbington"	1100
	"Corneys Chance"	100
	"Cumberland"	40
John Rigsby	"St. Peters Neck"	620
Jos. Allen (cnp)	"Marsh Ground" – owner unknown	33½
	"Sligoe" pt. "Little Belain"	270

	"Fortune"	60
	pt. "Smiths Folly"	100
51:1755:21 ...		
Maj. John Elzey	"Almoadington"	900
William Ballard	"Almoadington"	300
Gidean Tilghman	"Gideans Luck"	50
	"Williams Hope"	60
	"Tilghmons Care"	62
	"Plague without Profit"	143½
Whittington King	"Kings Chance" – land unknown	300
	"Chance"	90
	"Webly"	250
Thomas Laws	"Greenwich"	50
	"Northforlend"	200
	"Laws Defence"	90
	"Selfe Preservation"	29
51:1755:22 ...		
William Miles	"Desart"	100
	"Chance"	23
	"Fair Meadow"	109
	"Chance"	35
Mathew Goslin	"Sligoe" pt. "Little Belain"	50
William Turpin s/o John	"Totness"	250
	"Grays Improvement"	10
	"Long Lookt for" pt. "Daviss Choice"	175
	"Adventure"	100
	"Hors Hammock"	100
	"Fathers Care"	40
	"Loss & Gain"	44¼
	"First Choice"	39¾
	"Boyces Banks"	67½
Nehemiah Crockit	"Adventure"	26
	"Point Marsh"	3
	"Noble Quarter"	67
James Caldwell	"First Choice"	390
	"St. Giles"	10

51:1755:23 ...		
Magdalane Smith	"Stevenson" – land unknown	150
	"Brittingham" – land unknown	500
	"Borkin" – land unknown	300
	"Addition"	74
	"Hartlebury"	100
James Polk	"Moanan" – taken by elder survey	100
	"Racans" – land unknown	100
	"Dunnagall"	100
	"Williams Adventure"	64
	"Smiths Resolves"	251
	"Smiths Hope"	100
	"Double Purchase"	163
	"Addition to Smiths Hope"	190
Samuel Mathews	"Ellis's Lott"	50
	"Mathews Delight" pt. "Elgate"	50
	"Edwin"	40
	"Mathews Green"	48
John Ellis	"Barsheba" – land unknown	100
	"Bethsaida" – land unknown	100
	"Adventure"	70
51:1755:24 ...		
Samuel Mathews, Jr.	"Edwin"	100
	"Meadow"	25
Teague Reggan	"Middle Plantation"	175
	"Reggans Chance"	45
	"Last Choice"	18
Mary Reggin	"Prices Conclusion"	50
	"Edwin"	10
Charles Reggan	"Golden Lyon"	235
William Stevens	"Blakes Hope"	200
	"Wooten Underidge"	50
	"Cowley"	100
	pt. "Piney Point"	150
51:1755:25 ...		

William Vennables	"Mill Security"	70
	"Friends Good Will"	50
Purnell Newbold	"Acquintica"	200
	"Acquintica" – 300 a. per patent	200
	"Friendship"	100
	"Content"	77
Samuel Collins	"Tilghmans Adventure" – taken by elder survey	40
	"Late Discovery"	178
	"Collins's Addition"	223
	"Hamm"	50
	"Collins's Lott"	5½
	"Snow Hill" pt. "Late Discovery"	22
William Kersley	"Irish Grove"	62½
	"Discovery"	37½
	"Kersley Industry"	225
	"Shoomakers Meadow"	50
51:1755:26 ...		
Capt. John Williams for c/o William White	"Entrance" – denied	150
	"Caldicutt" tbc William Allen (62 a. WO)	500
	"Springfield"	486
	"Fair Meadow"	438
	"Rehoboth"	600
	"Entrance"	400
Capt. John Williams	"Little Bolton"	810
	"Flat Cap"	50
	"Mistake"	400
Maj. Sampson Wheatly	"Greenfield"	125
	"Irish Grove"	100
	"Merchants Treasure"	100
	"Wheatlys 2nd Addition"	45
John Perkins	"New Town"	265
	"Winter Harbour"	150
	"Chesnut Ridge"	50
John Cope	"Ennalls Frolick" – never patented	150
51:1755:27 ...		
Alexander Fullerton	"Poor Quarter"	100

Samuel Adams	"Shoomakers Meadow"	49
	"Haphazard"	25
	"Adams Folly"	301
	"Norfolk"	250
	"Brickles"	7
	"Irish Grove"	50
	"Turkey Tray"	100
	"Adams's Delight"	16½
	pt. "Bostons Purchase"	19⅔
h/o Collins Adams	"Snow Hill" pt. "Late Discovery"	178
	"Houstons Choice"	160
	"Late Discovery"	22
	"Collins Adventure"	119
Esaw Boston	"Sewards Purchase"	200
	"Nann Ellis Ridge"	40
Isaac Boston	"Sewards Purchase"	200
	"Boston Green"	25
	"Bostons Purchase" tbc Samuel Adams (19⅔ a.)	355
51:1755:28 ...		
Benton Harris	"Bear Point"	125
	"Pigg Pen Ridge"	8
	"Friends Choice"	18
	"Harrissons Venture"	263
	"Timber Grove"	262
	"Davis's Chance"	30
John Tull	"Bear Point"	175
John Harper	"Norfolk"	250
Tunstall Hack (VA)	"Long Meadow"	248
	"Bluff Hammock"	50
	"Spring Island"	25
	2 lots in Princess Ann Town	<n/g>
	"Pembertons Goodwill"	250
Charles Dickason	"Dickasons Hope"	40
	"Green Park"	200
	"Reggans Mine"	100
51:1755:29 ...		

Capt. John Dennis	"Piney Point"	175
	pt. "Double Purchase"	107⅓
Isaac Beauchamp	"Contention"	185
	"Puzle" containing: • "Contention" – 45 a. • "Discovery" – 50 a.	90
	"Remnent"	13
Margrett Fenton	"New Wood Hall" – in dispute	200
	"Wood Hall"	150
h/o Edward Beauchamp	"Ledburn" – owner unknown	200
	"Ledbourn"	266
h/o Samuel Handy	"Suffolk"	446
William Worwick	"Harpers Discovery"	100
	"Harpers Increase"	50
51:1755:30 ...		
Thomas Rensher	"Renshers Security"	63
	"Covingtons Meadow"	50
	"Errondley"	88
David Dreddon	"Hackhila"	120
	"Timber Grove"	37½
	"Cherry Gardin"	23
John Paden	"Hackhilla"	80
	"Cherry Garden"	63
	"Timber Grove"	37½
	"Chance"	20
Solomon Long	"Amity"	220
	"Adventure"	100
	"Sampier"	80
	"Cow Quarter"	50
John Laws	"Golden Quarter"	75
	"Long Delay"	137
	"Meadow"	25
51:1755:31 ...		
William Rensher (cnp)	"Errendley"	230
	"Covingtons Meadow"	145
	"Renshers Security"	37

	pt. "Comforts Adventure"	205
	pt. "Covingtons Meadow"	
h/o Robert Mitchell	"Good Suckcess"	150
James Weatherley	"Acworths Contrivance"	50
	"Snakey Island"	25
	"Addition"	200
	"Acworths Folly"	27
	"Prevention"	70
	"Weatherleys Marshes"	33⅔
Thomas Sceon	"New Invention"	212½
	"Barnabys Lott"	100
	"Salsbury"	110
	"Inucy"	104
	"Cones Chance"	100
	"Trouble"	50
51:1755:32 ...		
h/o Robert Givans	"Green Meadow" – taken by elder survey	75
	"Addition"	100
	"Begining" pt. "Pasturidge"	7
	"Incloased"	22
	"Denn Pasture"	100
	"Lyons Lott"	14
William Gyles	"Parremores First Choice"	300
	"Sallop"	250
	"Whetstone"	200
	"Agnewlow" & "Lergee"	116
h/o William Piper	"Toswondock" – land unknown	130
	pt. "Attawattaquaco" – land unknown	800
	"Salisbury Plains"	200
	"Wilton"	100
	"Marsh Hook"	75
	"Once Again"	75
	"Needless Cost"	150
James Larremore	"Cannons Choice"	283
51:1755:33 ...		

William Smith for h/o James Train	"Weatherleys Purchase"	225
	"Addition"	30
	"Slipe"	25
	"Weatherleys Purchase"	190
	"Compleat"	25
	"Marsh Hook"	25
	"Once Again"	25
Samuel Macclester	"Woodgate Dock"	100
	"Sweet Wood Hall"	400
Charles Acworth	"Manloves Delight" – land unknown	100
	"Hogg Quarter"	100
	"Acworths Delight"	158
	"Acworths Choice"	50
	"Ridges"	50
	"Marsh Point"	100
Martha Wallis	"Ware"	143
51:1755:34 ...		
Roger Nicholson	"Ellingsworths Hope"	100
John Wallis	"Middlesex"	300
	"Tarikil Hammock"	30
	"Addition"	180
Robert Collier	"Douteys Lott"	100
	"Parris"	100
Levin Moor	"Turkey Cock Hill"	100
Samuel Flewelling	"Tick Neel"	50
	"Prickle Cock Shot"	75
	"Milk More"	50
	"Clear of Cannon Shott"	50
	"Flewellings Purchase"	50
	"Cannons Lott"	50
	"Woolfs Quarter"	50
	"Cow Ridge"	100
	"Flewellings Settlement"	137
	pt. "Fishing Quarter" pt. "Bettys Inlargement"	120
	pt. "Cannons Choice"	5
	"Security"	50

51:1755:35 ...		
Lewis Beard	"Fishermans Quarter"	130
	"Bettyes Inlargement"	
	"Beards Advantage"	25
Daniel Henderson	"Turnstile"	100
John Shiles	"Might Have Had More"	400
	"Adventure"	46
	"Noble Quarter"	33
	"Sidney"	50
	"Finish"	58
Hezekiah Read for h/o William Langdale	"Woodstock"	100
George Dashiell	"Little Worth"	50
	"Beaudley"	500
51:1755:36 ...		
h/o Col. George Dashiell	"Contention"	95
	"Dashiells Lott"	435
	"Dashiells Meadow"	50
	"Turkey Ridge"	83
	"Satisfaction"	116
Joseph Dashiell	"Hazard" – taken by elder survey	30
	"Hazard"	70
	"Dashiells Folly"	118
	"Meeches Hope" & "Rich Swamp"	135
	"Shiles's Folly"	162½
	"Dashiells Addition"	25
	"Fair Ridge"	100
Levin Powell	"Hickory Ridge" pt. "Greenfield"	19
	"Gum Swamp Neck" pt. "Greenfield"	70
Edm. Tabb	"Nutters Adventure"	50
	pt. "Shields Choice"	220
Robert Hitch	"High Suffolk"	212
<two blank unnumbered pages>		
51:1755:37 ...		
John Hitch	"High Suffolk"	194
	"Fathers Neglect"	126

Henry Smith	"Bauld Ridge"	191
	"Dixons Choice Inlarged"	4½
Jessee Bounds	"Years Land"	37½
	"Easams Chance or Choice"	34
	"Collins's Ambition"	25
	"Barron Neck" tbc William Bounds	100
	"Anithing"	65½
h/o John Lecatt	"New Haven"	209
Henry Schofield	"Rehoboth"	200
51:1755:38 ...		
Jos. Calloway	"Cockland"	196
	"Anything"	50
William Brown	"Wilsons Mistake"	100
	"North Denn"	40
James Laws	"Addition"	100
	"Dogwood Ridge"	100
h/o Solomon Hitch	"High Suffolk"	305
	"Weatherleys Ridge"	100
John Dormon	"Tossater" called "Woolves Denn"	150
John Langford	"Weatherleys Adventure"	100
51:1755:39 ...		
John Goddart	"Bear Denn" – not yet patented	50
	"Dayes Begining"	239
George Benston	"Hap Hill" – not patented	100
	"Leatherland" – taken by elder survey	150
	"Winter Quarter" – disclaimed	40
	"Woolver"	100
Samuel Phebus	"Nicholsons Adventure"	41
	"Addition to Littleworth"	242
George Pollett	"Preston" – denied; owner unknown	30
	"Smithfield"	100
	"Tomroons Ridge"	100
	"Comby Chance"	10
Thomas Cooper	"Bedford"	300
51:1755:40 ...		

Isaac Cooper	"Quiaukason Neck"	164
	"Ebbyes Frollick"	10
Samuel Cooper	"Bedford"	50
Henry Potter	"Mitchells Choice"	180
	"Sunken Ground"	100
	"Cow Quarter"	10
	"Daniels Denn"	50
Jos. Stanford	"What You Please"	69
	"Denniss Addition"	50
	"Stanfords Finding"	50
Michael Disharoon, Jr.	"Second Purchase"	200
Thomas Pryer	"Dixons Kindness" – taken by elder survey	100
	"Bear Neck" – taken by elder survey	50
	"Mates Injoyment"	100
51:1755:41 ...		
h/o John Read	"Hogg Quarter"	175
	"Weston"	200
John Hillmon	"Brittain"	50
John Doherty	"Little Usk"	100
	"Meadow"	202
Thomas Glaster	"Maidens Lott"	100
Thomas Gilliss, Jr.	"Maidens Lott"	100
Jos. Gilliss, Jr.	"Maidens Lott"	100
51:1755:42 ...		
Henry Spear	"Dunnegall"	70
	"Bettey Shanney"	100
h/o James Collins	"Gilliss Adventure"	100
Archibald Richey	"Mount Hope"	40
	"Turnstile"	10
Ebinezar Cottman	"St. Gyles"	190
	"Weatherleys Adventure"	200
	"First Choice"	10
Jacob Mezeck	"Ellingsowrths Hope"	50
	"Pasturadge"	22½
	"Nantz"	50
	"James's Lott"	34

51:1755:43 ...		
Isaac Shurman	"Wrington"	88
	"Ægypt"	12
Thomas Gilliss	"Bedlem Green"	150
	"White Chappel"	100
	"End of Strife"	500
	"Addition"	52
	"Hermon"	150
	"Bears Quarter"	10
	"Second Choice"	10
	"Crambourn"	100
	"Horseys Chance" & "Canterbury"	100
	"Support"	137
	"Contention"	50
	"Coxes Advice"	200
h/o Ezekiel Gilliss	"Gilliss Addition"	100
Elijah Weatherley	"Acworths Folly"	115
	"Snakey Island"	26
	"Addition"	128
51:1755:44 ...		
h/o Richard Nicholson	"Agnewloe & Largee"	200
h/o Thomas Row	"Purgatory"	37½
	"Graves End"	300
	"Winsors Prevention"	60
h/o John Conway	"Fathers Care"	50
	"Wair Point"	50
	"Rumbling Point"	10
	"Webley"	20
	"Condoque"	50
h/o James Otley	"Morrisses Hope"	206
	"Boyards Security"	34
William Gray	"Kilmannum"	150
Rachel Caudory	"Cant Tel"	91
51:1755:45 ...		
Mary Maddux (cnp)	"Linseys Green"	25
	"Cow Quarter"	50

	"Daniels Denn"	50
	"Irish Grove"	22½
Levin Polson	"Troublesom"	100
William Duett	"Hope Still"	220
	"Ennemessex"	84
	"Musketo Creek"	100
	"Hopwell"	96
	"Mores Worth"	8
	"Hogg Land"	12
Robert Hastin	"Balla Magorrey"	50
William Hickman	"Old Castle"	50
	"Fair Meadow"	700
	"New Castle"	100
51:1755:46 ...		
Rev. Alexander Adams	"Barrowfield"	75
	"Eastwood"	234
	"Walleys Chance"	300
	"Crambourn"	250
	"Winsor"	100
	"Smiths Adventure"	433
	"Sana"	50
	"Glasgow Swamp"	300
	"Adams's Purchase"	18
	"Long Ridge"	50
	"Narrow Ridge"	25
	"Flat Ridge"	25
	"Trouble" now called "Unity to Glasgow"	230
	"Dantery" now called "Unity to Glasgow"	150
	"Huggs Purchase"	100
	"Wilsons Folly"	50
	"Guarnsey"	50
Southey Whittington (cnp)	"Goshen"	340
	"Scotland"	91
	"Scotts Folly"	50
	"Recovery"	200
	"Puzle"	170

	"Bridgets Lott"	100
	"Gillead"	285
	"Chance"	108
	"Baltemores Gift"	250
John Calloway	"Calloways Folly"	25
51:1755:47 ...		
Nehemiah King	"Good Luck"	320
	"Piney Island"	10
	"Barbados"	300
	"Double Purchase"	293
	"Addition to Collins Adventure"	111
	"Southforland"	50
	"Downs Lott" pt. "Double Purchase"	200
	"Closier" pt. "First Choice"	66
	"Conclusion"	1500
	"Kings Land" pt. "Double Purchase"	300
	"Conveniancy"	75
	"Collins Adventure"	500
	"Bear Swamp"	16
	"Kings Chance" & "Pimene"	112
	"New Addition" pt. "Double Purchase"	30
	½ lot in Princess Ann Town	<n/g>
	"Selfe Preservation"	175
	"Support"	37
	"Partners Choice" & "Kings Purchase United"	797½
	"Timber Tract"	347
	"Whartons Folly"	33½
	"Comby Chance" pt. "Double Purchase"	250
	pt. "Double Purchase"	60
	pt. "Double Purchase"	500
	"Dublin", "Kings Chance", & "Pimene"	163
Edward Kellem	"Cambridge"	205
51:1755:48 ...		
Thomas Maddux	"Inclosier"	590
Robert Nairn (cnp)	"Neighbourhood" – denied	250
	"Georges Marsh"	50

	"Tarsay"	150
	"Hogg Quarter"	250
Daniel Rhoades	"Shantavanah"	200
	"Worrington" now called "Rhoads Choice"	10
John Calloway, Jr.	"Golden Quarter"	50
	"Dany Neck" pt. "Days Begining"	6
James Trahair	pt. "Dixsons Lott"	55
	"Trahairns Lott"	55
51:1755:49 ...		
Henry Miles	"Harts Ease"	400
	"Marsh Ground"	50
	"White Oak"	125
	"Foscutt"	50
	"Hogpen Swamp"	50
	"Dixons Lott"	75
	"Neglect"	15
	"Hazard"	32
	"Fathers Care"	70
	"Hopwell"	37½
h/o William Cox	"Rook Prevented" – will give this up	144
	"Waterford"	450
	"Anglesey"	100
	"Cox Bit" now called "Calf Pasture"	35
John Davis	"Cow Quarter" – denied; land unknown	1150
	"Brickle How"	300
	"Hopwell"	50
	"Hopworths Pasture"	48
	"Davises Inlett"	50
	"Kirkminster"	225
	"Long Hedge"	250
	"Cow Quarter"	45
	"Appes Undvey"	400
	"Troublesom"	250
51:1755:50 ...		
Randal Long	"Hogg Hommock" & "Bears Neck"	208
	"Comby Chance"	86

Jonathan Mills	"Winter Quarter" – denied	100
	"Suffolk"	200
	"Somthing Better then Nothing"	75
Dennis Adams	"Long Ridge"	75
h/o Robert Scott	"Bears Neck"	52
	"Bears Neck" & "Hors Hommock"	68
David Adams	"Partners Agrement"	200
	"Planners Adventure"	100
	"Littleworth"	50
51:1755:51 ...		
Thomas Hayward	"Profitt"	250
	"Haywards Lott"	740
	"Blakes Hope" – 9 square poles	<n/g>
	"Addition"	45
	pt. "Plague Without Profit" & pt. "Tilghmans Luck"	½
Lewis Jones	"Laytons Conveniency"	70
	"Jones's Adventure"	25
	"Lunns Amendment"	100
	"Jones's Chance"	266½
	"Dows"	100
h/o Thomas Wright	"Long Lott"	50
	"Worst is Past"	150
	"Friend Agreement"	28
	"Friends Advice"	40
William Sausser	"Roodey"	200
	"New Port Pagnell"	50
	"Hanslop"	50
	"Woolf Harbour" pt. "Ignoble Quarter"	50
	"Sumthing Worth"	150
	"Saussers Folly"	100
	"Addition"	50
	"Saussers Lott"	50
51:1755:52 ...		
Charles Deane (cnp)	"Gladstons Industery"	170
	"Deanes Lott"	10

	"Deanes Chance"	20
Richard Green	"Maryes Choice"	200
	"Greens Recantation"	100
John Harris	"Chance"	316
	"Pasturage"	50
	"Winter Quarter"	10
Zachariah Harris	"Heaths Quarter"	100
	"Littleworth"	50
	"Liberty"	50
Robert Harris	"Bear Quarter"	20
51:1755:53 ...		
Jos. Reggan	"What You Will"	100
	"Reggans Content"	100
	"Harmsworth"	150
Col. George Gale	"Caryes Chance"	164
	"Addition"	1630
	"Stoney Ridge"	300
	"Satisfaction"	14
	"Denwoods Denn"	300
	"Wilsons Conclusion"	1001
William Staughton	"Chance"	50
	"St. Peters Neck"	100
	"Suckcess"	300
	"Bloyces Hope"	125
	"Penneywise"	95
	"Rainsbury"	345
	"Malbury"	
	"Chance"	
Jethro Vaughon	"Coxes Discovery"	250
51:1755:54 ...		
Isaac Hayman	"Woolf Pit Ridge"	115
	"White Oak Swamp"	30
	"Haymans Purchase"	25
John Leatherbury (cnp)	"Covingtons Vineyard"	300
	"Covingtons Folly"	70
	"Lott"	200

	"My Own Before"	61
h/o Elias Baley & William Baley	"White Chappell"	100
	"Glocester"	50
George Baley	"Glocester"	74
	"Baleys Chance"	41
Ezekiel Humphriss	"Hoggs Down"	170
51:1755:55 ...		
Francis Langake	"Comby Chance"	317
	"High Suffolk"	83
	"Georges Folly"	47
	"Stephens Freehold"	45
h/o Thomas Goslin	"Hoggs Down"	1200
Thomas Hairn	"Stains"	150
h/o William Hairn	"Stains"	425
Arthur Parks	"Pitchcroft"	75
51:1755:56 ...		
Col. Isaac Handy	"Pemberton"	620
	"High Suffolk" now called "Pemberton"	2
	"Friends Choice"	10
	"Spences Choice"	125
	"Breadys Chance"	171
	"Handys Pasture" pt. "Shiles Folly"	75
George Bozman	"More & Cas It"	200
	"Coalbourn"	216⅓
	pt. "Coalbourn"	4
h/o William Bozman	"More & Casit"	221
h/o Thomas Marvill	"Gladstones Adventer" tbc Joseph Raw	75
	pt. "Hord Shift" tbc Joseph Raw	25
Benjamin Richardson	"Casaway"	250
51:1755:57 ...		
Jacob Vinson	"Vinsons Choice"	125
Hiron Reddish	"Castle Hawn"	40
Ballard Bozman	"Double Purchase"	500
Rev. Hamelton Bell for h/o Rev. James Robertson	"Glanvills Lott"	440

Henry Newman	"Maryes Adventure"	40
	"Owens Choice"	17
	"Newmans Conclusion"	280
51:1755:58 ...		
John Dorman	"Dormans Chance"	100
	pt. "Covingtons Meadow"	42
	pt. "Comforts Adventure"	
Ralph Milbourn	"Dales Adventure"	200
	"Desire"	13
	"Prices Grove"	85
Aaron Tilghman	"Pools Hope"	60
	"Tilghmans Adventure"	180
	"Davis's Chance" pt. "Pools Hope"	100
	"Hogg Yard"	50
John Owens	"Golden Quarter"	150
	"Golden Quarter"	77
Visitors of the Public School	"Smiths Recovery"	99
51:1755:59 ...		
Absolem Ford	"Promis Land"	100
	"Vale of Misery"	88
William Gravenour	"Bass Legg"	150
William Wood	"Dublin"	180
	"Woods Contest"	161
William Adams	"Adventure" tbc Jacob Adams	91
	"Haphazard"	25
	"Addams's Conclusion"	155
	"Whittey" pt. "Hignalls Choice"	88
George Adams	"Adventure"	125
51:1755:60 ...		
h/o Benjamin Baley	"Hermon"	200
	"Baleys Purchase"	50
Spencer Harris	"Harrissons Adventure"	150
h/o Samuel Tayler	"Laytons Recovery"	100
Nathaniel Smullin	"Goshen"	150
William Jones for h/o Heathley Rider	"Meadfield"	190½

51:1755:61 ...		
William Mister	"Pitchcroft"	175
Jos. Leonard	"Plumton Salt Ash"	40
	"Levins Chance"	50
Samuel Acworth	"Acworths Purchase"	300
James Wainright	"Pasturadge"	130
	"Clear of Cannon Shott"	100
William Farrington	"Pasturage"	43
	"Weatherleys Purchase"	225
51:1755:62 ...		
John Tayler	"Weatherleys Contrivance"	150
	"First Choice"	100
	"Commons" now called "Taylers Addition"	50
John & Isaac Hopkins	"Cannons Shott"	300
	"Cajers Island"	75
	"Johns Chance"	100
	"Two Brothers"	100
Nicholis Dunn	"Shadwell" & "Late Discovery" – taken by elder survey	20
	"Shadwell"	100
h/o Thomas Smith	"Mile End"	75
Mary Shehon	"Malborough" – escheated to His Lordship for want of heirs	150
51:1755:63 ...		
Samuel Hall	"Point Patience"	143
Thomas Huffington	"Bacors Folly"	25
	"Huffingtons Lott"	20
h/o John Robertson	"Irelands Eye"	150
James Hayman	"Hopwell"	170
	"Addition"	80
	"Haymans Purchase"	58½
John Henry	"Phairsalia"	100
51:1755:64 ...		
Boaz Walston	"Double Purchase"	100
Archibald Stutt	"Dear Lott"	160
	"Smiths Polacey"	75

Jos. Ward	"Comby Chance"	100
	"Long Acre"	100
	"Paxon Hill"	100
Matthias Vincent	"Cockland"	100
Charles Dashiell	"Shiles Folly"	18
	"Venture"	50
	"Fathers Care"	166
	"Addition"	47
51:1755:65 ...		
Thomas Waller	"Parrish"	29
	"Cockland"	50
	"Worldsend Swamp"	25
	"Stepney"	59
	"Swamp Ridge"	50
William Tayler	"Round Pond"	100
Nathaniel Waller	"Swamp"	100
John Milbourn	"Late Discovery"	50
	"Prices Grove"	150
	"Venture"	80
William Calloway	"What You Please"	25
	"Iron Hill"	180
51:1755:66 ...		
h/o John Fowler	"Lotts Daughter" pt. "Lott"	100
	"Lotts Son" pt. "Lott"	140
Stephen Hopkins	"Samuels's Lott"	200
	"Cajors Island"	125
	"Mulbury Island"	50
William Hath	"Look" pt. "Wonsborough"	50
	"Haths Chance"	100
	"Addition to Smiths Hope"	30
William Kibble	"Bottom of the Neck"	103
	"Security"	113
Levin Larremore	"Cold Quarter"	125
William Outerbridge	"Mothers Care" & "Brothers Goodwill" pt. "Double Purchase"	200
51:1755:67 ...		

Thomas Gilliss for h/o Robert Dashiell	"Venture Priviledge"	62½
	"Recovery"	333
	"Improvement"	40
Capt. John Cox for h/o William Dashiell	"Venture Priviledge"	62½
	"Dashiells Purchase"	498
Mitch Dashiell	"Good Luck" – included in "Phairsalia"	31½
	"Phairsaila"	175
	"Venture Priviledge"	62½
Archabald White	"Prices Conclusion" – owner unknown	12½
	"Tulley Brisk" pt. "Manloves Lott"	118
	"Long Acre"	12½
	"Addition to Tulley Brisk"	76
	"Whites Desire"	11
Edward Cluff	"Blakes Hope"	200
	"Timber Grove"	75
	"New Town"	27
51:1755:68 ...		
Samuel Melson	"Partners Choice"	120
Ambroas Dixon	"Dixons Lott"	200
	"Security"	270
William Turpin for h/o Thomas Williams	"Winter Refuge" pt. "Dixons Lott"	150
	pt. "Williamstone"	230
	"Second Choice"	90
	pt. "Williams Conquest"	72
	"Thurd Choice"	20
	"Vaconsey"	19
Nicholas Evans	"Rice Land"	612
	"Troy"	50
	"Fox Hall"	50
	"Timber Grove"	100
	"Daniels Adventure"	150
	"Gilliss Care"	22
	"Darmas Improvement"	40
h/o John White (AN)	"Scotland"	70
	"Buck Ridge"	100
	"Poor Swamp"	100

51:1755:69 ...		
Capt. John Williams	"Williams's Lott"	200
	"Harford Broad Oak"	110
	"Middle Strand"	85
	"Capes Mouth"	12½
	pt. "First Choice"	21
	"North Border"	100
Thomas Evans	"Handys Meadow"	50
	"Owens Glendore"	285
	"Oyshtershell Bank" pt. "Dales Adventure"	9
Walter Darby	"Batchelors Choice"	50
h/o Edward Hairn	"Scotland"	97
George Irving	"Marioms Lott"	400
	"Hab Nab"	216
	"Georges Adventure"	1000
51:1755:70 ...		
Capt. Aaron Lynn	"Coxes Performance"	100
	"John's Folly"	55
	"Addition" – 22 years arrears	250
	"Carlyle" – 22 years arrears	300
James Quittermas	"Meedfield"	50
	"Poplar Neck"	200
h/o John Records	"Whetstone"	100
	"Good Luck"	40
	"Records Delight"	100
	"Sheppards Crook"	10
	"Turtle Ridge"	50
	"Givans Lott"	150
John Taytom	"Taytoms Habitation"	40
William Kinney	"Thurd Choice"	50
	"Desart"	100
	"Kenneys Chance"	50
	"Good Neighbourhood"	50
51:1755:71 ...		
John Mackdowell	"Georges Choice"	50

Isaac Williams	"Williamstone" – taken by elder survey	70
	"Thurd Choice" – taken by elder survey	44
Mathias Magloughlin	"Maglaughlins Chance"	50
h/o Margrett Lindow	"Piney Point"	539
Levin Woolford	"Woolford"	600
	"Woolfords Venture"	33⅔
	"Happy Addition"	66⅔
	"Meadow"	53½
John Winsor	"Coxes Performance"	250
51:1755:72 ...		
John Anderson	"Friends Discovery"	30
	"Greens Recantation"	20
James Winsor	"Comby Chance"	40
Thomas Langford	"Goodwill" pt. "Chance"	100
	"Chance"	33⅓
	pt. "Morriss's Lott"	30
John Walter	"Shadwells Chance"	281
John Jones (Goos Creek)	"Woolfords Chance"	36½
	"Enlargment"	50
	"Addition"	52
Thomas Parremore	"Good Luck at Last"	50
51:1755:73 ...		
John Huffington	"Barren Quarter"	250
	"Cambridge"	95
	"Which You Please"	50
Stephen Hobbs	"Hobbs Adventure"	100
	"Abbington"	100
	"Carneys Chance"	100
William Ralph	"Good Luck at Last"	100
Jobe Shurman	"Moors 2nd Choice"	50
	"Kinneys Ridge"	50
Vestry of Stepney Parish	"Spring Hill"	2
Vestry of Somerset Parish	"Somersett"	50
	"Davises Choice" called "Turners Purchase"	130
51:1755:74 ...		

James Nairn	"Nairns Adventure" – taken by elder survey; disclaimed	30
	"Entrance" – taken by elder survey	155
	"Tersay"	150
	"Nairns Addition"	57
	"Pimmo"	30
	"Northfield"	195
William Wright	"Chance"	66⅔
Thomas Dashiell	"Fathers Purchase" pt. "Noble Quarter"	100
	"Mount Alexander" pt. "Noble Quarter"	105
	"Shiles's Folly"	100
h/o Henry Dashiell	"Becknem"	150
	"Head of Tyaskin" originally "Cannons Peace"	100
	"Shiles's Folly"	116
Thomas Jones (MU)	"Jones's Choice"	175
	"Addition to Hogg Quarter"	446
51:1755:75 ...		
George Jones	"Golden Quarter"	70
	"Long Delay"	50
	"Jones's Priviledge"	80
Francis White	"Davids Disteny"	50
	"Ellits Choice"	50
	"Out Lett"	100
Michael Dorman	"Elliards Choice" – land unknown	200
	"Nelsons Choice"	55
	"Hunting Quarter"	100
	"Dormans Discovery"	171
Capt. Joseph Gilliss	"Oak Hall"	200
	"Manloves Adventure"	50
	"Chance"	300
	"More & Cas It"	158
h/o John Robertson	"Robertsons Lott"	147½
	"Cow Pasture"	25
51:1755:76 ...		
William Robertson (cnp)	"Robertsons Lott"	147½
	"Cow Pasture"	25

	"Parremores Double Purchase"	100
Ralph Lowe	"First Choice" pt. "Woodfield"	100
	"Woodfield"	150
h/o David Vance	"Cockmore"	100
h/o Col. Henry Ballard	"Nutters Purchase"	300
	"Turkey Ridge"	100
	"Friends Assistance"	200
	"Woolfs Denn"	66½
John Jurdin	"Turkey Cock Hill" – escheated for James Knight on 8 December 1749	40
51:1755:77 ...		
William Stewart	"Panters Denn"	100
	"Kendall"	60
William Turpin, Jr.	"Poyk"	10
	"Normondy"	25
	"Fountins Lott"	150
	"Hawtree Point"	100
	"Fathers Care"	90
	"Neighbours Agrement"	46
	"Turpins Choice"	100
Solomon Tull	"Peach & Pine"	50
	"Wallerton"	100
	"Wilsons Lott"	24
William Boston	"Forked Neck" pt. "First Choice"	50
	pt. "Bostons Lott"	86
	"Long Ridge"	60
Robert Beauchamp	"Discovery"	100
	"Beauchamps Chance"	206
51:1755:78 ...		
Joseph Tilghman	"Pools Hope"	50
	"Amity"	196
	"Beans Hall" pt. "Amity"	100
	"Mathews Ridge"	60
	"Josephs Folly"	66
	"Sapling Ridge"	19
Thomas Brereton (BA)	"High Meadow"	250

h/o Richard Brereton	"Cockmore"	100
Stephen Ward, Sr.	"Long Acre"	100
Cornelius Ward	"Prices Conclusion" – denied; has no right	275
	"White Oak Swamp" – denied; has no right	156
	"Cork"	50
	"Long Acre"	75
	"Littleworth"	25
	"Folly"	19
51:1755:79 ...		
Stephen Ward, Jr.	"Cork"	25
	"Littleworth"	50
Jonathan Reggan	"Cork"	25
Henry Cullin	"Exchange"	150
h/o Charles Roach	"Makepeace"	150
	"Exchange"	50
	"Meadland"	32
	"Force Put"	168
John Reggan	"Golden Lyon"	100
John Roach	"Meadland"	32½
	"Lott"	36
	"Long Town"	150
	"Johnstons Lott"	63
51:1755:80 ...		
Henry Caldhoon	"Cheasmans Chance"	60
	"Security"	100
Samuel Long, Jr.	"Wilsons Lott"	68
	"Rumbling Point"	22½
	"Holtwell"	100
	"Longs Delight"	60
	"Longs Chance"	25
Coalbourn Long	"Bostons Adventure"	55
	"Longs Prevention"	16
	"Longs Purchase"	40
Jeffery Long (cnp)	"Bostons Adventure"	197½
	"Longs Purchase"	83
	"Longs Prevention"	53

	"Marshells Inheritance"	129
	"Mother & Sons Injoyment" pt. "Bostons Adventure"	150
	"Conveniancy"	25
John Long	"Boston Town"	290
	"Bozworth"	154
	"Addition to Bozworth"	15
51:1755:81 ...		
John Evans	"Handys Hall" pt. "Dales Adventure"	100
	"Dales Adventure"	2
	"Tilghmans Adventure"	10
h/o John White (PO)	"Prices Conclusion" – owner unknown	12½
	"Sons Choice"	133
	"Long Acre"	12½
	"Addition" pt. "Pimmo"	105
h/o Capt. Samuel Wilson	"Kilglain"	500
	"Security"	150
	"Wilsons Discovery"	50
	"Tilbury"	50
	"Kings Purchase" pt. "Daviss Choice" – included in "Mothers Care" & placed here by mistake	25
	"Mount Ephraim"	375
	"Happy Addition"	100
	"Bozmans Addition"	148
	"Glasgow"	150
	"Gillead" pt. "Double Purchase"	26
	"Mothers Care"	795
	"Prospect"	449
Jonathan Bound	"Bounds Lott"	300
	"Stevens's Lott"	73
51:1755:82 ...		
John Evans	"Pitchcroft"	300
h/o Thomas Tyler	"Pitchcroft"	200
Margrett Smith	"Patricks Folly"	118
John Hall	"Pimmo"	200
	pt. "Priviledge"	12

Solomon Wright	"Solomons Delight"	100
James Nicholson	"Late at Night"	50
51:1755:83 ...		
James Ward	"Meekle Meadow" – denied; has no right	150
	"Jameses Town"	100
	"Agrement"	25
	"Muckle Meadow"	75
	"Apes Hole"	8
	"Prices Vineyard" pt. "James's Town"	50
	"Prices Conclusion"	150
	"Comby Chance"	17
	"Long Acre"	100
	"Wards Folly"	16½
Thomas Gilliss for h/o John Handy	"Belean"	317
	"What You Please"	25
Adam Carlisle	"Hopwell"	300
	"Addition"	100
	"Force Put"	50
William Byrd	"Hackhilla"	100
Richard Evans	"Pitchcroft"	200
51:1755:84 ...		
Mary Evans	"Pitchcroft"	100
Jacob Ward	"Prices Vineyard" pt. "James's Town"	150
	"Agrement"	50
	"Muckle Meadow"	75
	"Wards Folly"	52
Charles Hayman	"Hopwell"	80
	"Addition"	20
	"Fair Meadow"	24
	"Charles's Chance"	20
William Moor	"Turkeycock Hill"	50
	"Cross"	150
	"Titchfield"	100
Levin Gale (cnp)	"Coxes Lott"	100
	"Last Purchase"	70
	1 lot in Princess Ann Town	<n/g>

	"Bear Swamp"	15⅓
	"Priviledge"	7
51:1755:85 ...		
Richard Tulley	"Fairham"	78
	"Ægypt"	90½
	"Chelsey"	150
	"Commons"	83
Wilson Rider	"Weslocks Adventure or Venture"	200
	"Midfield"	9½
	pt. "Worwick"	100
John Roberts	pt. "Edwords Lott"	50
	pt. "Jeshimon"	50
Isaac Shurman	"Bettyes Choice"	100
Robert Malone	"Goddarts Folly" – taken by elder survey	100
h/o William Dashiell	pt. "Long Hill"	150
	"Greenwich"	50
	"Johnsons Addition"	274
51:1755:86 ...		
Levin Dashiell	"Mitchells Improvement"	250
	"Jones's Choice"	175
	"Shiles's Folly"	18
John Clifton	"Pissimmon Point"	50
	"Morriss Hope"	44
George Gale, Jr.	"Gales Purchase"	696
	"Vennason Pasture"	506
	"Warrington"	112
	"Aghew Lowe"	33⅓
	"Large"	166⅔
	"Chelsey"	15
	"Marsh & Land" (16 a.) pt. "Purchase"	20
Dudson Bacon	"Tatmans Folly"	50
	"Chance"	75
h/o Thomas Ward	"Agrement"	25
51:1755:87 ...		
Thomas Byrd (cnp)	"Jeshimon"	150
	"Elgits Lott"	100

	"Hackhilla"	50
	"Partners Choice"	150
Joseph Tulley	"Acworths Delight"	92
h/o Alexander Stewart	"Long Hill"	150
Benjamin Sharp	"Cannadee Island"	50
	"Desart"	71
John Knight	"Haphazard" pt. "Wilsons Discovery"	100
John Beard	"Calloways Addition"	50
	"Beards Advantage"	25
51:1755:88 ...		
Beauchamp Davis	"Ledbourn"	100
	"Mitchells Lott"	75
Isaac Moor	"Addition to Collins Adventure"	150
Bell Maddux	"Conveniency"	60
	"Ruscommond"	100
Thomas Phillips	"Greens Recantation"	80
Thomas Walston	"Winter Harbour"	40
	"London" pt. "Desart"	50
Teague Mathews	"Edwin"	100
	"Haphazard"	25
	"Worthless"	100
	"Adams Folly"	44
	"Meadow"	16
51:1755:89 ...		
John Mathews	"Edwin"	100
	"Meadow"	9
h/o John Kibble	"Wilsons Discovery" called "Delight"	75
Capt. Henry Lowes (cnp)	"Lowen Inlarge" – won't pay rent for this; pays for the original only	194
	"Coxes Performance"	250
	"Addition"	50
	"Sligoe" pt. "Little Belain"	140
	"Comby Chance"	100
	"Addition to Lowes's Prise House Lott" pt. "Kellems Folly" now "Bottom of the Neck"	15
	"Dowgate"	150

	"Sarahs Neck"	55
	"Dispence"	500
	"Robertsons Lott"	30
	"Relphs Prevention"	9
	"Hearafter"	200
	"Fathers Care"	250
	1 lot in Princess Ann Town – No. 20	<n/g>
	"Previlidge"	1
	"Chuckatuck"	1000
	"Dormans Delight"	250
	"Castle Haven"	160
	"Belean"	3½
	~~"Horseys Baliwick"~~	~~40~~
	pt. "Horseys Baliwick"	40
Thomas Beauchamp	"Ledbourn"	160
	"Beauchamps Venture"	145
51:1755:90 ...		
John Ward	"Cork"	75
	"Littleworth"	8
John Beauchamp	"Ledburn"	150
Thomas Lord	"Gullets Hope"	50
Mathew Oliphant	"Coxes Fork"	150
Thomas Martin	"Keep Poor Hall"	100
Jessee King	"Coxhead"	300
Stephen Horsey	"Coalbourn"	108¼
51:1755:91 ...		
Mathew Wallis	"Contention"	36
	"Gunners Range"	64
	"Golden Quarter"	53
	"Long Delay"	53
	"Meadow"	25
	"Friends Content"	67½
Isaac Knoble	"Timson"	150
Thomas Gyles	"Gyles's Lott"	350
Archabald Smith	"Pumton Salt Ash"	200
	"Murtle Grove"	50

Thomas Maddux	"Conveniency" – denied	52
	"Linseys Green"	25
James Quittermas	"Wilsons Discovery"	150
51:1755:92 ...		
Charles Cottingham	pt. "Boston"	23
	"Chance"	63
	"Mumford"	8
	"Rumbling Point"	15
Thomas Cottingham	"Vulcans Vineyard"	105
	"Rumbling Point"	37½
	"Cottinghams Chance"	40
	"Boston"	26
Teague Dickason	"Hopkins Gift" pt. "Ware"	140
	"Woolfe Quarter"	50
	"Force Put"	50
	"Previledge"	50
	"Townsends Situation"	53
	"Dickasons Hard Lott"	21½
Gilbert Huffington	"Tower Hill"	100
James Anderson	"Beckford"	225
51:1755:93 ...		
Caleb Milbourn	"Prices Grove"	150
Stephen Wainright	"Noble Quarter"	100
	"Whitteys Contrivance"	50
	"Ignoble Quarter"	32
Patrick Mackeinney	"Harts Contract"	50
	"Dixons Lott"	75
	"Patricks Folly"	100
Outerbridge Horsey	"Coalbourn"	195
	"Dixons Lott"	100
	"Coalbourn"	216⅓
	"Horseys Conclusion"	544
	"Horseys Lott"	51
	pt. "Dixons Kindness"	25
Alexander Madox (cnp)	"Greenfield"	181
	"Powells Addition"	50

	"Linseys Green"	25
51:1755:94 ...		
David Polk	"Tomroons Ridge"	100
	"Roxborough"	210
	"Comby Chance"	10
	"Fortune"	245
	"Hoggsdown"	55
John Kellem	"Dickason's Folly"	100
	"Chance"	50
Robert Twilly	"Woodstock"	100
William Flemming	"Unity"	20
	"Flemmings Purchase"	150
	"Minshalls Adventure"	200
	"Harrisons Venture"	150
Daniel Mackintire	"Handys Pasture" pt. "Shiles Folly"	50
	"End of Strife"	80
	"Daniels Previledge"	35
	"Hickory Ridge"	23
	"Safty"	23
	"Daniels Chance"	39½
51:1755:95 ...		
Zachariah Read	"Weatherleys Contrivance"	150
	"Acworths Delight"	100
	"Sons Choice"	50
Alexander Thomas Russell	"Trulocks Grange"	75
	"Good Suckcess"	50
	"Russells Liberty"	78
h/o Roger Kellet	"Horsey Baliwick"	100
	"Little Belain"	167½
	"Phillips Addition"	25
John Parker	"Davises Choice"	184
Thomas Marshell	"Marshells Inheritance"	309
Adam Price	"High Suffolk"	90
51:1755:96 ...		
h/o John Howard	"Dowgate"	50
	pt. "Brittaine"	50

h/o Henry Acworth	"Friends Discovery"	300
Thomas Records	"Sheppards Crook"	70
	"Morris's Lott"	300
	"Partners Choice"	100
	"Whetstone"	50
	"Morriss Lott"	100
h/o Obadiah Read	"Newbury"	300
Joseph Morris	"Security"	100
John Devorix	"Goddarts Folly" – taken by elder survey	90
51:1755:97 ...		
William Swulavan	"Winsor Castle"	100
h/o John Read, Jr.	"Hogg Quarter"	350
	"Green Meadow"	75
Ahab Coston	"Second Choice"	160
	"Bears Quarter"	70
	"Good Luck"	40
	"End of Strife" formerly "Second Choice"	10
	"Costins Trouble"	50
	"Costins Vineyard"	100
h/o Littleton Watters	"Halls Adventure"	1
John Scott	"Bears Neck"	52
h/o Benjamin Townsend	"Townsends Situation"	153
51:1755:98 ...		
Thomas Benston	"Middle"	100
	"Exchange"	100
	"Greenfield"	30
Thomas Pollet	"Daintery"	150
	"Trouble"	20
William Tompson	"Welcom" pt. "Double Purchase"	100
Pascue Bartlet	"Little Maseley"	100
Samuel Tayler (ACC)	"Discovery" pt. "Laytons Recovery"	100
Joshua Knight	"Harrisons Adventure"	175
51:1755:99 ...		
Thomas Jones (MO)	"Brigers Lott"	370
	"Friends Advice"	356
	"Winter Quarter"	274

Thomas Goddart	"Partners Choice"	150
	"Collins's Folly"	75
Peter Quinton	"Wilsons Discovery"	175
Samuel Kersley	"Irish Grove"	37½
	"Discovery"	12½
	"Kersleys Industery"	75
Jonathan Summors	"Summors's Hard Fortune" – taken by elder survey called "Annemessex"	25
	pt. "Annemessex"	54
	"Littleworth"	50
	"Jonathans Addition"	30
51:1755:100 ...		
Daniel Long	"Benjamins Advice"	50
	"Cunney Warrin"	125
	"Kings Glade"	58
Joseph Weatherley	"Acworths Folly"	50
	"Prevention"	20
	"Snakey Island"	24
	"Weatherleys Ridge"	100
John Evins	"Chance"	150
Capt. William Murray	"Vulcans Vineyard" – included in "Neathsdale"	29
	"Neathsdale"	289
Randall Mitchell	pt. "Double Purchase"	250
Rozanna Odear	"Tilghmans Lott" tbc Edward Watters (f. 143)	50
51:1755:101 ...		
h/o Daniel Dulaney	"Uniacks Chance"	50
Daniel Clifton	"Daniels Hazard"	50
Thomas Toadvine	"Guarnsey"	100
	"Jersey"	100
David Mackdonnold	"New Rumney"	244
John Grayham	"Long Acre"	200
	"Candorys Begining"	100
Matthias Costin	"Bares Hole"	50
	"Costins Trouble"	350
51:1755:102 ...		
Charles Harris	"Stevenson"	85

Alexander Maddox, Jr.	"New Town"	108
Thomas Acworth	"Acworths Delight"	200
	"Acworths Choice"	50
	"Ridges"	50
	"Marish Point"	100
James Dakes	"Hignalls Choice"	150
	"Buck Ridge"	150
John North	"Cascoway"	300
Samuel Bradley	"Tulleys Purchase"	50
51:1755:103 ...		
Aaron Sterling	"Johnstons Lot"	6
	"Barnet"	35
	"Marsh"	25
	"Haphazard"	64
	"Frusteration"	40
	"Industery"	5
	"Choice"	20
John Sterling	"Standreds Abby"	50
	"Sterlings Choice"	50
	"Marsh"	25
	"Sterlings Chance"	38
Henry Sterling	"Apes Hole"	192
	"Marsh"	25
Joseph Sterling	"Marsh"	26
Ann West	"Tribble Purchase" pt. "Double Purchase"	50
51:1755:104 ...		
John Bradley	"Taylers Chance"	50
Thomas Collins	"Stevens's Conquest"	300
Clemment Dashiell	pt. "Chance" now called "Good Luck"	15
	pt. "Dashiells Lott"	435
Louther Dashiell	pt. "Chance" now called "Good Luck"	30
	pt. "Dashiells Lott"	470
William Hitch	"High Suffolk"	202½
John Hitch, Jr.	"High Suffolk"	102½
51:1755:105 ...		
Robert Brown	"Which You Please"	150

William Ellis	"Andersons Invention"	200
Capt. Henry Waggaman	"Adventure"	200
	"Adventures Amendment"	37
	"Long Meadow"	78
	"Waggamans Lott"	384
	"Munsley"	111
	"Vennables Mistake"	100
	"Vulcans Vineyard"	75
	"Nicholsons Lott"	25
	"Mill Lott"	100
	"Waggamans Purchase"	947½
	"Nicholsons Lott" & "Vulcans Vineyard"	110
William Shores	"Balahack"	200
	"Forlorn Hope"	100
	"Polks Folly"	100
	"Clemnill"	100
	"Forlorn Hopes Addition"	90
	"Whitteys Lott"	50
	"Come at Last"	10
51:1755:106 ...		
Massey Beauchamp	"Niblets Lott"	28
	"Three Brothers"	522
Panter Laws	"Happy Addition"	54
	"Mill Point"	18½
	"Panters Denn"	240
Mitchel Dashiell, Jr.	"Venture Previledge"	62½
	"Recovery"	167
Richard Phillips	"Woodfield"	100
Jessee Dashiell	"Meeches Right"	300
	"Meehes Desart"	200
	"Woolf Trap Neck"	50
	"Shiles's Folly"	325
51:1755:107 ...		
Levin Goslin	"Trulocks Grange"	75
	"Ralphs Purchase" pt. "Trulocks Grange"	100

h/o Joseph Cottman	"Cottmans Point"	50
	"Taunton Deane"	186
William Waltom	"Waltoms Improvement"	294
George Macclester	"Adventure"	100
	"Adams Choice"	180
	"Point Marsh"	200
	"Rotterdam"	150
Thomas Mantgummery	"Dublin"	75
51:1755:108 ...		
Josephas Bell	"Worth Little" – taken by elder survey called "Watkins Point"	63
	"None Such" – taken by elder survey called "Watkins Point"	50
	"More Worth"	176
	"Bells Purchase"	100
	"Bells Discovery"	60
	"Bells & Horseys Conclusion"	117
	pt. "Watkins Point"	
George Vincent	"New Cary"	50
William Bratton	"Williams Hope"	119
William Stevens	"Whittingtons Choice"	150
Samuel Ward	"Cork"	250
	"Long Acre"	125
	pt. "Little Bolton"	40
51:1755:109 ...		
Isaac Dickason	"Late Discovery"	150
Elias Tayler	"Dublin"	75
h/o Brough Bratton	"Little Actton" pt. "Blakes Hope"	100
Jacob Morris	"Support"	50
Douty Collier	"Shadwell"	50
	"Turnstile"	50
	"Parris"	50
George Colliar	"Mount Hope"	45
	"Cannons Lott"	50
51:1755:110 ...		

John Willin	"Mount Hope"	65
	"Turnstile"	70
Peter Magee	"Rich Ridge"	70
h/o William Evans	"Island Glade"	50
Thomas Roberts	"Flowerfield"	165
	"Phairsalia"	50
	"Morris's Lott"	170
William Booth	"Coxes Discovery"	145
Francis Hains	"Hains's Grave"	50
51:1755:111 ...		
Thomas Collins (cooper)	"Good Hope"	100
Hill Cox	"Alderbury"	72
	"Plumton Salt Ash"	28
George Bennit	"Chelsey"	100
William Smullin	"Goshen"	150
Samuel Jones	"Laytons Conveniency"	70
	"Jones's Adventure"	25
	"Lunns Amendment"	151
	"Jones's Chance"	266½
	"Chance"	22
51:1755:112 ...		
Rebecca Levins	"Cascoway"	150
Col. Joseph Ennalls	"Desart"	100
	"Caldwells Lott"	15
	"Incloased" now called "Wileys Frolick"	40
	"Givans Lott"	100
Thomas Wallis	pt. "Cony"	150
h/o William Laws	"Somthing Worth" – lies in DO	325
	"Littleworth"	50
	"Taylers Hill"	200
William Jones	"Jones's Delight"	65
Ezekiel Hall	pt. "Walls Choice"	152
	"Halls Hammock"	50
	"Halls Pasture"	50
51:1755:113 ...		

Purnall Outton	"Condoque"	50
	"Outtens Addition"	25
	"Wairpoint Inlarged"	34
Samuel Jackson	"Abbergaveny"	50
	"Small Lott"	50
	"Warrington"	35
	"Warwick"	33⅓
William Frigs	"Glasgow"	50
	"Triggs Chance"	180
John Caudory	"Goddarts Lott"	100
William Moor	"Coxes Discovery"	100
51:1755:114 ...		
George Wales	"Golds Delight"	200
Bloyce Harris	"Evans Purchase" pt. "Stannaway"	140
Daniel Waller & Jonathan Hickman	"Townsends Situation" formerly "Hartford"	50
h/o John Anderson	"Andersons Adventure"	114
Hiron Reddish for h/o Samuel Johnston	"Friends Choice"	87½
h/o Noble Hoobs	"Abbington"	100
	"Combys Chance"	50
51:1755:115 ...		
Nehemiah Hairn	"Stains"	125
	"Sandy Hill"	74
	"Fairfield"	37
	"Cascoway"	100
James Wallis	"Meadow"	25
	"Friends Content"	67½
John Nicholson	"Dudley"	80
	"Colliars Good Success"	320
	"Bits's Previledge"	50
Isaac Calloway	"Pick & Cull"	100
	"Calloways Venture"	25
George Hairn (cnp)	"Stains"	150
	"Goshens Addition"	97
	"Goshen"	50

	"Hogg Quarter"	50
	"Maidenhead"	50
51:1755:116 ...		
John Moor s/o William	"Gordens Delight"	100
h/o William Dormon	"Nelsons Choice"	175
Isaac Jones	"Jones's Venture"	50
	"Jones's Choice"	50
William Phillips	"Beverley"	107¼
Jarvice Jenkins	"Hogg Neck"	100
Jos. Langford, Jr.	"Vulcans Vineyard"	9
	"Langfords Content"	89
51:1755:117 ...		
Henry Wright	"Contention"	50
	"Intent"	162
	<n/g> from (N) Robertson	100
	<n/g> from (N) Staughton	50
Joseph Scroggin	"Fairfield"	142
Benjamin Calloway	"Calloways Venture"	30
	"Calloways Hard Fortune"	50
Jonathan Pollet	"Long Ridge"	125
	"Tomroons Ridge"	50
Robert Walter	"Walters Chance"	50
	"Roberts Lott"	25
	"Poor Choice"	40
51:1755:118 ...		
Stacey Miles	pt. "Boyces Banks"	100
Elihue Mezeck	"Ellingsworths Hope"	50
	"Pasturidge"	22½
	"Nantz"	50
Teague Reggan	"Meadow Ground"	100
	"Reggans Amendment"	285
William Haynie	"Lawsons Adventure"	52
	"Joas Ridge"	10
	"Beards Ballens"	3½
	"Long Acre"	8
John Maddux	"Rowley Ridge"	100

Joshua Edge	“Good Luck”	50
	“Batchollers Folly”	50
51:1755:119 ...		
Capt. William Winder	“Pembertons Good Will” –survey is erroneous & rent refused	350
	“Commons”	117
	“Lyons Lott”	86
	“Twilleys Ridge”	134
	“Hongars Quarter”	71
h/o Col. Peter Presley	“Janes Island”	100
	“2 Brothers”	100
	“Buck Ridge”	1
	“Ceadar Hammock”	4
Phillip Adams	“Adventure”	110
	“Haphazard”	25
	“Adams’s Venture”	21
Samuel Miles	“White Oak”	125
	“Security”	172
John Phillips	“Dudley”	50
	“Rowley Hill”	100
	“Grays Purchase”	100
	“Security”	51
51:1755:120 ...		
Jane Strawbridge	“Ridges”	60
	“Addition”	82
	“Conveniency”	100
	1 lot in Princess Ann Town – No 2.	<n/g>
	“Widdows Chance”	1059
Thomas Maddux	“Tilghmans Care”	76
	“New Town”	50
Richard Wallis	“Caldwells Lott”	200
William Williams	“Bay Bush Hall”	100
William Nelson (cnp)	“Wrights Choice”	50
	“Wrights Venture”	52½
	“Noble Quarter”	100
	“End of Strife”	9

	"Handys Discovery"	33
John Crouch	"High Suffolk"	100
51:1755:121 ...		
John Williams	"Puzle" – lies in WO & is sold but not conveyed	100
	"Sligoe" pt. "Little Belain"	80
David Mathews	"Golden Lyon"	150
	"Cow Quarter"	100
Dennis Dulaney	"High Suffolk"	30
	"Comby Chance"	70
Capt. Ephraim King	"Kings Misfortune"	1704
	pt. "Good Neighbourhood"	194
	"Kings Choice"	50
John White	"Andersons Adventure"	140
	1 lot in Princess Ann Town	<n/g>
51:1755:122 ...		
Major Dorman	"Charleston"	50
Joshua Turpin	"Doe Better"	150
Henry Lord	"Troublesom" pt. "Chesnut Ridge"	25
	pt. "Cork"	50
h/o Randall Lord	"Puzle" pt. "Chesnut Ridge"	75
Jos. Ellis	"Turkey Trap Ridge"	50
h/o Paul Alloson	1 lot in Princess Ann Town	<n/g>
Joseph Melson	"Partners Choice"	60
51:1755:123 ...		
John Collins	"Orphans Lott"	30
Solomon Mackcreddy	"Mathews Adventure"	35
	"First Choice"	100
	"Mackcreddys First Choice"	17¾
William Skerving	"Owins Choice"	283
	"Browns Lott"	182
	"No Name"	57
John Morris	"Bettys Choice"	100
	"Mealeys Begining"	87
James Spicer	"White Oak Swamp"	100
Capt. John Fitz (DO)	"Peckingoe Ridge"	250
51:1755:124 ...		

Thomas Dixon	"Boston Town"	30
	"Dixons Addition"	31
	"Dixons Lott"	100
	"Dixons Choice Inlarged"	216
Robert Kersley	"Kersley Joake"	60
	"Kersley in Earnest"	27½
Isaac Dixon	"Bauld Ridge"	9
	"Dixons Lott"	150
	"Dixons Addition"	136
	"Damquarter"	64
	"Dixons Choice Inlarged"	209
Richard Harris	"Elizabeths Choice"	100
George Weatherley	"Mathews Adventure"	50
51:1755:125 ...		
Isaac Maccreddy	"Mathews Adventure"	50
John Mears	"Moorfields"	130
Benjamin Mitchell	"Poorfields"	150
Daniel Goslin	"Ægypt"	33
	"Fairham"	22
William Nutter	"Delight"	194
	"Marsh Ground"	100
	"Nutters Adventure"	232
	"Dormans Delight"	50
	"Middle Trout"	50
51:1755:126 ...		
John Sceon	"Belain"	280
John Parsons	"Swans Luck"	50
	"Plumton Salt Ash"	10
Covington Mezeck	"Covingtons Habitation"	100
Dennis Morris	"Morris's Adventure"	50
Stephen Tulley	"Commons" tbc Richard Tulley (f. 85)	83
James Bradley	"Addition to Collins Adventure"	159
51:1755:127 ...		
James West	"North Wales"	200
Margret Olipher	"Rich Ridge"	30
	"Drummany"	50

William Furnice	pt. "Double Purchase"	245
	"Amity"	100
Levin Huffington	"Lazey Hill"	85½
John Phebus	"Nicholsons Adventure"	97
	"Brothers Agrement"	79
Joshua Jackson	"Boadly"	100
51:1755:128 ...		
Thomas Langake	"Francis Solomon"	50
Isaac Parremore	"Purchase"	50
	"Weatherleys Purchase" pt. "Weatherleys Reserve"	18
George Sharp	"Hogg Neck"	100
Jabis Pitts	"Enterance" – denied	255
	"Enterance"	145
	"Owens Glandon"	15
	pt. "Dales Adventure"	1¼
	"Milbourns Mistake"	1⅛
Robert Elzey	"Manloves Discovery"	250
	"Grays Adventure"	110
Vestry of Coventry Parish	"Mitchells Lott"	150
51:1755:129 ...		
Robert Willin	"Hogg Quarter"	25
	"Saifty"	27
	"Daniels Choice"	39½
	"Daniels Previledge"	23
James Smith	pt. "Laytons Recovery"	100
Thomas Gibbins	"Hopwell"	150
	"Thomas's Chance"	91
John Gibbans	"Hopwell"	150
	"Givans's Chance"	74
Charles Leatherbury	"Oldberry"	400
	"Young Simson"	168
51:1755:130 ...		
Peter Spencer Hack	"Bluff Hammock"	50
	"Spring Island"	25
Robert Banks	"Sarah Security"	350
	"Halls Adventure"	168

Zorobabel King	pt. "Cloverfield"	60
	"Kings Glade"	320
	"Gullets Advisment"	100
Jos. Ward, Jr.	"Little Swamp"	29½
	"Crooked Ridge"	25
	"Winter Swamp"	70½
John Johnson	"Doe Park"	50
	"Rich Swamp"	50
Thomas Ralph	"Ralphs Delight"	20
51:1755:131 ...		
Thomas Gibbans, Jr.	"Granfathers Gift"	100
John Polk (whele right)	"Labour in Vain"	171
John Bratton	"Addition"	40
	"Williams Hope"	61
	"Hogg Quarter"	50
Isaac Mitchell	"Middlesex"	180
	"Williams Hope"	62½
John Wales	"Golds Delight"	200
Robert Colliar, Jr.	"Colliars Enlargment"	90
	"Josephs Lott"	12
	"Bettys Choice"	100
51:1755:132 ...		
William Bennett	"Titchfield"	50
	"Fartham"	50
Ephraim Vaughan	"Coxes Discovery"	150
John Culver	"Beverley"	92¾
Thomas Cox	"Wilton"	50
	"Plumton Salt Ash"	30
h/o Samuel Jackson	"Jacksons Lott"	50
Noble Tull	"Coalmans Adventure"	250
	"Bickles"	93
51:1755:133 ...		
William Beauchamp	"Hoggyard"	95
	"Ledbourn"	5
	"Three Brothers"	200

Rev. John Hamilton	"Chance"	29
	"Cyprus Swamp"	15
	"Little Derry"	175
George Summors	"Summors's Hard Fortune" – taken by elder survey called "Ennemssex"	25
	"Ennemessex"	54
	"Littleworth"	50
Hannah Goldsmith	"Coaldrain"	50
Stephen Tull	"Providence"	36
	"Chance"	111
Robert Downs	"Mitchels Choice"	250
51:1755:134 ...		
Rev. Hamilton Bell	"Vulcans Forge"	100
	"Manloves Venture"	100
	"Friends Kindness"	100
	"Hazard"	160
	"Davis's Choice" called "Georges Delight"	146
	pt. "Davis's Choice" called "Gleab Land"	120
	land from John Parkes not patented	4
William Donohoe	"Anything"	63½
Winder Dashiell	"Woolfe Troy Ridge"	50
	pt. "Shiles Folly"	162½
	"Winders Addition"	102
Isaac Handy	"Handys Discovery"	270
Jonathan Tull	"Coalmans Adventure"	250
	"Beckles"	100
	"Chance"	50
51:1755:135 ...		
Col. Robert Jenkins Henry (cnp)	"Marys Lott" pt. "Rehobath"	400
	"Henrys Addition"	50
	"Conveniency" pt. "Dickasons Hope"	134½
	"Limbrick"	133½
	"Friends Assistance"	300
	"High Land"	100
	"Dickasons Hope"	125½
	"Goos Marsh"	50

	"Cow Marsh"	50
	"Conveniency"	375
	"Good Suckcess" pt. "Conveniency"	200
	"Long Meadow"	646
	"Glasgow"	72
	pt. "Manloves Lott"	138
	"Providence"	200
	"Whitly" pt. "Hignalls Choice"	62
	"Providence"	200
Hope Adams	"Adventure"	90
	"Good Hope"	38
	"Chance"	68
John Covington	"Covingtons Choice"	150
51:1755:136 ...		
David Jenkins	"Second Purchase"	100
Hezekiah Dorman	"Morriss Lott"	100
Isaac Dashiell	"Meekes Hope"	75
	"Rich Swamp"	40
	"Shiles's Folley"	100
	"Chance"	80
	"Years Land"	75
	"Fairsalia"	175
	"Good Luck"	31½
Arnald Elzey	"Chance"	60
	"Boazmans Adventure"	133
Mathias Benston	"Hockley"	50
51:1755:137 ...		
h/o Abraham Covington	pt. "Double Purchase"	200
Abraham Harris	"Middleton"	85
	"Harrissons Venture"	50
	"Flemmings Loss"	30
George Green	"New Haven"	208
Neale Macclester	"White Chappell"	300
	"Oak Grove"	200
Moses Owen (cnp)	"Adams Purchase"	50
	"Turkey Troy"	100

	"Chance"	50
	"Adams Gardin"	50
51:1755:138 ...		
Thomas Dixon, Jr.	"Second Choice"	215
	"Dixons Lott"	50
Benjamin Wales	pt. "Quiaukeson Neck"	100
William Owen	"Hogg Island"	50
John Carmicle	"Warrington"	190
Jacob Airs	"Airs's Purchase"	323
Robert Heron, Esq.	1 lot in White Haven Town	<n/g>
51:1755:139 ...		
John Stilley	"Stilleys Cost"	66¼
	pt. "Glasgow"	100
	"Previledge"	50
Thomas Langford, Jr.	"Cubeys Choice"	50
Michael Raglin	"Comby Chance"	100
	"Raglins Chance"	50
Stephen Handy	"Middlesex"	200
	"Hap at a Venture"	101
William Adams	"Industery"	75
Thomas Adams	"Industery"	75
51:1755:140 ...		
Revill Horsey	pt. "Double Purchase"	100
Ralph Milbourn, Jr.	"Cork"	200
Phillip Adams	"Adams Garden"	8
	"Adams Green"	50
Thomas Stevens	pt. "Dudley" now called "Stevens Inheritance"	20
	"Late Discovery" now called "Stevens Inheritance"	50
	"Shadwell" now called "Stevens Inheritance"	50
William Pollett	"Wilsons Finding"	68
	"Wansborough"	50
	"Pollitts Victory"	198
William Macclemmey	"Coalbrook"	200
51:1755:141 ...		
Thomas Waller, Jr. (cnp)	"Ludgate Hill"	100
	"Sharps Chance"	50

	"Pleasant Grove"	50
	"Hogg Pallace"	50
William Adams	"Evershamp" called "Glasgow Grove"	500
	"Suffolk" now called "Bremelow"	200
	"Fathers Care"	200
John Adams	"Toneys Vineyard"	84
	"Horseys Chance"	101
	"Sportingfields"	50
	"Johns Desire"	82
Ezekiel Gibbans	"Spittle"	22
	"Deep"	150
Joshua Moor	"Moors Advantage"	75
51:1755:142 ...		
Daniel Kinnakin	"Ridge Glade"	50
William Adams s/o William	"Hickory Ridge"	55
	"Adams's Conclusion"	198
Wrixham White	"Batcholers Delight"	50
Mary Whittingham	"Mores Barrow"	323
James Read	"End of Strife"	272
David Hopkins	"Cannons Shot"	200
51:1755:143 ...		
h/o Joshua Morris	pt. "Partners Choice"	150
Edward Waters	pt. "Whartons Folly"	66½
	pt. "Timber Tract"	312
	"Tilghamns Lott"	50
Elizabeth Dixon	"Dixons Lott"	100
	"Security"	135
James Robertson	"Irelands Eye"	150
James Beard	pt. "Laytons Recovery"	100
Jos. Ward (AN)	pt. "Cork"	25
51:1755:144 ...		
Ezekiel Hitch	"Graveley Hill"	50
Arthur Hickman	"Poor Choice"	10
Thomas Sloss (cnp)	"Conclusion"	138
	1 lot in Princess Ann Town – No. 22	<n/g>
	"Bellfast"	75½

	pt. "Golden Quarter"	23
Thomas Noble	pt. "Middle Neck"	100
Capt. John Kellem	"Acworths Folly"	108
	"Discovery"	160
Joshua Jones	"Jones's Delight"	50
51:1755:145 ...		
Capt. Ephraim King for David Wilson	"Smiths Recovery"	600
	"Cloverfields"	990
	"Kilglain"	250
	"Security"	75
	"Tilbury"	25
	"Wilsons Discovery"	25
	"Glasgow"	75
William Wheatly	"Cabbin Swamp"	150
	"Roaches Folly"	74
Ephraim Wilson	pt. "Samuels"	64
	"Wilsons Lott"	688
	"Wilsons Conclusion"	318
	"Winders Purchase"	160
	"Nava Franswa"	100
Samuel Wilson	"Great Hope" pt. "Double Purchase"	165
	"Wilsons Lott" pt. "Double Purchase"	100
	pt. "Double Purchase"	94⅔
	"Kilglain"	250
	"Security"	75
	"Tilbury"	25
	"Wilsons Discovery"	25
	"Glasgow"	75
51:1755:146 ...		
James Knight	"Harrissons Adventure"	120
	"Nights Suckcess"	206
Stephen Ward, Jr.	"Harmsworth"	150
Samuel Miles	"Miles's Lott"	150½
Capt. John Handy (cnp)	"Delight"	194
	"Nutters Adventure"	468
	"Nutters Contrivance"	219

	"Bottom"	143
	"Middle Tract"	50
	"Cheverley"	100
	"Handys Cear"	235
	"Lott"	200
Benjamin Bird	"New Haven"	100
51:1755:147 ...		
Rev. Hugh Henry	pt. "Phairsalia"	91
William Benston	"Whittingtons Neglect"	156
Samuel Pryer	"Pryers Adventure"	24
	"Kings Glade"	100
Richard Waller	"Williams Green"	50
	"Conlet"	380
	pt. "Stepney"	41
	pt. "Parrish"	41
John Langford	"Langfords Content"	50
Jacob Carter	"Mount Charles"	50
51:1755:148 ...		
Abraham Barklet	"Barklets Lott"	14
John Betsworth	"Cole Pit"	50
	"Betsworths Choice"	62½
David Hale	"Whittingtons Choice"	150
Joseph Read	"Addition to Littleworth"	200
William Austin	"Elizabeths Choice"	100
Thomas Dashiell, Jr.	"Summers Pasture"	135
	"Lott"	100
	"Bottom of the Neck"	80
	"Dashiells Lott"	400
51:1755:(unnumbered) **<blank>**		
51:1755:149 ...		
John Mastin	"What You Please"	25
James Harris	"Middleton"	90
	"Flemmings Loss"	30
Mary Woolford (cnp)	"Thornton"	400
	"Jeshimon"	33⅔
	"Hackhilla"	200

	"Woolford"	300
	"Woolfords Venture"	16½
	"Happy Addition"	33⅓
	"Meadow"	26½
Levin Woolford for Charles Woolford	"Thornton"	200
	"Jeshimon"	16⅓
	"Hackhilla"	100
51:1755:150 ...		
William Polk	pt. "Illchester"	150
Capt. George Handy	pt. "Pemberton"	350
	"Surveyors Mistake"	30
Thomas King	pt. "Longs Lott" now called "Addition to Late Purchase"	44
	pt. "Ledbourn" now called "Addition to Late Purchase"	16
Thomas Ward	"Coalbourns Ridge"	100
	pt. "Scotland"	17
	pt. "Bears Neck"	3
h/o Sarah Bannester	pt. "Double Purchase"	43
Solomon Harris	"Lergee"	84
	"Purchase"	16
51:1755:151 ...		
Thomas Whitney	"Woolfs Denn"	53¼
Jacob Spear	pt. "Dunnegall"	130
Joseph Cottman	"Collins Venture" now called "Winter Quarter"	78
Joshua Whittington	"Givans's Security"	300
Solomon Collins	"Kinkins Folly"	49
Thomas Flint	"Uncles Advice"	50
51:1755:152 ...		
James English	"Englishes Adventure"	47
William Knoles	"Widdows Hope"	13
Ann Pryer	"Conclusion"	47
William Miles	"Pleasure"	49½
Mathew Mangarife	"Mangarifes Choice"	82½
William White	"Previledge" tbc John Hall	27½
51:1755:153 ...		

Francis Crowder	"Cow Quarter"	100
John Barklet	"Hogg Quarter"	79
	"Stannaway"	160
	"St. Albins"	140
	pt. "Townsends Situation" for Meckley Hartford	50
Samuel Handy	"Barbers Rest"	150
	"Daniels Adventure"	150
Pewsey Langford	"Langfords Content"	69
	"Dam Quarter"	36
Phillip Adams s/o William	pt. "Adventure"	34
	"Adams's Conclusion"	182
51:1755:154 ...		
William Dreddon	"Davids Disteny"	100
Jacob Crouch	"Poor Quarter"	50
John Robertson	"Long Delay"	100
George Lewis Gastinue	"Chance"	100
Mathew Dorman	"Weatherleys Purchase" pt. "Weatherleys Reserve"	250
	"Slipe"	25
John Parremore	"Crooked Ridge"	50
51:1755:155 ...		
Benjamin Parremore	"Parremores Misfortune"	50
	"Addition"	31
William Walston	"Loss & Gain" – denied	14
	"First Choice" – denied	16
	"Winter Harbour"	40
	"London" pt. "Desart"	50
Robert Hollond	"Ferry Bridge"	100
William Robertson	"Redbourn"	140
David Wilson	pt. "Darby"	175
51:1755:156 ...		
James Wilson	pt. "Darby"	175
Jonathan Stott	"What You Please"	225
	"Black Watter"	25
	"Supply"	25
	"Dear Lott"	96
Isaac Vincent	"Cockland"	100

Kirk Gunby	"Chance" – disclaimed	40
	"Middle Ridge"	248
	"Discovery"	3
	"Chance"	10
	"Kirks Chance"	32
William Tulley	"Tulleys Choice"	50
51:1755:157 ...		
Sarah Blair	pt. "Wood Hall"	50
George Phebus	"Nicholdsons Adventure"	12
	"Addition to Littleworth"	98
h/o Richard Phillips	"Ægypt"	65½
Morgan Caudory	"Quiaukeson Neck"	50
John Waters, Jr.	"Salsbury"	90
	"Envy"	478
51:1755:158 ...		
John Richardson	"Norths Situation"	481
h/o John Leatherbury	"Small Lott"	50
	"Abergaving"	50
	"Worwick"	66⅔
	"Warrington"	15
	"Leatherburys Fancey"	8
Robert Hopkins	"Carneys Chance"	50
John Robertson	pt. "Boazmans Adventure"	133
	"Ignoble Quarter"	182
John Magee	"Kings Luck"	50
Allen Gray	"Harrissons Adventure"	55
51:1755:159 ...		
Michael Owen	"Board Tree Ridge"	100
Arnald Ballard	"Suckcess"	121
John Powell	"Powells Chance"	165½
Henry Grayham	"Tarr Kill Ridge"	60
John Waller	pt. "Parish"	30
John Elzey, Jr.	"Second Purchase"	250
	"Lotts Daughter"	30
	"Ellises Choice"	100
51:1755:160 ...		

Zorobabel Hall	"Desart"	175
Alexander Robertson	"Akham"	1514
David Marvell	"Hard Shift"	100
Nicholas Evans Colliar	pt. "Last Choice"	100
Thomas Wright	pt. "Contention"	50
	pt. "Intent"	155
	"Discovery"	44
51:1755:161 ...		
Isaac Costin	"Bear Point"	200
	"Flat Land"	100
	"Costins Trouble"	50
Thomas Hayward, Jr.	pt. "Double Purchase"	249
Francis Roberts	pt. "Ellits Choice"	100
William Tayler	"Knights Loss"	39
George North	1 lot in Princess Ann Town – No. 24	<n/g>
William Roberts	pt. "Davids Disteny"	250
51:1755:162 ...		
Thomas Moor	pt. "Conveniency"	96
	"Moors Previledge"	100
Jarvice Ballard	"Derry"	77
	"Goldsmiths Delight" pt. "Illchester"	100
	"Smiths Resolve"	100
Thomas Robertson	"More & Cas It"	12
	"Bozmans Addition"	52
	"More & Cas It"	420
Michael Disharoon	"Ascues Choice"	58
William Disharoon	"Frizels Injoyment"	150
William Bounds	"Barron Lott"	100
51:1755:163 ...		
Samuel Murray	"Cloverfields"	200
Gidean Tilghman, Jr.	pt. "Lott"	50
	pt. "Timber Lott"	15
Stephen Tilghman	pt. "Lott"	50
	pt. "Timber Lott"	15
Jonathan Hath	"Hogg Ridge"	100
William Stanford	pt. "Stanfords Finding"	50

Cannon Wainright	"Woolhope"	75
	pt. "Pasturidge"	130
51:1755:164 ...		
John Owen, Jr.	"Golden Quarter"	50
John Willin	"Ignoble Quarter"	50
Thomas Willin, Jr.	"Ignoble Quarter"	50
Levin Willin	"Shiles's Meadow"	60
William Brown, Jr.	pt. "Wilsons Mistake"	100
James Brown	"Algate"	150
51:1755:165 ...		
George Brown	"Bacors Folly"	75
John Brown	"What You Please"	50
Richard Huffington	pt. "Bacors Folly"	50
John Finch	pt. "Bedford"	100
Thomas & Samuel Cooper, Jr.	"Gladstones Adventure"	75
	"Hardshift"	75
William Cooper	"Bedford"	50
51:1755:166 ...		
Joshua Huffington	"Youngs Purchase"	150
John Jenkins	pt. "Crouches Choice"	50
Joseph Jenkins	pt. "Crouches Choice"	50
Jane Lewcas	"Conveniency"	13
	pt. "Cascoway"	250
Elisha Long	"Longs Chance"	100
George Miles	"Davids Adventure"	99
51:1755:167 ...		
Richard Acworth	pt. "Hogg Quarter"	100
James Acworth	pt. "Acworths Delight"	50
Littleton Dennis (cnp)	"Good Suckcess"	150
	pt. "Williams Hope"	137½
	"Chance"	15
	"Many Owners"	50
	"Cow Meadow"	25
	"Hap at a Venture"	75
	pt. "Timber Tract"	150
	pt. "Carters Lott"	50

	pt. "Cowley"	25
	"Security"	267
James Williss	"Good Luck"	53
John Tilghman	"Beauchamps Priviledge"	79
51:1755:168 ...		
Cornelius English	"Tarr Kill"	45½
James Jones	"Pleasure"	50
Isajah Tilghman	"Beaverdam Branch"	52
James Deane	"Deanes Venture"	50
James Tull	"Accident"	37
Jonathan Jenkins	"Fox Island"	67
51:1755:169 ...		
Robert Geddes	"Support"	50
Isaac Winsor	"Woolwedge"	150
	"Long Delay"	90
James Curtis	pt. "Armstrongs Lott"	183¼
William Coalbourn, Jr.	pt. "Pomfret"	249
	"Discovery"	92
Ebinezar Calloway	"Calloways Folly"	25
	"Calloways Venture"	25
Joseph Rawls	"Gladstones Choice"	150
51:1755:170 ...		
William Waller	"Hogg Pallace"	50
Benjamin Coalbourn	pt. "Pomfrett"	172
Isaac Coalbourn	pt. "Pomfrett"	234
Andrew Fr. Cheney	1 lot in Princess Anne – No. 30	<n/g>
Thomas Laws, Jr.	"Northforland"	100
Day Givan	"Lyons Folly"	150
	"Wales"	50
	pt. "Weatherleys Reserve"	32
	"Givans Discovery"	5
51:1755:171 ...		
Obed Reggan	"Calfe Pasture"	212
John Done	1 lot in Princess Ann Town – No. 15	<n/g>
Robert Swan (cnp)	"Walbrook"	260
	"Aarons Folly"	150

	"Carters Lott"	100
Sewell Handy	"Armstrongs Purchase"	320
	"New Invention"	212½
Samuel Collins Adams	"Adams's Purchase"	50
51:1755:172 ...		
William Geddis	1 lot in Princess Ann Town – No. 7	<n/g>
Isaac Kenney	pt. "Desart"	50
Jacob Gyles	pt. "Gyles Lott"	50
	pt. "Partners Choice"	50
Isaac Gyles	pt. "Gyles Lott"	50
William Revill	pt. "Double Purchase"	100
h/o David Caudory	pt. "Partners Choice"	20
51:1755:173 ...		
Elijah Weatherly	"Acworths Folly"	115
	"Snakey Island"	26
	"Addition"	28
Nehemiah Hitch	"Quiet Entrance"	100
Daniel Cox	"Plumton Salt Ash"	50
Rachel Caudory	"Cant Tel" – charged on f. 44	91
Betty Game	"Georges Pleasure"	50
Patrick Quittermus	"Hogg Quarter"	100
51:1755:174 ...		
Nehemiah Covington	"Sweet Wood"	178
	"Sowerwood"	122
	pt. "Comforts Adventure"	51
	pt. "Covingtons Meadow"	
Phillip Covington	pt. "Sweet Wood"	22
	"Second Choice"	200
	"Sowerwood"	48
	"Henrys Enjoyment"	50
	"Amity"	50
	"Sassafras Neck"	206
	"Comforts Adventure"	57
John Weatherly (cnp)	"Weatherleys Conveniency" – land not known	200
	"Acworths Contrivance"	50
	"Fathers Delight"	100

	"Addition"	122
	"Quiaukeson Neck"	86
	"Snakey Island"	25
	"Weatherleys Marshes" – vide, abstract if not 33¾ a.	3¾
William Bounds	"Barren Neck"	100
Joshua Hall	"Schoolhous Ridge"	98
51:1755:175 ...		
Jacob Adams, Jr.	pt. "Adventure"	125
51:1755:176 **accounts returned by Mr. Charles Dickenson (farmer, DO) as the lands lying in WO.**		
h/o Thomas Hick (SO)	pt. "Three Brothers"	45
h/o Denwod Hicks	pt. "Three Brothers"	46
Col. John Henry	pt. "Three Brothers"	16
Ann Lookerman (widow)	pt. "Three Brothers"	16
James Muir	"Muirs Venture"	150
51:1755:177-195 <missing>		
51:1755:<unnumbered> <blank>		
51:1755:196 ...		
William Scott	"Ryland" – taken by elder survey	150
	"Jones's Caution" – land unknown	200
	"Scotlands Addition" – taken by elder survey	65
Thomas Everender	"Hopkins Disteny" – cut of by the water	50
	"Londons Advisment" – land unknown	50
Mary King	"Hogg Ridge" – owner unknown	100
Mary Price	"Macker Meadow" – said to be in dispute & no owner appears	150
John Long	"Longs Lott" – land unknown	200
Thomas Davis	"Enlargment" – land unknown	100
George Downs	"Chance" – land unknown	150
51:1755:197 ...		
Thomas Dashiell	"Chance" – land unknown	150
Ephraim Polk	"Locust Hammock" – land unknown	50
George Hutchins	"Manloves Grove" – land unknown	250
Thomas Shaw	"Masons Adventure" – taken by elder survey	100
Nehemiah Covington (cnp)	"White Marsh" – land unknown	100
	"Suffolk Neck" – land unknown	150

	"Snow Hill" – land unknown	200
John Panter	"Ignoble Quarter" – belongs to his heirs in ENG	50
Robert Polk	"Polks Lott" – land unknown	50
Thomas Carny	"Carneys Delight" – land unknown	300
51:1755:198 ...		
Daniel Hull	"Hold Fast" – belongs to his heirs in VA	400
Alexander Carlisle	"Friends Advice" – land unknown	30
John Davis	"Sallop" – land unknown	100
	"Battlefield" – land unknown	50
	"Marsh Ground" – owner unknown	40
Adam Hitch	"Fortune" – land unknown	50
William Rodulphas	"Chance" – land unknown	200
John Johnson	"Angola" – land unknown	44
Philip Askue	"Turkey Hall" – land unknown	116
John Richardson	"Would Have Had More" – disclaimed	50
Cornelius Anderson	"Bilboa" – land unknown	50
51:1755:199 ...		
Magdalane Polk	"Richins Addition" – land unknown	100
David Brown	"Browns Chance" – land unknown	55
Michael Gray	"Grays Improvement" – heir in VA	140
James Johnston	"Long Guile" – land unknown	50
James Conner	"Coalrain" – land unknown	200
	"Slooping Pine" – land unknown	50
Arthur Smith	"Suffolk" – land unknown	150
	"Fludders" – land unknown	50
John Mears	"Durham" – land unknown	150
Henry Ellitt	"Wassawomack" – land unknown	250
51:1755:200 ...		
William Stevens	"Ment More" – taken by elder survey	400
John Lawrance	"Lawrances" – land unknown	200
James Jolley	"Cobham" – land unknown	100
	"Jolleys Delight" – cut of by line of VA	700
Mary Games	"Lannom Deveroys" – land unknown	300
Pearce Bray	"Clonmell" – land unknown	40
Henry Peasley	"Thornbury" – land unknown	1000
John Manlove	"Manloves Improvment" – taken by elder survey	300

Samuel Young	"Coventry" – land unknown	300
William White	"Kings Norton" – land unknown	100
51:1755:201 ...		
Timothy Pead	"West Ridge" – land unknown	150
Dockit Beauchamp	"Contention" – owner unknown	65
William Twyford	"Hickory Levill" – land unknown	40
Richard Whitemarsh	"Whitemarshes Chance" – land unknown	200
Michael Williams	"Fanningham" – land unknown	300
James Weatherley	"Weatherleys Purchase" – owner unknown	110
h/o James Givan	"Largey" – heir went to Carrolina	100
Charles Nutter	"No Name" – land unknown	50
	"Nutters Rest" – land unknown	450
	"Rich Ridge" – land unknown	239
William Wainright	"Doutys Lott" – owner unknown	50
51:1755:202 ...		
widow of John Aylworth	"St. Albins" – owner unknown	64
Peter Doutty	"St. Jermon" – land unknown	50
	"Douttys Previledge" – land unknown	50
Oliver Smith	"Monmoth" – land unknown	40
John Marrett	"Lyons Denn" – land unknown	200
	"Ferry Hall" – land unknown	100
John Cheasman	"Coopers Hall" – land unknown	200
Thomas Chappell	"Kingston" – land unknown	100
John Gladston	"Glads Tower" – land unknown	100
	"Gladstons Delight" – land unknown	100
	"John Gladstons Land" – land unknown	300
James Wyth & Marmaduke Masters	"Batcholers Delight" – land unknown	250
	"Batcholers Intention" – land unknown	250
	"Batcholers Contrivance" – land unknown	150
51:1755:203 ...		
William Keen	"Partners Choice" – owner unknown	50
	"Washwatter" – taken by elder survey	36
James Warrington	"Chance" – land unknown	300
John Hall	"Somthingworth" – land unknown	200
David Harris	"Hearts Content" – taken by elder survey	300
John Lamee	"Pasturage" – land unknown	50

Richard Russell	"New Ireland" – land unknown	500
John Frizell	"Island Marsh" – owner unknown	50
Andrew Whittington	"Monmoth" – land unknown	50
Thomas Holster	"Liverpool" – land unknown	500
51:1755:204 ...		
Peter Calloway	"Harlington" – taken by elder survey	200
	"Little Britain" – land unknown	200
John Holder	"Chance" – land unknown	32
Thomas Huggett	"Carpenters Folly"	190
John Rutter	"Tower Hill" – land unknown	150
John Peter Frank	"Lozange" – disclaimed; land unknown	100
John Parker	"Cambridge" – land unknown	300
William Aylford	"First Lott" – land unknown	600
Rebecca Price	"Prices Purchase" – land unknown	100
Jos. & Benjamin Hardy	"Orphans Lott" – Jos. went to sea & never returned & as no division has been made, Benjamin refuses to pay the rent	333⅔
51:1755:205 ...		
Jeremiah Barrinclue	"Peace" – land unknown	200
William Phillipson	"What You Will" – land unknown	200
William Aylward	"Aylwards Addition" – taken by elder survey	100
	"Aylwards First Lott" – taken by elder survey	425
James Bradey	"Wallis's Adventure" – land unknown	200
Thomas Potter	"Owens Lott" – taken by elder survey	100
William Yaulding	"Hanslo" – land unknown	50
John Wilson	"Batcholers Choice" – land unknown	100
Edward Dixon	"Contention" a/s "Dixton" – land unknown	300
Mathew Armstrong	"Skippers Plantation" – land unknown	600
51:1755:206 ...		
Raymon Stapleford	"Staplefords Neck" – land unknown	250
Peter Kersley	"Townsend Neck" – land unknown	150
Edward Price	"Prices Hope" – land unknown	200
Cornelias Ward	"Bear Point" – land unknown	200
Daniel Curtis	"Curtis Improvement" – land unknown	150
William Furnice	"Furnis's Adventure" – land unknown	200
William Watters	"Friends Choice" – land unknown	600

Andrew Calloway	"Recovery" – land unknown	288
Richard Lewis	"Stepney" – land unknown	150
Alexander Thomas	"Happy Enjoyment" – land unknown	144
51:1755:207 ...		
Robert Wair	"Increase" – taken by elder survey	182
h/o Col. John Rider	"Three Brothers" – heirs in DO	136
Benjamin Nesham	"Benjamins Good Success" – land unknown	16
Thomas Cottingham	"Contention" – owner unknown	65
William Beauchamp	"First Choice" – taken by elder survey	59
Joseph Cottman	"Nobles Lott" – taken by elder survey	75
Jarrat Bashaw	"Hoggs Down" – heirs in VA if any	125
Daniel Lingoe	"Pembertons Good Good Will" – in dispute	100
	"Plumton Salt Ash" – owner unknown	100
Ebinezar Handy	"Coxes Fork" – owner unknown	75
51:1755:208 ...		
Samuel Tayler (ACC)	"Harrissons Adventure" – owner unknown	50
Heneritta & Ann Bondler	"Prestons Addition" – heirs in ENG	125
James & William Weatherley	"Weatherleys Marshes" – owners unknown	102⅓
Daniel Sheridon	"Sheridons Desire" – owner unknown	20
John Trahairn	"Holders Chance" – owner unknown	65
Stephen Kenney	"Kenneys Luck" – land unknown	50
George Tull (DO)	"James's Choice"	150
Richard Wallis	"Folly" – land unknown	50
John Twyford (DO)	"Prickle Pair Island"	5
	"Cow Quarter"	5
51:1755:209 ...		
Robert Dorman	"Josephs Choice" – land unknown	50
Francis Martin	"Chery Hinton" – land unknown	24
Samuel Alexander	"Monmoth" – land unknown	100
Henry Hayman	"Shapleys Neglect" – land unknown	50
	"Haymans Hill" – land unknown	200
	"Bagshot" – land unknown	200
	"Twittingham" – land unknown	200
Henry Smith	"Davis Choice" – owner unknown	140
	"Smiths Hope" – taken by elder survey	1002
Moses Owens	"Moses's Lott" – land unknown	100

51:1755:<unnumbered> No. 1 – Lands resurveyed in SO.				
Name of Land	**Surveyed for**	**Resurveyed for**	**Acres**	**Folio**
"Dixons Choice"	Ambroas Dixon	William Dixon	550	1
"Hearts Ease"	Robert Heart	Henry Miles	200	1
pt. "Watters River"	William Watters	John Watters	302½	1
"Straights"	Cornelius Johnston	Robert King	600	2
"Johns Town"	George Johnston	Robert King	300	2
"Boston Town"	Henry Boston	William Planner	350	2
"Cheap Price"	Thomas Price	William Planner	500	2
"Ware Point"	Germon Gillit	John Outton	100	2
"Dixons Lott"	Ambroas Dixon	George Wilson	245	2
"Desart"	Stephen Horsey	Thomas Walston	400	4
"Maddux Hope"	Lazarus Maddux	Daniel, Thomas & Lazarus Maddux	100	4
"Coalbourns Purchase"	William Coalbourn	William Stevens	300	5
"Long Acre"	Alexander Draper	Cornilius Ward	100	6
"Prices Vineyard"	James Price	<n/g>	200	7
"Middle Ridge"	William Stevens	Kirk Gunby	200	7
"Undue"	William Stevens	John Davis	300	7
"Vulcans Vineyard"	Thomas Cottingham	Jos. Langford	86	7
"First Choice"	Thomas Dixon	William Dixon	200	7
"Wood Street"	John Emmett	Thomas Jones	300	8
"Hopwell"	John Garratt	John Coldwell	50	10
"Pomfrett"	William Coalbourn	William Coalbourn	1400	10
pt. "Mitchells Lott"	William Stevens	Thomas Marshall	100	10
"Bay Bush Hall"	William Stevens	William Williams	100	11
"Hackland"	John Vanhack	Betty Gale	1000	13
"Bozmans Choice"	William Bozman	Betty Gale	300	13
"Panters Denn"	John Panter	Robert Laws	200	15
"Bells Previledge"	George Bell	George Irving	100	14
"Lunns Improvment"	William Stevens	Lewis Jones & Martha Wilson	250	15
"Friends Choice"	Persquel Read	John White & Richard Wallis	300	15
"Lunns Increase"	Edward Lunn	Martha Wilson	150	16
pt. "Washford"	Henry Hayman	Henry Waggaman	75	16
pt. "Washford"	Henry Hayman	Henry Waggaman	75	16

"Hab Nab"	George Bell	Francis Wilson	50	16
"Coxes Mistake"	William Green	James Jones	200	17
"Stanidge"	Nicholas Smith	Levin Denwood	50	17
"Hope"	John White	Lewis Jones	100	18
"Noble Quarter"	John Tayler	Nicholas Rice & Thomas Shiles	1000	19
"Rice Land"	Nicholas Rice	Levin Gale	388	19
"Dispence"	David Spence	Thomas Walker	500	19
"Kellems Folly"	Robert Ingram	for several	550	19
"Errendly"	John Elzey	Thomas & Underwood Rensher	350	20
pt. "Tinson"	William Bozman	John Leattesbury	150	20
"Bennetts Adventure"	Richard Bennett	George Dashiell	2500	20
"Horseys Baliwick"	Stephen Horsey	Robert Ridgley & Edward North	400	21
"Johnsons Lott"	George Johnston	Robert King	300	21
"Vulcans Vineyard"	Thomas Cottingham	William Murray	29	21
"Averys Policey"	John Avery	for several	300	21
"Mitchels Lott"	Alexander Mitchell	William Elgitt	300	22
"Coxes Choice"	Thomas Cox	Daniel Jones	150	23
51:1755:<unnumbered> ...				
"Sunken Ground"	James Jones	Levin Gale	500	25
"Munsley"	William Elgitt	Murray, Hall, & Brady	243	25
"Second Choice"	Samuel Smith	Thomas Gilliss	130	25
"Hickory Ridge"	William Stevens	John Shiles	50	26
"Little Belain"	Robert Ridgley	David Polk	100	28
"Canterbury"	John Parsons	Alexander Adams & Peter <unr>	50	28
"Dantery"	John Parsons	William Alexander	150	28
pt. "Smiths Adventure"	Samuel Smith	Thomas Gilliss	369	33
pt. "Lott"	William Thomas	Thomas Dashiell	78	33
"Toneys Vineyard"	Stephen Horsey	Alexander Adams	300	33
"Pemberton"	(N) Pemberton	Isaac Handy	900	36
"More & Cas It"	William Bozman	George Bozman	188	37
"Canes Choice"	James Carne	Daniel, Thomas, & Lazarus Maddux	200	37
"Berrors Lott"	Phillip Berror	David Wilson	600	37

"Glanvills Lott"	William Glenvell	James Robertson	500	38
"Davis's Conquest"	William Davis	Levin Wilson	300	38
"First Choice"	Richard Acworth	David Wilson	210	38
"St. Peters Neck"	Peter Elzey	Lewis Rigsby	400	38
"Almoadington"	John Elzey	Arnald Elzey	1000	38
"South Betherton"	William Thorn	Thomas Brown	300	38
"Nutters Delight"	Christopher Nutter	David Wilson	150	38
"Winders Purchase"	John Winder	Nicholas Fountin	200	39
"Thorns Intention"	David Brown	David Wilson	50	39
"Woolfords Chance"	Roger Woolford	George Bozman	260½	40
"Small Hopes"	William Stevens	Aaron Tilghman	100	40
"New Rumney"	John Winder	Nicholas Fountin	150	40
"Ellitts Improvment"	Thomas Manlove	Michael Dorman	200	40
"Bridgers Lott"	Jos. Bridgers	H. Waggaman & Thomas Jones	11000	41
"Friends Choice"	Thomas Jones	David Wilson	300	41
"Contention"	John Bozman	Daniel, Thomas, & Lazarus Maddux	100	42
"Maddux Adventure"	John White	Daniel, Thomas, & Lazarus Maddux	150	43
"Cross"	William Green	Robert King	36	43
"Turkey Cock Hill"	John King	James Knight	125	43
"Davises Choice"	John White	Levin Wilson	100	44
"Norwich"	Thomas Shanks	William Pollett	100	44
"Woolfords Land"	Roger Woolford	Roger Woolford	700	44
"Maidstone"	William Stevens	David Wilson	70	44
"Shipways Choice"	William Stevens	Heber Whittingham	227	44
"Maddux Inclosier"	William Stevens	Daniel, Thomas, & Lazarus Maddux	100	44
"Woodland"	William Stevens	David Wilson	150	44
pt. "Illchester"	Henry Smith	Jane Strawbridge	650	46
"Corporals Ridge"	Charles Jones	William Walston	50	45
"Partners Choice"	Arnald Elzey	Robert King	150	47
"Gullets Asshurance"	William Gullet	Michael Dorman	100	46
"Crawleys Folly"	John Crawley	William Pollett	100	47
"Hartlebury"	Abraham Hath	William Waltom	50	48
"Blakes Hope"	Joel Blake	Thomas Hayward	200	48

"Arracoca"	William Price	William Merrell	250	45
pt. "Elgate"	William Elgate	Jacob Adams	100	50
pt. "Golden Lyon"	Thomas Horwood	Col. Robert Jenkins Henry	365	50
"Williams Hope"	William Smith	Henry Smith	1000	50
"Kings Neck"	Jenkin Price	Southey Littleton	300	50
pt. "Dublin"	John Marvill	Robert Tayler	25	51
51:1755:<unnumbered>	...			
"Hillards Discovery"	John Hilands	Teague Riggin	150	54
"Allens Contest"	Richard Allen	William Wood	100	53
"Ledbourn"	William Stevens	Edward Beauchamp	350	58
"Houstons Choice"	Robert Houston	Thomas Hayward & Phillip Quinton	150	60
"Shoomakers Meadow"	John Powell	Jacob Adams	109	61
"White Marshes Delight"	Richard Whitemarsh	John Lyon	300	62
"Meeches Hope"	Thomas Meech	William Dashiell	150	62
"Runsell"	Samuel Jackson	John Macclester	100	63
"Bently"	Thomas Walker	Ephraim King	300	65
"Hartford"	Charles Hutchins	Benjamin Townsend	200	65
"Shadwell"	Charles Hutchins	John Waller	100	65
"Batcholers Adventure"	Robert Collier	Ephraim King	200	66
"Cannons Choice"	Stephen Cannon	<n/g>	12	66
"Covent Garden"	Robert Collier	Ephraim King	200	68
"Close Fork"	Richard Whittey	Thomas Brereton	500	74
"Gettesamany"	William Stevens	Christopher Nutter & John Jones	300	75
"Carters Lodge"	George Carter	James Read	350	76
"Supply"	Isaac Foxcroft	Ephraim King	750	76
"Meadow"	Nathaniel Doherty	John Doherty	50	78
"Happy Addition"	Roger Woolford	Roger Woolford	250	81
"Wrights Venture"	William Wright	Isaac Handy	52½	83
"Drownd Cow"	William Coalbourn	William Coalbourn	200	88
"Elgates Purchase"	William Elgate	William Elgate	70	89
"Littleworth"	George Phebus	Samuel Phebus	200	91
"Hogg Quarter"	William Alexander	John Alexander	100	97

"Maddux Inclosier"	Lazarus Maddux	Daniel, Thomas, & Lazarus Maddux	250	101
pt. "Partners Desire"	Richard & John Waller	John Waller	95	103
"Everdon"	Thomas Everton	Robert King	500	104
"Saplin Ridge"	Peter Benton	Benton Costin	50	109
"Coopers Mistake"	Samuel Fluelling	Jacob Airs	100	111
"Unexpected"	Arthur Denwood	David Wilson	40	113
"Little Bolton"	Alexander Draper	Thomas Jones	250	114
"Crouches Choice"	Ambroas Crouch	John Anderson	254	115
pt. "Daviss Choice"	Thomas Davis	David & Levin Wilson	275	115
"Davis's Lott"	Richard Davis	Levin Wilson	300	116
"Undue"	Steven Horsey	William Stevens	200	116
"Might Have Had More"	James Jones	James Jones	200	119
"Hastfords Purchase"	George Hastford	Isaac Boston	200	120
"White Marshes Delight"	John Lyon	Robert Givan	300	123
pt. "Williams Hope"	Henry Smith	Thomas Hayward	562	126
pt. "No Name"	David Brown	David Wilson	293	127
"Edwards Lott"	Ann Roberts	Edward Roberts	220	131
pt. "Increase"	Robert Wair	Southey Whittington	168	140
"Contention"	Alexander Leckie	Levin Gale	556	141
"Addition"	Jos. Macclester	John Gale	713	141
"Benstons Lott"	Thomas Benston	Edward North	50	145
"Runsell"	John Macclester	William Dashiell	120	148
"Nantwick"	John & Lewis Disharoon	William Vennables	300	150
"Porters Island"	Jos. Gray	Sarah King & Jos. Waters	50	152
"Timber Tract"	Robert King	Robert King	280	153
"Timber Grove"	Phillip Covington	Henry Waggaman	150	154
"Chance"	Samuel Fluelling	Samuel Fluelling	25	154
"Cox Bill"	Edward Rook	Thomas Hayward	167	156
51:1755:<unnumbered> ...				
"Chance"	Daniel Long	David Long	125	157
"Meadow"	William Adams	William Adams	316	157
"Jeshimon"	William Stevens	Ephraim King	300	57

"Ross"	John Evans	John Handy	50	68
pt. "Weslocks Neck"	John Spann	Jos. Macclester	233	70
"Kings Purchase"	Robert King	Robert King	300	157
"Henrys Vineyard"	Henry Newmon	Henry Newmon	50	166
"No Name"	John Hewit	Levin Gale	1550	165
"Fountins Lott"	Samuel Fountin	David Wilson	100	169
"Lott"	James Polk	Henry Wright	200	176
"Waggamans Purchase"	Henry Waggaman	Henry Waggaman	436	178
"Liberty"	Henry Waggaman	Henry Waggaman	163	180
"Indien Bones"	Upsher King	Zorobabel King	100	181
"Dixons Bull"	Thomas Dixon	Thomas Dixon	70	191
"Little Derry"	John Russell	Justices of Somerset Co.	200	61
"Kings Lott"	John King	Isaac Adams	96	17
pt. "Wrights Choice"	Bloyce Wright	Isaac Handy	50	29
"Eason"	Thomas Bloyce	Isaac Handy	50	39
"Salkerk"	James English	George Irving	50	67
"Comby Chance"	Christopher Newgent	John Polk	150	67
"St. Gyles"	George Bell	George Irving	200	68
pt. "Minshalls Adventure"	Jeffery Minshell	Caleb Harris	60	54
"Chance"	Roger Woolford	Robert Harris	300	54
"Hudsons Folly"	Henry Hudson	Jacob Adams	200	55
"Years Land"	John Bounds	William Dashiell	37½	64
"Tick Neal"	Leonard Jones	Jacob Aires	51	68
"Cow Quarter"	George Phebus	George Irving	60	96
"Jones's Meadow"	Samuel Jones	Lewis Jones	300	103
"No Name"	William Elgitt	William Murray	450	113
"Clenneth"	Edward Horson	Edward Howard	400	116
"Prices Vineyard"	James Price	<n/g>	201	116
"Briscoes Lott"	Arthur Brisco	Robert Ridgley	600	119
"Covington" a/s "Sassafras Neck"	William Stevens	Phillip Covington	150	123

51:1755:<unnumbered>	No. 2 – Lands taken by elder survey.			
Name of Land	**Surveyed for**	**Included in**	**Acres**	**Folio**
pt. "William Ston"	Thomas Williams	<n/g>	70	1
pt. "Bears Neck"	William Stevens	<n/g>	67	6
pt. "Hopwell"	John Garrat	<n/g>	50	10
"Rigland"	assigned to William Scott	<n/g>	150	12
"Unity"	Samuel, Nathaniel, & Isaac Horsey	<n/g>	100	12
"Glaucester"	John Okean	"White Chappell"	25	23
"Goddarts Folly"	John White	"Horseys Baliwick"	300	27
"Chance"	John White	"Bennets Adventure"	295	28
"Hogsdown"	Richard Stevens	"Bennets Adventure"	150	34
"Monsham"	John Christopher	"Horseys Baliwick"	100	35
pt. "Diep"	John Shipway	"Shipways Choice"	150	37
"Crambrook"	Catherine Price	<n/g>	300	52
pt. "Tilghmans Adventure"	Gideon Tilghman	<n/g>	40	60
"Scotlands Addition"	William Scott	<n/g>	65	145
"Conners Grove"	Phillip Conner	<n/g>	200	53
"Manloves Improvment"	John Manlove	<n/g>	300	53
"Need More"	William Stevens	<n/g>	400	53
pt. "Minshells Adventure"	Jeffery Minshell	<n/g>	140	54
"Little Actton"	John Freeman	<n/g>	100	55
pt. "Dales Adventure"	David Dale	<n/g>	88	56
pt. "Middlesex"	William Stevens	<n/g>	70	58
pt. "Ware"	William Woodgate	<n/g>	17	66
"Hearts Content"	David Harris	<n/g>	300	77
pt. "Branford"	Robert Catlin	<n/g>	56	79
"Nobles Lott"	Isaac Knoble	"Toneys Vineyard"	73	80
"Masons Adventure"	William Mason	<n/g>	100	81
"Smiths Hope"	Henry Smith	<n/g>	1002	84
"Leatherhead"	George Benston	<n/g>	150	88
"Wash Water"	William Keen	<n/g>	36	89
"Harrington"	William Keen	<n/g>	200	89
"Aylwards Addition"	William Aylward	<n/g>	100	96
pt. "Prices Conclusion"	Edward Price	<n/g>	25	97

"None Such"	Anthony Bell	"Watkins Point"	50	98
pt. "Dixons Kindness"	George Hough	<n/g>	75	99
pt. "Bozmans Addition"	John Bozman	"More & Cas It"	50	99
pt. "Williams Adventure"	Michael Williams	<n/g>	17	103
"Aylwards First Lott"	William Aylward	<n/g>	425	105
"Newfound Land"	Francis Roberts	<n/g>	125	106
"Timber Lott"	Walter Tayler	<n/g>	250	109
"Desart"	Thomas Walston	<n/g>	25	111
pt. "Late Delay"	Ephraim Polk	<n/g>	34	114
pt. "Catlins Lott"	Robert Catlin	<n/g>	279	115
"Hillards Adventure"	John Hillard	<n/g>	100	117
pt. "First Choice"	William Stevens	<n/g>	73¼	121
"Owens Lott"	Moses Owen	<n/g>	100	127
51:1755:<unnumbered>	**...**			
"Rich Swamp"	Jos. Macclester	"Meeches Hope"	50	133
"Atkins Fancy"	William Coalbourne	"Pomfrett"	200	144
"Raymons Chance"	Jonathan Raymon	"Smiths Adventure"	69	145
pt. "Good Luck"	John Coldwell	<n/g>	31½	156
pt. "Increase"	Robert Wair	<n/g>	182	155
pt. "Nairns Addition"	John Coldwell	<n/g>	30	143
"Ruck Prevented"	William Cox	<n/g>	145	160
"Colliers Desire"	Thomas Collier	"Daniels Adventure"	50	165
"Thurd Choice"	Isaac Williams	<n/g>	44	165
"Hard Fortune"	Thomas Larrimore	<n/g>	40	156
"Shoemakers Meadow"	Jacob Davis	<n/g>	10	168
"Diep"	Henry Dorman	"Shipways Choice"	36	170
pt. "Chance"	Kirk Gunby	<n/g>	40	171
"Worth Little"	Josephus Bell	"Watkins Point"	63	182

51:1755:<unnumbered>	**No. 3 – Lands in SO where no rent is paid with reason.**			
Land	**Surveyed for**	**Reason**	**Acres**	**Folio**
"Hopkins Distoney"	George Johnston	cut of by water	50	6
"Ignoble Quarter"	George Andrews	belongs to h/o John Panter in ENG	50	14
"Hogg Down"	Edward Southern	belongs to h/o Jarrat Bashaw if any	125	24
pt. "Sarahs Neck"	John Winder	escheat; no claimant	46	29
"Pembertons Good Will"	John Winder	survey is erroneous & not half the quantity	700	32
pt. "Smiths Adventure"	Samuel Smith	not contained within the bounds	133	33
pt. "Prices Grove"	William Price	cut of by Pocomoke River	15	49
"Acquintica"	Jenkin Price	only 200 a.	100	52
"Benstons Lott"	Henry Smith	belongs to Jos. Benston (VA)	100	55
pt. "Winsor Castle"	William Winslow	owner went into PA & died; no claimant	100	59
"Fathers Delight"	John Manlove	belongs to h/o James Weatherley but not conveyed	100	69
"Little Munmoth"	Thomas Brereton	patent vacated	100	70
"Witipevant"	Stephen Horsey	patented to Stephen Conner by another name & quantity	600	74
"Crain Ridge"	James Weatherley	given up	550	75
"Thomas's Court"	Thomas Gordon	patent vacated	500	77
"Newwod Hill"	Richard Forwell	in dispute	200	79
pt. "Addition"	James Weatherley	John Weatherley supposed to be heir – denied	122	85
"Goslins Lott"	John Goslin	land can't be found	100	88
"Nop Hill"	George Benston	has no patent	100	88
"Malborough"	Edward Wheler	escheat for want of heirs	150	89
"Troublesom"	John Richens	escheat for want of heirs	100	91
"Holdfast"	Richard Hull	heir in VA	400	93
"Wilsons Lott"	Thomas Wilson	heir in VA	100	93

pt. "Orphans Lot"	Gabriel Cooper	one of owners out of country	333⅔	93
"Grays Improvment"	Michael Gray	heir in VA	140	94
pt. "What You Please"	Phillip Askue	sold but not conveyed	80	98
"Weatherleys Conveniency"	James Weatherley	heir says he knows no such land	200	106
pt. "Crouches Choice"	Ambroas Crouch	escheat if to be found	246	115
"Doe Better"	Thomas Gilliss	disclaimed; patent for 200	1850	119
"Danbury"	Samuel Jackson	patent vacated	300	120
"Would Have Had More"	John Richardson	disclaimed by Richardson	50	30
"Plain Harbour"	Nathaniel & Isaac Horsey	patent vacated	500	128
pt. "New Haven"	Thomas Everenden	belongs to (N) Baley (VA)	517	129
"Largee"	James Givan	heir went to Carolina	100	131
"Glasgow"	Thomas Gorden	disclaimed by John Smith	150	132
"Three Brothers"	John Rider	belongs to h/o (N) Rider (DO)	136	146
"Cow Quarter"	William Twiford	belong to his heirs in DO	5	146
"Partners Choice"	John Flemming	patent vacated	100	164
"Discovery"	Benjamin Langford	patent vacated	50	167
51:1755:<unnumbered> **<blank>**				

51:1755:<unnumbered>	**No. 4 – Surveyed lands that are unknown.**		
Land	**Surveyed for**	**Acres**	**Folio**
"Londons Advisment"	William Furnice	50	4
"Johnstons First Choice"	William Stevens	200	5
"Martins Hope"	William Green	100	9
"Horseys Denn"	William Stevens	150	11
"Cherry Hinton"	William Stevens	150	11
"Rest"	Jos. Gray	150	12
"Chance"	Stephen Horsey	300	14
"Worst is Past"	James Nicholson	50	14
"Carneys Order"	Thomas Carney	100	15
"Shipleys Neglect"	Henry Hayman	50	16
"White Marsh"	Nehemiah Covington	100	17
"Roberts's Lott"	Francis Roberts	100	17
"Locust Hammock"	John Pilkey	50	19
"Jones Hole"	James Jones	250	19
"Haymans Hill"	(N) Haymon	200	22
"Carneys Delight"	Thomas Carney	300	22
"Newbury"	William Stevens	150	26
"Winterburn"	John White	100	26
"Berks"	John White	150	27
"Angola"	William Green	44	28
"Lime Hous"	William Stevens	40	29
"Suffolk"	William Stevens	150	31
"Addition"	Richard Keen	100	32
"Bilboa"	Cornelius Anderson	50	32
"Carys Adventure"	Edward Cary	50	34
"Rhodey"	John Singleton	350	35
"Sallop"	John Davis	100	35
"Battlefield"	John Davis	50	35
"Ellords Choice"	Stephen Ellord	200	38
"Double Purchase"	Nicholas Fountin	80	44
"Longuile"	John Johnson	50	45
"Richins Addition"	John White	100	45
"Turkey Cock Hill"	Edward Sidbury	120	48
"Coalrain"	James Conner	200	48

"Durham"	John Mears	150	48
"Fludders"	Arthur Smith	50	49
"Wassawomack"	Henry Elliott	250	49
"Cobham"	James Jolley	100	49
"Lawrances"	John Lawrance	200	50
"Lannum Devoroy"	Richard Games	300	50
"Seamans Choice"	Thomas Ball	150	51
"Hudsons Fortune"	Henry Hudson	100	51
51:1755:<unnumbered> ...			
"Thornbury"	Henry Peasley	1000	52
"Kent"	Col. Edward Cones	1500	52
"Jones's Caution"	Walter Lane	200	54
"Kings Norton"	Thomas White	100	53
"Coventery"	Samuel Young	300	53
"Bringingham"	William Smith	500	53
"Lyons Penn"	John Lyon	200	67
"Acton"	John Freeman	300	55
"Wests Ridge"	Timothy Pead	150	60
"Bengill"	John Marks	100	61
"White Marshes"	Richard Whitemarsh	200	62
"Long Hill"	Samuel Jackson	300	62
"Fanningham"	Richard Acworth	300	64
"Manloves Delight"	Richard Acworth	100	66
"Ferry Hall"	John Smith	100	71
"Weatherleys Chance"	James Weatherley	250	72
"Kingston"	Thomas Chappell	100	73
"Manloves Grove"	William Stevens	500	73
"Toswendock"	William Stevens	130	73
"Attawattaquaquo"	William Stevens	1200	74
"Venture"	Samuel Jackson	300	74
"Glads Tower"	John Gladston	100	75
"Batcholers Delight"	James Wyth & Marmaduke Masters	250	75
"Batcholers Invention"	James Wyth & Marmaduke Masters	250	75
"Batcholers Contrivance"	James Wyth & Marmaduke Masters	150	75
"Chance"	John Parremore	300	76
"Gladstons Delight"	John Gladston	100	76

“John Gladstons Land”	John Gladston	300	76
“Vale of Easom”	John Mark	200	77
“Srewsbury”	John Roggers	150	77
“Molleytuck”	Richard Webb	200	77
“Slooping Pine”	James Conner	50	77
“Coopers Hall”	William Merrett	200	77
“Monmoth”	Andrew Whittington	50	78
“Liverpool”	Thomas Holster	500	79
“No Name”	Christopher Nutter	50	80
“Enlargment”	Thomas Davis	100	80
“Carpenters Folly”	Thomas Huggett	190	81
“Polks Lott”	Robert Polk	50	81
“Tower Hill”	Manasses Morris	150	82
“Nutters Rest”	Christopher Nutter	450	82
“Darby”	Henry Holson	200	83
“Browns Chance”	John Brown	55	83
“Lozange”	John Peter Frank	100	84
“Cuckolds Delight”	William Layton	500	86
“Hendersons Chance”	John Henderson	70	86
“Cambridge”	John Parker	300	86
“Middle Neck”	William Brereton	300	87
“Harlington”	John Tayler	200	88
“First Choice”	William Aylford	600	89
51:1755:<unnumbered> ...			
“Chance”	John Renshaw	200	89
“Sand Ridge”	John Tayler	100	89
“Little Brittain”	John Hewitt	200	90
“Taunton”	Walter Read	110	90
“Snow Hill”	Nehemiah Covington	200	91
“Bagg Shott”	Henry Hayman	200	92
“Twillingham”	Henry Hayman	200	92
“White Chappell”	Robert Crouch	100	92
“Peace”	John Richins	200	94
“Woods Land”	John Wood	150	94
“Roaches Priveledge”	John Roach	57	95
“Parkers Peace”	Francis Martin	130	96

"Plumton"	Thomas Cox	450	96
"Salt Ash"	Thomas Cox	480	96
"Coopers Purchase"	Richard Cooper	100	96
"Troublesom"	Francis Martin	130	98
"Turkey Hall"	Phillip Askue	116	100
"Hounsloe"	William Yaulding	100	100
"Prices Purchase"	Alexander Price	100	101
"Wallises Adventure"	James Wallis	200	101
"White Chappell"	Robert Crouch	200	104
"Grays Lott"	James Gray	250	109
"Grays Lott"	James Gray	50	109
"Moses Lott"	Moses Owen	100	110
"Purgatory"	Thomas Rowe	160	110
"Batcholers Choice"	John Wilson	100	111
"Wilsons Lott"	John Wilson	50	111
"Doutys Priveledge"	Peter Douty	50	111
"Wilsons Lott"	John Wilson	38	112
"Contention" a/s "Dixton"	Edward Dixon	300	114
"Johnston"	George Johnston	300	115
"Skippers Platation"	Nathaniel Armstrong	600	115
"Hackworths Charity"	Richard Hackworth	600	115
"Taylers Choice"	Walter Tayler	600	115
"Kings Choice"	John King	300	116
"Staplefords Neck"	Raymond Stapleford	250	116
"Townsends Neck"	John Townsend	150	116
"Prices Hope"	Edward Price	200	116
"No Name"	Stephen Horsey	500	117
"Bear Point"	Cornelius Ward	200	117
"Clarks Marsh"	John Clark	50	117
"Curtis's Improvment"	William Stevens	150	117
"Chance"	Richard Preston	600	118
"Last Choice"	Ambroas London	10	118
"Berkin"	William Smith	300	118
"Bershaba"	John Ellis	100	118
"Bethsada"	William Stevens	100	118
"Furnis's Adventure"	William Furnice	200	118

"Friends Choice"	William Watters	600	119
51:1755:<unnumbered> ...			
"Kingsale"	Josias Seward	150	120
<unr>	William Stevens	150	123
"Recovery"	John Forr	288	124
"Fairfield"	Thomas Pemberton	900	124
"Morris's Advisment"	William Stevens	150	125
"Hopwell"	William Furnice	300	126
"Happy Enjoyment"	Alexander Thomas	144	126
"Lanes Caution"	Walter Lane	220	126
"St. Jermons"	Peter Douty	50	129
"Clonmell"	Pierce Bray	40	108
"Annomesex Marsh"	James Gray	250	129
"What You Will"	Phillip Hunnings	200	132
"Friends Advice"	Alexander Carlisle	30	133
"Taylers Choice"	James Bounds	200	134
"Gideans Luck"	John Caldwell	100	136
"Pasturidge"	John Lamee	50	137
"Hickory Levill"	William Twyford	40	137
"Chance"	John Read	20	140
"Bacnar"	William Polk	100	144
"Benjamins Good Success"	Benjamin Easham	16	144
"Worcester"	John Jones	100	144
"Hopwell"	Roger Woodcroft	200	144
"Asconoakin"	Phillip Calvert, Esq.	2000	144
"Long Lott"	Samuel Long	200	144
"Prestons Addition"	Heneritta & Ann Bondle	125	145
"Security"	John Stevens	35	145
"Chance"	John Holder	32	145
"Dispute"	James Lindow	40	152
"Folly"	Richard Wallis	50	162
"Conveniance"	Thomas Wheatly	52	168
"Josephs Choice"	Joseph Hughs	50	173
"Flat Land"	<n/g>	50	78
"Good Neighbourhood"	<n/g>	200	78
"New Irland"	Lawrance Young	500	78

51:1755:<unnumbered> No. 5 – Lands for which the owner is unknown.			
Land	**Surveyed for**	**Acres**	**Folio**
pt. "Contention"	Edward Dixon	65	4
pt. "Armstrongs Lott"	Mathew Armstrong	50	4
pt. "Double Purchase"	Randolph Revill	385	8
pt. "Merchants Purchase"	Stephen Costin	50	9
"White Oak Swamp"	William Stevens	150	11
pt. "Mackee Meadow"	James Price	150	12
"White Oak Swamp"	Richard Cary	100	16
"Island Marsh"	William Brereton	50	34
"Barnabys Lott"	James Barnaby	40	36
pt. "Davis's Choice"	James Davis	140	37
pt. "Hogg Ridge"	Thomas Manlove	100	47
pt. "Kendall"	Barnard Ward	40	49
pt. "Morris's Hope"	Morris Lister	100	55
pt. "Harrissons Adventure"	John Harrisson	47	56
pt. "Entrance"	Edward Howard	305	59
pt. "Weatherleys Purchase"	James Weatherley	82	63
pt. "St. Albins"	William Woodgate	60	66
pt. "Douteys Lott"	Stephen Cannon	50	66
pt. "Fairsalia"	John White	9	69
pt. "Partners Choice"	William Keen	50	76
"Coxes Fork"	Thomas Cox	150	80
"Bear Ridge"	Thomas Manlove	200	82
pt. "Quiaukeson Neck"	James Weatherley	100	91
pt. "Green Meadow"	James Givan	75	93
pt. "Prices Conclusion"	Edward Price	275	97
pt. "Marsh Ground"	Richard Davis	40	101
pt. "Noble Quarter"	Nicholas Rice	45	118
pt. "Scotland"	William Stevens	25	121
pt. "Holders Chance"	John Holder	65	140
"Weatherleys Marshes"	James & William Weatherley	101⅓	146
"Sheridons Desire"	Daniel Sheridon	20	146
"Loss & Gain"	Edward Beauchamp	15¾	152
"Ledbourn"	Edward Beauchamp	200	157
"Barnets Choice"	James Barnet	98	185

"Shiels's Ridge"	John Moor	75	193
pt. "Suffolk"	William Stevens	354	56

51:1755:<unnumbered> No. 6 – Lands that are twice charged.			
Land	**Surveyed for**	**Acres**	**Folio**
"First Choice"	William Stevens	150	9
"Beards Neck"	Robert Dukes	350	12
"Mile End"	William Stevens	25	30
"Supply"	Isaac Foxcroft	750	35
"Chance"	Roger Woolford	300	59
"Middle Plantation"	William Planner	150	60
"Balley Buggan"	John Coldwell	200	87
"No Name"	David Brown	345	89
"Crouches Desart"	Robert Crouch	100	92
"Hold Fast"	Richard Hull	400	104
"Quiankeson Neck"	James Weatherley	500	104
"Addition"	Phillip Askue	50	109
"Wilsons Discovery"	James Weatherley	500	104
"Josephs Lott"	Benjamin Wailes	70	114
"Covingtons Folly"	Samuel Covington	70	114
"Irish Grove"	Morris Lyster	150	116
"Bloyces Hope"	Thomas Bloyce	150	117
"Londons Advisment"	William Furnice	50	117
"Discovery"	William Cheasman	150	118
"Suffolk"	William Morris	1000	120
"Recovery"	Thomas Brereton	100	121
"Marsh Hook"	James Weatherley	100	123
"Cascoway"	William Stevens	1000	123
"Island Marsh"	William Brereton	50	124
"Quiankeson Neck"	James Weatherley	500	127
"Fathers Care"	John Conner	50	129
"Pastureidge"	James Mackmoris	260	130
"Long Delay"	Ephraim Polk	274	130
"Adventure"	Richard Crocket	70	131
"Unexpected"	Arthur Denwood	40	131
"Batcholers Choice"	John Wilson	100	132
"Stonidge"	Levin Denwood	300	132
"Shields Folly"	James & Thomas Dashiell	1225	111
"Comby Chance"	Adam Hitch	560	137

"Hardship"	John Anderson	200	144
"Middle Tract"	Christopher Nutter	100	160
"No Name" a/s "Lott"	Robert Ridgley	200	163
"Foscutt"	Henry Miles	50	166
"Security"	John Calhoon	100	171
"Coxes Advice"	Anthoney Underwood	200	187
"Chance"	Aaron Sterling	20	195

51:1755:<unnumbered> No. 7 – Lands that are overcharged.			
Land	**Surveyed for**	**Acres**	**Folio**
"Yoorkshire Island"	William Stevens	150	2
"Double Purchase"	William Stevens	150	9
"Holl Well"	William Stevens	100	9
"Ferry Bridge"	William Coalbourn	200	13
"Friends Choice"	William Layton	300	33
"Contention"	John Renshaw	200	16
"Greenwich"	William Stevens	50	29
"Furnis's Choice"	William Furnice	300	37
"Webley"	Henry Smith	250	43
"Manloves Lott"	William Manlove	300	55
"Adams Gardin"	William Stevens	100	56
"Georges Marsh"	William Stevens	50	58
"Entrance"	Edward Howard	850	59
"Good Suckcess"	James Round	300	61
"Weatherleys Purchase"	James Weatherley	750	63
"Acworths Delight"	Richard Acworth	100	64
"Bedford"	William Stevens	500	71
"Prevention"	James Weatherley	90	85
"Hopworths Pasture"	John Hopworth	48	95
"Meadow"	Robert Catlin	100	102
"Cheap Price"	William Planner	725	103
"Meadland"	John Rosen	64	108
"Desart"	Thomas Walston	529	111
"Watterton"	John Watters	100	111
"Almoadington"	Arnald Elzey	1200	120
"Boston Town"	William Planner	500	124
"Williams Hope"	Henry Smith	1002	126
"Chance"	Robert Geddes	29	172
"Timber Lott"	Gidean Tilghman	30	176
"Riggans Amendment"	Teague Riggan	285	196
"Collins Lott"	William Collins	21	200
"Friends Choice"	William Layton	300	33
"Sidney"	William Stevens	50	28
"Covingtons Meadow"	Phillip Covington	460	107

51:1755:<unnumbered> No. 8 – Lands that are undercharged.

Land	Surveyed for	Acres	Folio
"Teague Down"	Ambroas London	16	5
"Salsbury Plains"	Isaac Noble	200	63
"Little Bolton"	Thomas Jones	850	87
"Downs Choice"	Robert Downs	62	93
"Caldwells Chance"	John Caldwell	27	94
"Mitchels Choice"	Thomas Potter	180	98
"Collins Adventure"	Samuel Collins	223	108
"Eashams Chance"	Benjamin Easham	34	144
"Last Choice"	Day Scott	450	179

51:1755:<unnumbered> No. 9 – Lands that are undercharged due to quantity of acres.

Land	Surveyed for	Acres	Folio
"Lazey Hill"	Josias Rotten	50	146

51:1755:<unnumbered> No. 10 – Lands that are paid for more than patent expresses.

Land	Surveyed for	Acres	Folio
"Armstrongs Purchase"	Mathew Armstrong	120	4
"Ignoble Quarter"	Thomas Shiles	14	119
"Rehoboth"	William Stevens	200	51
"Cannons Shott"	Stephen Cannon	200	66

51:1755:<unnumbered> No. 11 – Lands that are overcharged as to quantity of acres.

Land	Surveyed for	Acres	Folio
"Worthless"	William Mathews	10	100
"Meadow"	Robert Catlin	50	102
"Watterton"	John Watters	20	111
"Errondley"	Thomas & Underwood Rensher	63	186

51:1755:<unnumbered> <blank>

51:1755:<unnumbered> <blank>

45:1759:1 ...		**Acres**
Isaac Addams	"Addams First Choice"	208
	"Kings Lott"	204
	"Addams Garden"	42
Joseph Allen	"Sligoe" pt. "Little Belean"	270
	"Fortune"	60
	pt. "Smiths Folly"	100
	"Marsh Ground"	33½
	"Sligoe" pt. "Little Belean"	80
Samuel Addams	"Shoe Makers Meadow"	10
	"Hap Hazard"	25
	"Addams Folly"	301
	"Norfolk"	250
	"Brickles"	7
	"Irish Grove"	50
	"Turkey Trap"	100
	"Addams Delight"	16½
	~~"Bostons Pasture"~~	~~49⅔~~
	pt. "Norfolk"	10½
h/o Collins Addams	"Snow Hill" pt. "Late Discovery"	178
	"Houstons Choice"	160
	"Late Discovery"	22
	"Collins Adventure"	119
Charles Ackworth	"Hogg Quarter"	100
	"Ackworths Delight"	158
	"Ackworths Choice"	50
	"Ridges"	50
	"Marsh Point"	100
45:1759:2 ...		
Rev. Alexander Addams (cnp)	"Barrow Field"	75
	"East Wood"	234
	"Wallys Chance"	300
	"Crambourn"	250
	"Windsor"	100
	"Smiths Adventure"	433
	"Sana"	50

	"Glasgow Swamp"	300
	"Addams Purchase"	18
	"Long Ridge"	50
	"Narrow Ridge"	25
	"Flat Ridge"	25
	"Trouble" now called "Unity to Glasgow"	230
	"Dantary"	150
	"Huggs Purchase"	100
	"Wilsons Folly"	50
	"Guarnsey"	50
	"Guarnsey"	100
	"Jersey"	100
Dennis Addams	"Long Ridge"	75
David Addams	"Partners Agreement"	200
	"Planners Advent"	100
	"Littleworth"	50
William Addams	"Haphazard"	25
	"Addams' Conclusion"	155
	"Whittey" pt. "Hignalls Choice"	88
	pt. "Adventure"	91
45:1759:3 ...		
Samuel Ackworth	"Ackworths Purchase"	300
John Anderson	"Friends Discovery"	30
	"Greens Recantation"	20
James Anderson	"Beckford"	225
h/o Henry Ackworth	"Friends Discovery"	300
Thomas Ackworth	"Ackworths Delight"	200
	"Ackworths Choice"	50
	"Ridges"	50
	"Marsh Point"	100
	"Addition"	116
h/o John Anderson	"Andersons Adventure"	107
Phillip Addams	"Adventure"	110
	"Haphazard"	25
	"Addams Venture"	21
h/o Patrick Alleson	1 lot in Princess Ann Town	<n/g>

45:1759:4 ...		
Hope Addams	"Adventure"	90
	"Good Hope"	38
	"Chance"	68
Jacob Ayres	"Aires's Purchase"	323
	pt. "Shiles Folly"	40
William Addams	"Industery"	75
Phillip Addams	"Addams Garden"	8
	"Addams Green"	50
Thomas Addams	"Industery"	75
William Addams	"Evershamp" called "Glasgow Green"	500
	"Suffolk" now called "Brambles"	200
	"Fathers Care"	200
	"Hazard"	29
John Addams	"Toneys Vineyard"	84
	"Horsey Chance"	101
	"Sportingfield"	50
	"Johns Desire"	82
45:1759:5 ...		
William Addams s/o William	"Hickory Ridge"	55
	"Addams Conclusion"	198
William Austin	"Elizabeths Choice"	100
Phillip Addams s/o William	pt. "Adventure"	34
	"Addams Conclusion"	182
Richard Ackworth	pt. "Hogg Quarter"	100
James Ackworth	pt. "Ackworths Delight"	50
	"Batchelders Purchase"	50
Samuell Collins Addams	"Addams Purchase"	50
Jacob Addams, Jr.	pt. "Adventure"	125
~~h/o John Aylworth~~	~~"Saint Albans"~~	~~64~~
45:1759:6 ...		
Robert Austin	"Carneys Chance"	50
45:1759:7 ...		
David Bird	"Hills Folly"	150
h/o Thomas Bannester (cnp)	pt. "Double Purchase"	127
	"Woolf Harbour"	150

	"Bears Chance"	15
	"Low Lands"	100
Mary Benston	"Westlock Neck"	300
Charles Ballard	"Hazard"	400
	"Covingtons Meadows"	100
h/o William Brereton	"Smiths Adventure"	67
	"Breretons Chance"	300
	"Mile End"	250
h/o Graves Boaman	"Ralphs Venture"	100
	"Gales Purchase"	17
	"Good Success"	50
45:1759:8 ...		
Jonathan Bailey	"Rich Ridge"	100
	"Baileys Lott"	50
	"Pleasant Green"	50
William Ballard	"Almoadington"	300
Esau Boston	"Sewards Purchase"	200
	"Nann Ellis Ridge"	40
Isaac Boston	"Bostons Chance"	260½
	"Bostons Green"	25
Isaac Beauchamp	"Contention"	185
	"Puzle" containing: • "Contention" – 45 a. • "Discovery" – 50 a.	90
	"Remnant"	13
h/o Edward Beauchamp	"Ledbourn"	100
	"Ledbourn"	266
Lewis Beard	"Fishermans Quarter"	130
	"Betty Enlargement"	
	"Beards Advantage"	25
Jessee Bounds	"Years Land"	37½
	"Easams Chance or Choice"	34
	"Collins Ambition"	25
	"Anything"	68½
45:1759:9 ...		

William Brown	"Wilsons Mistake"	100
	"North Denn"	40
George Benston	"Woolver"	100
h/o Elias Bailey & William Bailey	"White Chaple"	100
	"Glocester"	50
George Bailey	"Glocester"	74
	"Baileys' Chance"	41
George Bozman	"More & Cas It"	200
	"Coulbourn"	216⅓
	pt. "Coulbourn"	4
h/o William Bozman	"More & Cas It"	221
Ballard Bozman	"Double Purchase"	500
Rev. Hamilton Bell for h/o Rev. James Robertson	"Glanvills Lott"	440
45:1759:10 ...		
h/o Benjamin Bailey	"Hermon"	200
	"Baileys Purchase"	50
h/o Col. Henry Ballard	"Woolfs Denn"	66½
William Boston	"Forked Neck" pt. "First Choice"	50
	"Bostons Lott"	86
	"Long Ridge"	60
Robert Beauchamp	"Discovery"	100
	"Beauchamps Chance"	206
Jonathan Bound	"Bounds Lott"	300
William Byrd	"Hachilla"	100
Dudson Bacon	"Tatmans Folly"	50
	"Chance"	75
	"Levil Ground"	21½
Thomas Byrd	"Jeshemon"	150
	"Elgats Lott"	100
	"Hachilla"	50
	"Partners Choice"	150
45:1759:11 ...		
John Beard	"Callaways Addition"	50
	"Beards Advantage"	25

Thomas Beauchamp	"Ledbourn"	160
	"Beauchamps Venture"	145
	pt. "Ledbourn"	50
John Beauchamp	"Ledbourn"	150
	pt. "Ledbourn"	50
Paskue Barnett	"Little Marsely"	100
Samuell Bradley	"Tulleys Purchase"	50
John Bradley	"Taylors Chance"	50
Robert Brown	"Which You Please"	150
Massy Beauchamp	"Nobblets Lott"	28
	"Three Brothers"	522
William Bratton	"Williams Hope"	119
45:1759:12 ...		
Josephus Bell	"More Worth"	176
	"Bells Purchase"	100
	"Bells Discovery"	60
	"Bells & Horseys Conclusion" pt. "Hopkins Point"	117
	"Worth Little"	63
	"None Such"	50
	"Addition"	6
h/o Brough Bratten	"Little Acton" pt. "Blakes Hope"	100
William Booth	"Coxes Discovery"	145
George Bennett	"Chelsey"	100
James Bradley	"Addition to Collins Adventure"	159
Robert Banks	"Sarahs Security"	350
	"Halls Adventure"	168
John Bratten	"Addition"	40
	"Williams Hope"	61
	"Hogg Quarter"	50
William Bennett	"Titchfield"	50
	"Fairham"	50
45:1759:13 ...		
William Beauchamp	"Hogg Yard"	95
	"Ledbourn"	5
	"Three Brothers"	200

Rev. Hamilton Bell	"Hameltons Fortune"	882
	"Davis's Choice" pt. "Glebe Land"	120
	<n/g> land from John Parker not patented	4
	"Waltoms Improvement"	55½
Mathias Benston	"Hockley"	50
James Beard	"Laytons Recovery"	100
Benjamin Bird	"New Haven"	100
William Benston	"Whittingtons Neglect"	156
	pt. "Nights Success"	100
John Betsworth	"Providence"	215½
	"Betsworth Choice"	62½
Abraham Barklett	"Barkletts Lott"	111
h/o Sarah Bannester	pt. "Double Purchase"	43
45:1759:14 ...		
John Barklett	"Hogg Quarter"	75
	"Stanaway"	160
	"St. Albans"	140
	pt. "Townsends Salutation" formerly "Hartford"	50
Arnold Ballard	"Success"	121
Joshua Ballard	"Deny"	77
	"Goldsmith Delight" pt. "Ilchester"	100
	"Smiths Resolves"	100
William Brown, Jr.	pt. "Wilsons Mistake"	100
James Brown	"Algate"	150
George Brown	"Bacors Folly"	75
John Brown	"What You Please"	50
William Bounds	"Barren Neck"	100
Sarah Blair	pt. "Wood Hall"	50
45:1759:15 ...		
~~Levin Ballard~~	~~"Dormans Purchase"~~	~~150~~
	~~"Dormans Priviledge"~~	~~30~~
	~~"Dormans Addition"~~	~~104~~
Thomas Benston, Jr.	pt. "Exchange"	35
	"Greenfield"	32
	pt. "Middle"	11

John Burk	"Ross"	56
	"Chance"	12
William Benston s/o Thomas	"Middle"	89
	"Exchange"	65
45:1759:16 ...		
Benjamin Cottman	"Boyers Banks"	32½
	pt. "Costons Vineyard"	91½
	pt. "Costons Trouble"	47
Jacob Cullen	"Johnstons Lott"	137
	"Point Next the Worst"	25
	"Haphazard"	6
	"Peacemaker"	3½
William Catlin	"Hartford Broad Oake"	290
	"Brandford"	44
	"Catlins Venture"	50
	"Catlins Lott"	21
h/o Charles Curtis	"Armstrongs Lott"	66½
	"Curtis's Lott"	75
John Cottingham	"Boston"	154
	"Rumling Point"	15
William Coulbourn	"Pomfritt"	918
45:1759:17 ...		
James Covington	"Mannings Resolution"	130
h/o Thomas Covington	"Covingtons Choice"	150
William Cannon for his wife	"Vulcans Vineyard" & "Nicholson Lott"	161
h/o Benjamin Cottman	"Coxes Discovery"	100
Joshua Caldwell	~~"Maiden Head"~~	~~300~~
	"Caldwells Chance"	27
	~~"Bally Buggan"~~	~~197~~
	"Purchase"	134
	"Anything"	100
	"Bear Swamp"	16
Benjamin Cottman	"Tauntin Dean"	114
	"Shurmas Land"	30
	pt. "Young Timson"	120
h/o John Crouch	"Hogg Neck"	100

45:1759:18 ...		
John Christopher	"White Chappell Green"	50
	"Mousham"	100
Nehemiah Crockitt	"Adventure"	26
	"Point Marsh"	3
	~~"Noble Quarter"~~	~~69~~
	"Meeches Hope"	75
	"Rich Swamp"	40
	"Shiles's Folly"	35
	"Chance"	80
	"Years Land"	75
James Caldwell	"First Choice"	290
	"St. Giles"	10
Samuell Collins	"Late Discovery"	178
	"Collins Addition"	223
	"Hamon"	50
	"Collins's Lott"	5½
	"Snow Hill" pt. "Late Discovery"	22
	"Tilghmans Adventure"	40
John Cope	"Ennalls Frollick"	150
Robert Colliar	"Doughtys Lott"	100
	"Parris"	100
45:1759:19 ...		
Thomas Cooper	pt. "Bedford"	166
Isaac Cooper	"Quoackeson Neck"	164
	"Ebbys Frollick"	10
Samuell Cooper	"Bedford"	50
h/o James Collins	"Gilliss's Adventure"	100
Ebenezar Cottman	"St. Giles"	190
	"Weatherleys Adventure"	200
	"First Choice"	10
h/o John Conway	"Fathers Care"	50
	"Wair Point"	50
	"Rumbling Point"	10
	"Webbley"	20
	"Condoque"	50

Rachel Caudory	"Cant Tell"	91
45:1759:20 ...		
John Callaway, Sr.	"Callaways Folly"	25
John Callaway, Jr.	~~"Golden Quarter"~~	~~50~~
	"Day Neck" pt. "Day Bigg"	6
h/o William Cox	"Waterford"	450
	"Anglesey"	100
	"Cox Bill" now called "Calf Pasture"	35
William Callaway	"What You Please"	25
	"Iron Hill"	180
Capt. John Cox for h/o William Dashiell	"Ventures Priviledge"	62½
	"Dashiells Purchase"	498
Edward Cluff	"Blakes Hope"	200
	"Timber Grove"	75
	"New Town"	27
Henry Caldhoon	"Cheasmans Chance"	60
	"Security"	100
45:1759:21 ...		
John Clifton	"Pissimmon Point"	50
	"Morriss Hope"	44
Charles Cottingham	"Boston Point"	23
	"Chance"	63
	"Mumford"	8
	"Rumbling Point"	15
Thomas Cottingham	"Vulcans Vineyard"	105
	"Rumbling Point"	37½
	"Cottinghams Chance"	40
	"Boston"	26
h/o Ahab Coston	"Seccond Choice"	160
	"Bears Quarter"	70
	"Good Luck"	40
	"End of Strife" formerly "Seccond Choice"	10
	pt. "Costons Trouble"	3
	pt. "Costons Vineyard"	9
Mathais Coston	"Bears Hole"	50
	"Costons Trouble"	350

Thomas Collins	'Stevens's Conquest"	300
45:1759:22 ...		
h/o Joseph Cottman	"Cottmans Point"	50
	"Taunton Dean"	186
Doughty Colliar	"Shadwell"	50
	"Turnstile"	50
	"Parris"	50
George Colliar	"Mount Hope"	45
	"Cannons Lott"	50
Thomas Collins (cooper)	"Good Hope"	100
John Caudory	"Godart Lott"	100
Isaac Callaway	"Callaway Venture"	25
	"Pick & Cull"	100
Benjamin Callaway	"Callaways Venture"	30
	"Callaways Hard Fortune"	50
John Crouch	"High Suffolk"	100
45:1759:23 ...		
John Collins	"Orphans Lott"	30
Robert Colliar, Jr.	"Colliars Enlargement"	90
	"Josephs Lott"	12
	"Bettys Choice"	100
John Culver	"Beverly"	92¾
Thomas Cox	"Wilton"	50
	"Plumton Salt Ash"	30
h/o Abraham Covington	pt. "Double Purchase"	200
John Carmical	"Warrington"	190
Joseph Cottman	"Costons Venture"	140½
Solomon Collins	~~"Kinkins Folly"~~	~~49~~
	"Glasgow"	100
45:1759:24 ...		
Jacob Crouch	"Poor Quarter"	50
Morgan Caudory	"Quiaukeson Neck"	50
Nicholas Evans Colliar	pt. "Last Choice"	100
Isaac Coston	"Bear Point"	200
	"Flat Land"	100
	"Costons Trouble"	50

Thomas & Samuell Cooper, Jr.	"Gladstones Adventure"	64
	"Hard Shift"	86
William Cooper	"Bedford"	50
James Curtis	pt. "Armstrongs Lott"	183½
William Coulbourn, Jr.	pt. "Pomfith"	249
	"Discovery"	92
45:1759:25 ...		
Ebenezar Callaway	"Callaways Folly"	25
	"Callaways Venture"	25
Benjamin Coulbourn	pt. "Pomfritt"	172
Isaac Coulbourn	pt. "Pomfritt"	234
Andrew Francis Cheney	1 lot in Princess Ann Town – No. 30	<n/g>
	1 lot in Princess Anne	1
h/o David Cordory	pt. "Partners Choice"	20
Daniel Cox	"Plumton Salt Ash"	50
Nehemiah Covington	"Sweet Wood"	178
	~~"Sowerwood"~~	~~122~~
	~~pt. "Comfort Adventure"~~	~~81~~
	~~pt. "Covingtons Meadow"~~	
	pt. "Comforts Adventure"	9
45:1759:26 ...		
Phillip Covington	pt. "Sweetwood"	22
	~~"Second Choice"~~	~~200~~
	~~"Sowerwood"~~	~~48~~
	~~"Henrys Enjoyment"~~	~~50~~
	~~"Amity"~~	~~50~~
	~~"Sassafras Neck"~~	~~206~~
	~~"Comforts Adventure"~~	~~57~~
	"Covingtons Conclusion"	348
Benjamin Callaway	"Smalls Chance"	6
Levin Callaway	"Levins Folly"	33
Moses Callaway	"Chance"	50
Hill Cox	"Alderburry"	72
	"Plumton Salt Ash"	28
~~Francis Crowder~~	~~"Cow Quarter"~~	~~100~~

Fenton Catlin	"Newwood Hall"	200
	"Wood Hall"	100
45:1759:27 ...		
Thomas Denwood	"Weatherlys Chance"	90
	"Brown Stone"	300
	"Denwood Inclusion"	21
Nehemiah Dorman	~~"Nelsons Choice"~~	~~70~~
	"Shipways Choice"	22½
	"Dormans Purchase"	150
	"Dormans Addition"	104
Charles Dickason	"Dickasons Hope"	40
	"Green Park"	200
	"Riggans Mine"	100
Capt. John Dennis	"Piney Point"	175
	pt. "Double Purchase"	107¼
David Dreddon	"Hachila"	120
	"Timber Grove"	37½
	"Cherry Garden"	23
George Dashiell	"Littleworth"	50
	"Beaudly"	500
45:1759:28 ...		
h/o Col. George Dashiell	"Contention"	95
	"Dashiells Lott"	435
	"Turkey Ridge"	83
	"Satisfaction"	116
Joseph Dashiell	"Hazard"	70
	"Dashiells Folly"	108
	"Meches Hope" & "Rich Swamp"	135
	"Dashiells Addition"	25
	"Fair Ridge"	100
	"Hazard"	30
	"Sheridons Desire"	20
John Dorman	"Tosseler" called "Woolfs Denn"	150
Michael Disheroone, Jr.	"Second Purchase"	200
John Doherty	"Little Usk"	100
	"Meadow"	202

William Duet	"Hope Still"	220
	"Ennemessix"	84
	"Musketo Creek"	100
	"Hopewell"	96
	"Moresworth"	8
	"Hogg Land"	12
45:1759:29 ...		
Charles Dean	"Gladstons Industry"	170
	"Deans Lott"	10
	"Deans Chance"	20
John Davis	"Brickle How"	300
	"Hopewell"	50
	"Hopeworth Pasture" – denied	48
	"Davis's Inlett"	50
	"Kirkminster" – denied	225
	"Long Hedge" – denied	250
	"Cow Quarter"	45
	"Upper Unduey" – denied	400
	"Troublesome"	250
John Dorman	"Dormans Chance"	100
	pt. "Covingtons Meadow"	42
	pt. "Comforts Adventure"	
Nicholas Dun	"Shadewell" & "Late Discovery"	20
	"Shadewell"	100
Charles Dasheill	"Shiles Folly"	18
	"Venture"	50
	"Fathers Care"	166
	"Addition"	47
Mitchell Dasheill	"Pharsalia"	175
	"Venture"	62½
	"Good Luck"	31½
45:1759:30 ...		
Ambrose Dixon	pt. "Dixons Lott"	50
	"Security"	270
Walter Derby	"Batchellors Choice"	50
	"Derbys Addition"	146

Thomas Dasheill	"Fathers Purchase" pt. "Noble Quarter"	100
	"Mount Allexander" pt. "Noble Quarter"	105
	pt. "Shiles Folly"	75
h/o Henry Dasheill	"Buknam"	150
	"Head of Tyaskin" originally "Cannons Peace"	100
	"Shiles Folly"	116
Michael Dorman	"Nelsons Choice"	55
	"Hunting Quarter"	100
	"Dormans Discovery"	171
	pt. "Golden Quarter"	25¾
h/o William Dasheill	pt. "Long Hill"	150
	"Greenwich"	50
	"Johnsons Addition"	274
Levin Dasheill	"Mitchells Improvement"	250
	"Jones Choice"	175
	"Shiles Folly"	16
45:1759:31 ...		
Beauchamp Davis	"Ledbourn"	100
Teague Dickason	"Hopkins Gift" pt. "Ware"	140
	"Woolf Quarter"	50
	"Force Put"	50
	"Priviledge"	50
	"Townsends Situation"	53
	"Dickasons Hard Lott"	21½
	"Saint Albans"	60
John Devorix	"Godarts Folly"	90
James Dakes	"Hignalls Choice"	150
	"Buck Ridge"	150
h/o Clement Dasheill	pt. "Chance" now called "Good Luck"	15
	"Dasheills Lott"	435
Louther Dasheill	pt. "Chance" now called "Good Luck"	30
	pt. "Dasheills Lott"	470
	"Chance"	60
Mitchell Dasheill, Jr.	"Venture Priviledge"	62½
	"Recovery"	167
45:1759:32 ...		

Jessee Dasheill	"Meeches Right"	300
	"Meeches Desart"	200
	"Woolf Trap Neck"	50
	"Shiles Folly"	325
	"Shiles Folly"	162½
Isaac Dickason	"Late Discovery"	150
	pt. "Late Discovery"	50
Dennis Dulany	"High Suffolk"	30
	"Comby Chance"	70
~~Major Dorman~~	~~"Charleston"~~	~~50~~
Thomas Dixon	"Boston Town"	30
	"Dixons Addition"	31
	"Dixons Lott"	100
	"Dixons Choice Ilarged"	216
	pt. "Dixons Addition"	20½
Robert Downs	"Mitchells Choice"	250
William Donohoe	"Anything"	68½
Winder Dasheill	"Woolf Trap Ridge"	50
	pt. "Shiles Folly"	162½
	"Winders Addition"	102
45:1759:33 ...		
Ezekiel Dorman	"Morriss Lott"	100
~~Isaac Dasheill~~	~~"Pharsalia"~~	~~175~~
	~~"Good Luck"~~	~~31⅓~~
Thomas Dixon, Jr.	"Seccond Choice"	215
	"Dixons Lott"	50
Elizabeth Dixon	"Dixons Lott"	100
	"Security"	135
Thomas Dasheill	pt. "Desheills Lott"	400
William Dreadon	"Davids Disteny"	100
Matthew Dorman	"Weatherly Purchase" pt. "Weatherlys Refuse"	250
	"Slipe"	25
h/o Michael Disheroon	"Asever Choice"	58
45:1759:34 ...		
William Disheroone	"Puzels Injoyment"	150

Littleton Dennis	"Good Success"	150
	"Williams Hope"	137½
	"Chance"	15
	"Many Owners"	50
	"Cow Meadow"	25
	"Hapata Venture"	75
	pt. "Timber Tract"	150
	pt. "Cowley"	25
	"Security"	267
	pt. "Carters Lott"	50
James Dean	"Deans Venture"	50
John Done	1 lot in Princess Ann Town – No. 15	<n/g>
	"Labour in Vain"	133¼
	pt. "Golden Quarter"	23
	pt. "Golden Quarter"	51¼
	pt. "Golden Quarter"	15¼
	"Beard Tree Ridge"	83½
	pt. "Golden Quarter"	108¾
	pt. "Golden Quarter"	76
Ester Dasheill	"Grandfathers Care"	548½
	"Ventures Priviledge"	62½
Abraham Dean	"Punch Bole"	1
45:1759:35 ...		
John Duet	pt. "Poor Swamp"	60
	pt. "Buck Ridge"	60
	pt. "Scotland"	65
David Dredon, Jr.	"Powells Chance"	165½
Henry Dasheill, Jr.	pt. "First Choice"	100
Isaac Denston	"First Choice"	66
Joseph Dasheill, Jr.	"Summer Pasture"	135
	"Lott"	100
	"Bottom of the Neck"	80
	"Dasheills Meadow"	50
Isaac Dixon (cnp)	"Bauld Ridge"	9
	"Dixons Lott"	150
	pt. "Dixons Addition"	115½

	pt. "Dam Quarter"	25¼
	"Dixons Choice Enlarged"	209
	"Dixons Bull"	70
45:1759:36 <blank>		
45:1759:37 ...		
Maj. John Elzey	"Almoadington"	900
John Ellis	"Adventure"	70
Nicholas Evans	"Rice Land"	612
	"Troy"	50
	"Fox Hall"	50
	"Timber Grove"	100
	"Daniels Advent"	150
	"Gilliss Care"	22
	"Dormans Improvement"	40
Thomas Evans	"Handys Meadow"	50
	"Owens Glandore"	285
	"Oystershell Bank" pt. "Dales Adventure"	9
John Evans	"Handys Hall" pt. "Dales Adventure"	100
	"Dales Adventure"	2
	"Tilghmans Adventure"	10
John Evans	"Pitchcroft"	300
Richard Evans	"Pitchcroft"	200
45:1759:38 ...		
John Evans	"Chance"	150
William Ellis	"Anderton Invention"	200
Joshua Edge	"Good Luck"	50
	"Batchellors Folly"	50
Joseph Ellis	"Turkey Trap Ridge"	50
	"Quiet Entrance"	100
Robert Elzey	"Manloves Discovery"	250
	"Grays Adventure"	110
Arnold Elzey	"Bozmans Advent"	133
James English	"Englishes Adventure"	47
	"Kings Luck"	50
John Elzey, Jr. (cnp)	"Second Purchase"	250
	"Lotts Daughter"	30

	"Elliss's Choice"	100
Cornelius English	"Tar Kill"	45½
45:1759:39 ...		
James Furnice	"Brothers Agreement" pt. "Amity"	200
	"Something Worth"	44
Mary Fountain	"Fountains Lott"	150
	"Normondy"	25
	"Newfound Land"	10
	"Marsh Ground"	55
	"Fishing Island"	10
Alexander Fullaton	"Poor Quarter"	100
~~Margaret Fenton~~	~~"Newwood Hall"~~	~~200~~
	~~pt. "Wood Hall"~~	~~50~~
h/o John Fowler	"Lotts Daughter" pt. "Lott"	100
	"Lotts Son" pt. "Lott"	140
Samuell Flewelling	"Tick Nell"	50
	"Prickle Lock Shott"	75
	"Milk Moor"	50
	"Clear of Cannon Shott"	50
	"Flewellings Purchase"	50
	"Cannons Lott"	50
	"Woolfs Quarter"	50
	"Cow Ridge"	100
	"Flewellings Settlement"	137
	pt. "Fishing Quarter"	120
	pt. "Bettys Inlargement"	
	"Cannons Choice"	5
	"Security"	50
45:1759:40 ...		
Absolam Foard	"Promise Land"	100
	"Vale of Misery"	88
William Farrington	"Pastureadge"	43
	"Weatherlys Purchase"	225
William Flemming (cnp)	"Unity"	20
	"Flemmings Purchase"	150
	"Minshalls Adventure"	200

	"Harrissons Venture"	150
Capt. John Fitz (DO)	"Peckingoe Ridge"	250
William Furnice	pt. "Double Purchase"	245
	"Amity"	100
John Finch	pt. "Bedford"	100
William Furnice	"Furnices Adventure"	200
John Freney	"Uncles Advice"	50
William Fountain	pt. "Conveniency"	45
Thomas Fletcher	"Little Naylseye"	200
	"Bells First Choice"	200
45:1759:41 ...		
James Gunby	"Meadow"	100
	"Kirks Purchase"	200
	"Gunbys Venture"	75
	"Low Swamp"	100
h/o John Goslin	"Goslins Lott"	50
	"What You Please"	50
Mathew Goslin	"Sligoe" pt. "Little Belean"	50
h/o Robert Given	"Green Meadow"	75
William Giles	"Parremores First Choice"	300
	"Sallop"	250
	"Whettstone"	200
	"Agnewlow" & "Lergee"	116
John Godart	"Days Beginning"	289
45:1759:42 ...		
Thomas Glaster	"Maidens Lott"	100
Thomas Gilliss, Jr.	"Maidens Lott"	100
Joseph Gilliss, Jr.	"Maidens Lott"	100
William Gray	"Kilmannum"	150
Thomas Gilliss (cnp)	"End of Strife"	500
	"Bears Quarter"	10
	"Seccond Choice"	10
	"Cranbourn"	100
	"Horseys Chance"	100
	"Canterberry"	
	"Support"	138

	"Contention"	50
	~~"Coxes Advice"~~	~~200~~
	"Gillises Double Purchase"	303
	"White Chaple"	502
Richard Green	"Moryes Choice"	200
	"Greens Recantation"	100
Col. George Gale	"Careys Choice"	164
	"Addition"	1630
	"Stoney Ridge"	300
	"Satisfaction"	14
	"Denwoods Denn"	300
	"Wilsons Conclusion"	1001
45:1759:43 ...		
h/o Thomas Goslin	"Hoggs Down"	100
William Gravenour	"Bass Legg"	150
Capt. Joseph Gilliss	"Oake Hall"	200
	"Manloves Venture"	50
	"Chance"	300
	"More & Casit"	158
Capt. Thomas Gilliss for h/o John Handy	"Belean"	317
	"What You Please"	25
Levin Gale	"Coxes Lott"	100
	"Last Purchase"	70
	1 lot in Princess Ann Town	<n/g>
	"Bear Swamp"	15⅓
	"Priviledge"	7
George Gale, Jr.	"Gales Purchase"	696
	"Venason Pasture"	506
	"Warrington"	112
	"Aghew Lowe"	33⅓
	"Lerge"	166⅔
	"Chelsey"	15
	marsh & land (16 a.) pt. purchased	20
45:1759:44 ...		
Thomas Gyles	"Gyles Lott"	350

Thomas Godart	"Partners Choice"	150
	"Collins Folly"	75
John Graham	"Long Acre"	200
	"Caudorys Beginning"	100
Levin Goslin	"Trulocks Grange"	75
	"Relphs Purchase" pt. "Trulocks Grange"	100
Daniel Goslin	"Ægypt"	38
	"Fairham"	22
Thomas Gibbens	"Hopewell"	150
	"Thomas's Chance"	91
John Gibbens	"Hopwell"	150
	"Givens Chance"	74
Thomas Gibbens, Jr.	"Grandfathers Gift"	100
Hannah Goldsmith	"Coldrain"	50
45:1759:45 ...		
George Green	"New Haven"	208
Ezekiel Gibbens	"Spittle"	22
	"Deep"	150
George Lewis Gastinue	"Chance"	100
Allen Gray	"Harringsons Adventure"	55
Kirk Gunby	"Middle Ridge"	248
	"Discovery"	3
	"Chance"	10
	"Kirks Chance"	32
	"Chance"	40
	"Dixons Lott"	150
Henry Graham	"Tarr Kill Ridge"	60
Robert Geddess	"Support"	30½
Day Givens	"Lyons Folly"	150
	"Wales"	50
	pt. "Weatherlys Reserve"	32
	"Givens's Discovery"	5
45:1759:46 ...		
William Geddess	1 lot in Princess Ann Town – No. 7	<n/g>
Jacob Gyles	"St. Gyles Lott"	50
	"Partners Choice"	50

Isaac Gyles	"St. Gyles Lott"	50
Betty Game	"Georges Pleasure"	50
George Gullet	"Ridger"	60
John Gupton	"Glade Side"	50
	"Ware"	145
h/o Ezekiel Gilliss	"Gilliss Addition"	100
45:1759:47 ...		
Smith Horsey	pt. "Coulbourn"	108¼
	"Yorkshire Island"	150
	"Horseys Venture"	41
h/o Absolum Hobbs	"Hamons Chance"	50
	"Chance"	100
h/o John Horsey	pt. "Double Purchase"	200
Richard Hall	"Halls Choice"	148
	"Halls Adventure"	249
	"Halls Hammock"	50
	"Halls Posture"	50
Stephen Horsey, Sr.	"More Worth"	24
	"Cow Quarter"	105
	"Double Purchase"	401
	"Horseys Fancy"	150
	"Horseys Down"	150
Isaac Holland for h/o William Furnice	"Fair Spring"	300
	"Pools Hope"	100
Michael Holland	"Pomfrit"	50
	"Ferry Bridge"	100
45:1759:48 ...		
Thomas Humphriss	"Keens Lott"	150
	"Green Hill"	25
Joshua Humphriss	"Keens Lott"	150
	"Green Hill"	25
Elgate Hitch	"High Suffolk"	141
	"Comeby Chance"	173
Thomas Holbrooke	"Harrington"	200
	"Priviledge"	106½
	"Last Vacancy"	60

William Harris	"Lott"	452
~~Abraham Hath~~	~~"Welsh"~~	~~15~~
	~~"End of Strife"~~	~~37~~
Mathelias Hobbs	"Abbington"	100
	"Carneys Chance"	100
	"Cumberland"	40
	"Carneys Chance"	50
Benton Harris	"Bear Point"	125
	"Pigg Pen Ridge"	8
	"Friends Choice"	18
	"Harrissons Venture"	263
	"Timber Grove"	262
	"Davis Chance"	30
45:1759:49 ...		
John Harper	pt. "Norfolk"	239½
h/o Samuel Handy	"Suffolk"	446
Daniel Henderson	"Turnstile"	100
Robert Hitch	"High Suffolk"	212
John Hitch, Sr.	"High Suffolk"	194
	"Fathers Neglect"	126
h/o Solomon Hitch	pt. "High Suffolk"	100
	"Weatherlys Ridge"	100
John Hillmon	"Brittain"	50
William Hickman	"Old Castle"	50
	"Fair Meadow"	700
	"New Castle"	100
Thomas Hayward, Jr.	"Profitt"	250
	"Haywards Lott"	740
	"Blakes Hope"	9 s.p.
	"Addition"	45
	pt. "Pledged Without Proffitt" & pt. "Tilghmans Luck"	½
45:1759:50 ...		
John Harris	"Chance"	316
	"Pasturadge"	50
	"Winter Quarter"	10

Zachariah Harris	"Heaths Quarter"	100
	"Littleworth"	50
	"Liberty"	50
Robert Harris	"Bear Quarter"	20
Isaac Hayman	"Woolf Pitt Ridge"	115
	"White Oake Swamp"	30
	"Haymans Purchase"	25
Ezekiel Humphriss	"Hoggs Down"	170
Thomas Hairn	"Staines"	150
Elijah Hairn	"Staines"	275
Col. Isaac Handy	"Pemberton"	620
	"High Suffolk" now called "Pemberton"	2
	"Friends Choice"	10
	"Spences Choice"	1125
	"Bradys Chance"	171
	"Handys Pasture" pt. "Shiles Folly"	75
45:1759:51 ...		
Spencer Harriss	"Harrissons Advent"	150
John & Isaac Hopkins	"Cannon Shott"	300
	"Cajus Island"	75
	"Johns Chance"	100
	"Two Brothers"	100
Thomas Huffington	"Bacors Folly"	25
	"Huffingtons Lott"	20
James Hayman	"Hopewell"	170
	"Addition"	80
	"Haymans Purchase"	58½
John Henry	"Pharsalia"	100
Stephen Hopkins	"Samuels Lott"	200
	"Cajus Island"	125
	"Mulberry Island"	50
William Heath	"Look" pt. "Wansborough"	50
	"Haths Chance"	100
	"Addition to Smiths Hope"	30
h/o Edward Hairn	"Scotland"	97
45:1759:52 ...		

John Hoffington	~~"Barren Quarter"~~	~~250~~
	~~"Cambridge"~~	~~98~~
	~~"What You Please"~~	~~50~~
	"Ill Neighbourhood"	658
	"Partners Choice"	80
Stephan Hobbs	"Hobbs Adventure"	100
	~~"Abbington"~~	~~100~~
	~~"Carneys Choice"~~	~~100~~
John Hall	"Pimino"	200
	pt. "Priviledge"	12
Charles Hayman	"Hopewell"	80
	"Addition"	20
	"Fair Meadow"	24
	"Charles Chance"	20
Stephen Horsey	"Coulbourn"	108¼
Gilbert Hoffington	"Tower Hill"	100
Outterbridge Horsey	"Dixons Lott"	100
	"Coulbourn"	216⅓
	"Horseys Conclusion"	544
	"Horseys Lott"	51
	"Dixons Kindness"	25
	"Dam Quarter"	20½
	"Hogg Palace"	50
	"Ludgate Hill"	100
	"Sharpes Chance"	50
	"Horseys Prevention"	283¼
	"Dixons Choice Enlarged"	4½
45:1759:53 ...		
h/o John Howard	"Dowgate"	50
	"Brittain"	50
Charles Harris	"Stevenson"	85
Ezekiel Hall	"Halls Hammock"	50
	"Halls Pasture"	50
	"Halls Kindness"	258
Bloyce Harriss	"Evans Purchase" pt. "Stanaway"	140

Nehemiah Hairn	"Hains"	125
	"Sandy Hill"	75
	"Fair Field"	37
George Hairn	"Hains"	150
	"Goshens Addition"	97
	"Goshen"	50
	"Hogg Quarter"	50
	"Maidenhead"	50
Richard Harriss	"Elizabeths Choice"	100
Levin Hoffington	"Lazey Hill"	35½
45:1759:54 ...		
Rev. John Hamilton	"Chance"	29
	"Cypress Swamp"	15
	"Little Derry"	176
Isaac Handy	"Handys Discovery"	270
Col. Robert Jenkins Henry	"Marys Lott" pt. "Rehoboth"	400
	"Henrys Addition"	50
	"Conveniency" pt. "Dickensons Hope"	134½
	"Lanbrick"	133½
	"Friends Assistance"	300
	"High Land"	100
	"Dickensons Hope"	125½
	"Goos Marsh"	50
	"Cow Marsh"	50
	"Conveniency"	375
	"Good Success" pt. "Conveniency"	200
	"Fair Meadow Rectified"	535
	"Long Meadow"	646
	"Glasgow"	72
	pt. "Manloves Lott"	138
	"Providence"	200
	"Whitty" pt. "Hignalls Choice"	62
	"Golden Lyon"	278
Abraham Harriss	"Middleton"	85
	"Harrisson Venture"	50
	"Flemings Loss"	30

Robert Heron, Esq.	1 lot in White Haven Town	<n/g>
45:1759:55 ...		
h/o Stephen Handy	"Midlesex"	200
	"Hap at a Venture"	101
Revill Horsey	"Double Purchase"	100
David Hopkins	"Cannon Shott"	200
	"Hopkins's Choice"	25
Ezekiel Hitch	"Gravely Hill"	50
h/o Capt. John Handy	"Delight"	194
	"Nutters Adventure"	468
	"Nutters Contrivance"	219
	"Bottom"	143
	"Midle Tract"	50
	"Handys Care"	235
Rev. Hugh Henry	pt. "Pharsalia"	91
David Hale	"Whittingtons Choice"	150
John Hastin	"What You Please"	25
	"Balla Magerrey"	50
45:1759:56 ...		
James Harriss	"Middleton"	90
	"Flemmings Loss"	30
Capt. George Handy	"Pemberton"	350
	"Surveyors Mistake"	30
Solomon Harriss	"Lergee"	84
	"Purchase"	16
Samuel Handy	"Bacbus Rest"	150
	"Daniels Adventure"	150
	"Cheverly"	100
	"Lott"	200
Robert Holland	"Ferry Bridge"	100
Robert Hopkins	~~"Carneys Chance"~~	~~50~~
	"Poor Fields"	150
Zorobable Hall	"Desart"	175
Thomas Hayward, Jr.	pt. "Double Purchase"	249
Richard Huffington	pt. "Badors Folly"	50
45:1759:57 ...		

Joshua Hoffington	"Youngs Purchase"	150
Sewell Handy	"Armstrongs Purchase"	320
	"New Invention"	212½
	"Bear Ridge"	200
	"Armstrongs Lott"	50
Joshua Hall	"School House Ridge"	98
Thomas Hairn, Jr.	"Eagle Tower"	100
Ebenezar Hairn	"Flanders"	66
David Haines	"Haines Grave"	50
William Hayward	"Nutters Purchase"	300
	"Turkey Ridge"	100
	"Friends Assistance"	200
	pt. "Nelsons Choice"	75
	"Dormans Priviledge"	30
Doctor Harry	"Covingtons Choice"	150
45:1759:58 ...		
Wilson Heath	"Wilsons First"	100
Samuell Handy	"Strugle"	200
	"Small Lott"	8
	"Loss & Gain"	40
	"Last Choice"	10
William Haine	"Lawsons Adventure"	52
	"Jons Ridge"	10
	"Beards Ballens"	3½
	"Long Acre"	8
Ebenezar Handy	"Coxes Fork"	75
Isaac Hairn	pt. "Staines"	150
45:1759:59 ...		
Daniel Jones	"Mannings Resolution"	400
	"Jones Purchase"	127
	pt. "Sweet Wood"	100
	"Coxes Choice"	80
	pt. "Mannings Resolution"	20
Mary Jones	"Mannings Resolution"	250
	"Jenkins Mistake"	163

Capt. John Jones	"Jones Chance"	331
	"Downs Choice"	62
Capt. Robert Jones	"Jones's Choice"	350
Purnal Johnson	"Spences Choice"	125
	"Friends Choice"	115
Lewis Jones	"Laytons Conveniency"	70
	"Jones's Adventure"	25
	"Lunns Amendment"	100
	"Jones's Chance"	266½
	"Downs"	100
45:1759:60	...	
William Jones for h/o Heathly Rider	"Meadfield"	190½
George Irving	"Maccoms Lott"	400
	"Habb Nabb"	216
	"Georges Adventure"	1000
John Jones (Goose Creek)	"Woolfords Chance"	36½
	"Enlargement"	50
	"Addition"	52
Thomas Jones (MU)	"Jones Choice"	175
	"Second Addition to Hog Quarter"	776
	"Comforts Adventure"	125
	"Sasswafrax Neck"	206
	"Covingtons Meadow"	10
George Jones	"Golden Quarter"	70
	"Long Delay"	50
	"Jones's Priviledge"	80
Thomas Jones (MO)	"Bridgers Lott"	370
	"Friends Advice"	356
	"Winter Quarter"	255¾
45:1759:61	...	
Samuell Jones	"Jones's Adventure"	25
	"Lunns Amendment"	151
	"Jones's Chance"	266½
	"Chance"	22
	"Laytons Chance"	130½

Samuell Jackson	"Abergaveny"	50
	"Small Lott"	50
	"Warrington"	35
	"Warwick"	33⅓
Jervice Jenkins	"Hogg Neck"	100
Joshua Jackson	"Boadley"	100
John Johnson	"Doe Park"	50
	"Rich Swamp"	50
h/o Samuel Jackson	"Jacksons Lott"	50
David Jenkins	"Seccond Purchase"	100
45:1759:62 ...		
Joshua Jackson	"Jones Delight"	50
John Jenkins	pt. "Crouches Choice"	50
James Jones	"Pleasure"	50
Jonathan Jenkins	"Fox Island"	67
Joseph Jenkins	pt. "Crouches Choice"	50
Winder Jacobs	pt. "Wallaces Virtue"	352½
Mitchell Jones	"Pharsalia"	175
	"Good Luck"	32
45:1759:63 ...		
h/o Mathew Kemp	"Gethsemany"	300
	"Levins Grief"	12
Whittington King	"Chance"	90
	"Webby"	250
	"Kings Chance"	300
William Kersley	"Irish Grove"	62½
	"Discovery"	37½
	"Kersleys Industery"	225
	"Shoe Makers Meadow"	50
Edward Killum	"Ill Neighbourhood"	255
William Kibble	"Bottom of the Neck"	103
	"Security"	113
William Kinney	"Third Choice"	50
	"Desart"	100
	"Kenneys Chance"	50
	"Good Neighbourhood"	50

45:1759:64 ...		
Nehemiah King	"Good Luck"	320
	"Piney Island"	10
	"Barbados"	300
	"Double Purchase"	293
	"Addition to Collins Advent"	111
	"South Foreland"	50
	"Downs Lott" pt. "Double Purchase"	200
	"Closiar" pt. "First Choice"	66
	"Conclusion"	66
	"Kings Land" pt. "Double Purchase"	300
	"Conveniency"	75
	"Collins Adventure"	500
	"Bear Swamp"	16
	"Kings Choice" & "Pimini"	112
	"New Addition" pt. "Double Purchase"	30
	½ lot in Princess Ann Town	<n/g>
	"Self Preservation"	175
	"Support"	37
	"Partners Choice" & "Kings Purchase United"	797½
	"Whartons Folly"	33½
	"Comby Chance" pt. "Double Purchase"	250
	pt. "Double Purchase"	60
	pt. "Double Purchase"	500
	"Dublin", "Kings Chance", & "Pimini"	163
	"Timber Tract"	522
	pt. "Longs Lott" now called "Addition to Late Purchase"	44
	pt. "Ledbourn" now called "Addition to Late Purchase"	16
h/o John Kibble	"Wilsons Discovery" called "Delight"	75
45:1759:65 ...		
Jessee King	"Oxhead"	300
Isaac Knoble	"Timson"	150
John Killum	"Dickasons Folly"	100
	"Chance"	50

h/o Roger Killett	"Horseys Bailywick"	100
	"Little Belain"	167½
	"Phillips Addition"	25
Joshua Knight	"Harrison's Adventure"	175
Samuell Kersley	"Irish Grove"	37½
	"Discovery"	12½
	"Kersleys Industery"	75
Capt. Ephraim King	"Kings Misfortune"	1704
	"Good Neighbourhood"	194
	"Kings Choice"	50
45:1759:66 ...		
Robert Kersley	"Kersleys Joke"	60
	"Kersley in Earnest"	27½
	pt. "Dam Quarter"	19¼
Zorobable King	pt. "Cloverfield"	60
	"Kings Glade"	320
Daniel Kinnakin	"Ridge Glade"	50
Capt. John Killum	"Ackworths Folly"	108
	"Discovery"	160
	"Aghenlow"	100
	"Lergee"	100
Capt. Ephraim King for David Wilson	"Smiths Recovery"	601
	"Cloverfields"	990
	"Kilglain"	250
	"Security"	75
	"Tilbury"	25
	"Wilsons Discovery"	25
	"Glasgow"	75
James Knight	"Harrisons Adventure"	120
	pt. "Nights Success"	13
45:1759:67 ...		
William Knowles	"Widows Hope"	13
Isaac Kinney	pt. "Desart"	50
Benjamin Langford (cnp)	"Boston Town"	180
	"Galloway"	150
	"New Brittain"	50

	"Discovery Enlarged"	64
	pt. "Wattkins Point"	33
	pt. "Longs Chance"	260
Jesse Lister	"Boyces Banks"	100
	"Addition"	40
Thomas Linsey	"Boston"	8
	"Cheasmans Chance"	40
	"Mumford"	92
45:1759:68 ...		
Thomas Laws	"Greenwich"	50
	"Northforland"	200
	"Laws Defence"	90
	"Self Preservation"	29
Solomon Long	"Amity"	220
	"Adventure"	100
	"Sampiar"	80
	"Cow Quarter"	50
John Laws	"Golden Quarter"	75
	"Long Delay"	137
	"Meadow"	25
James Larrimore	"Cannons Choice"	283
James Laws	"Addition"	100
	"Doggwood Ridge"	100
John Langford	"Weatherlys Adventure"	100
Randall Long	"Hogg Hammock" & "Bears Neck"	208
	"Comby Chance"	86
45:1759:69 ...		
John Leatherbury	"Covingtons Vineyard"	300
Fran. Langake	"Comby Chance"	317
	"High Suffolk"	83
	"Georges Folly"	47
	"Stephens Frehold"	45
Joseph Leanord	"Plumton Salt Ash"	40
	"Levins Chance"	50
h/o Margaret Lindow	"Penny Point"	539

Relph Lowe	"First Choice" pt. "Woodfield"	100
	"Woodfield"	150
Samuell Long, Jr.	"Wilsons Lott"	68
	"Rumbling Point"	22½
	"Holtwell"	100
	"Long Delight"	60
	"Longs Chance"	25
Coulbourn Long	pt. "Longs Chance"	131½
45:1759:70 ...		
Jeffery Long	"Conveniency"	25
	pt. "Longs Chance"	739½
John Long	"Boston Town"	290
	"Bozworth"	154
	"Addition to Bozworth"	15
Capt. Henry Lowes (cnp)	"Lowes Inlarged"	194
	"Coxes Performance"	250
	"Addition"	50
	"Sligoe" pt. "Little Belain"	140
	"Comeby Chance"	100
	"Addition to Lowe's Prize House Lott" pt. "Killums Folly" now called "Bottom of the Neck"	15
	"Dowgate"	150
	"Sarah's Neck"	55
	"Dispence"	500
	"Robertsons Lott"	30
	"Relphs Prevention"	9
	"Hereafter"	200
	"Fathers Care"	250
	1 lot in Princess Ann Town – No. 20	<n/g>
	"Priviledge"	1
	"Chuckatuck"	1000
	"Dormans Delight"	250
	"Castle Haven"	160
	"Belain"	3½
	pt. "Horseys Baliwick"	40
	"Fishing Island"	100

	"Good Will" pt. "Chance"	100
	"Morriss Lott"	30
	"Flowerfield"	576
	"Cockland"	196
	"Anything"	50
45:1759:71 ...		
Thomas Lord	"Gullets Hope"	50-
Panter Lawes	"Happy Addition"	54
	"Mill Point"	18½
	"Panters Denn"	288½
Rebecca Levins	"Cascoway"	150
h/o William Laws	"Littleworth"	50
	"Taylors Hill"	200
	"Something Worth"	325
Joseph Langford	"Vulcans Vineyard"	9
	"Langfords Content"	89
Robert Leatherbury	"Covingtons Folly"	70
	"Lott"	200
	"My Own Before"	61
John & Relph Lowe	"Cascoway"	100
Lazarus Langford	pt. "Chance"	4
45:1759:72 ...		
Henry Lord	"Troublesome" pt. "Chesnutt Ridge"	25
	pt. "Cork"	50
h/o Randall Lord	"Puzell" pt. "Chesnutt Ridge"	75
Charles Leatherbury	"Oldbury"	400
	"Young Timson"	158
Thomas Langford, Jr.	"Cubys Chance"	50
John Langford	"Langfords Content"	50
Pewsey Langford	"Langfords Content"	69
	"Dam Quarter"	36
h/o John Leatherbury	"Small Lott"	50
	"Aberganing"	50
	"Warwick"	66⅔
	"Warrington"	15
	"Leatherburys Fancy"	8

Jane Lucas	"Conveniency"	13
	pt. "Cascoway"	250
45:1759:73 ...		
Thomas Laws, Jr.	"Northforland"	100
Judith Langford	"Chance"	33⅓
45:1759:74 ...		
Lazarus Maddux	"Lazurus's Lott"	641
William Maddux	"Whitefield"	350
Alexander Maddux	"Whitefield"	350
Daniel Maddux	"Barnabys Lott"	6
	"Security"	310
Thomas Moor	"Mitchells Lott" now called "Fathers Gift Secured"	75
Whitty Macclemmey	"Cole Brook"	350
Isaac Mitchell	"Amity"	200
James Mackmurray	"Whittys Invention"	300
	"Whittys Latter Invention"	100
45:1759:75 ...		
h/o John Magraw	"Owens Improvement"	150
	"Owens Delight"	100
	"Middle"	100
	"Refuge"	50
William Miles	"Desart"	100
	"Chance"	23
	"Fair Meadow"	109
	"Chance"	35
Samuell Mathews	"Ellis's Lott"	50
	"Matthews Delight" pt. "Elgate"	50
	"Edwin"	40
	"Matthews Green"	48
Samuell Mathews, Jr.	"Edwin"	100
	"Meadow"	25
h/o Robert Mitchell	"Good Success"	150
Samuell Macclester	"Woodgate Dock"	100
	"Sweet Wood Hall"	400
45:1759:76 ...		
Levin Moor	"Turkey Cock Hill"	100

Jacob Mezeck	"Ellingsworths Hope"	50
	"Pasturage"	22½
	"Nantz"	50
	"James's Lott"	34
Mary Maddux	"Linseys Green"	25
	"Cow Quarter"	50
	"Daniels Denn"	50
	"Irish Grove"	22½
Thomas Maddux	"Inclosiser"	590
h/o Jonathan Mills	"Suffolk"	200
	"Something Better than Nothing"	75
Henry Miles	"Harts Ease"	400
	"Marsh Ground"	50
	"White Oake"	125
	"Foscull"	50
	"Hogg Penn Swamp"	50
	"Dixons Lott"	75
	"Neglect"	15
	"Hazard"	32
	"Fathers Care"	70
	"Hopewell"	37½
45:1759:77 ...		
~~h/o Thomas Merrill~~	~~"Gladstones Adventure"~~	~~75~~
	~~pt. "Hardship"~~	~~25~~
Ralph Milbourn	"Dales Adventure"	200
	"Desire"	13
	pt. "Prices Grove"	38
William Mister	"Pitchcroft"	175
John Milbourn	"Late Discovery"	50
	"Prices Grove"	150
	"Venture"	80
Samuell Melson	"Partners Choice"	40
John MackDowell	"Georges Choice"	50
William Moor	"Turkey Cock Hill"	50
	"Titchfield"	100
	"Cross"	266

45:1759:78 ...		
Robert Melone	"Godarts Folly"	100
Isaac Moor	"Addition to Collins Advent"	150
Teague Matthews	"Edwin"	100
	"Haphazard"	25
	"Worthless"	100
	"Adams's Folly"	44
	"Meadow"	16
Bell Maddux	"Conveniency"	60
	"Ruscommond"	100
John Matthews	"Edwin"	100
	"Meadow"	9
Thomas Martin	"Keep Poor Hall"	100
Caleb Milbourn	"Prices Grove"	150
	"Linseys Green"	50
45:1759:79 ...		
Daniel Mackintire	"Handys Pasture" pt. "Shiles Folly"	50
	"End of Strife"	80
	"Daniels Priviledge"	35
	"Hickory Ridge"	23
	"Safety"	23
	"Daniels Chance"	39½
	"Daniels Hope"	80
Patrick Mackinney	"Harts Comfort"	50
	"Dixons Lott"	75
	"Patricks Folly"	100
Alexander Maddux	"Greenfield"	181
	"Powells Addition"	50
	"Linseys Green"	25
Thomas Marshall	"Marshall Inheritance"	309
	"Mitchells Lott"	75
	"Shoe Makers Meadow"	39⅔
	"Bostons Purchase"	19
Jo. Morriss	"Security"	100
	"Stevens Lott"	73

Capt. William Murray	"Vulcans Vineyard"	29
	"Neaths Dale"	289
	pt. "High Suffolk"	310
45:1759:80 ...		
Randall Mitchell	pt. "Double Purchase"	250
David McDonald	"New Rumney"	244
~~Alexander Maddux, Jr.~~	~~"New Town"~~	~~108~~
George Macclester	"Adventure"	100
	"Addams Choice"	180
	"Point Marsh"	200
	"Rotterdam"	150
Thomas Mantgummery	"Dublin"	75
	"Half Quarter"	35
Jacob Morriss	"Support"	50
Peter Magee	"Rich Ridge"	70
William Moor	"Coxes Discovery"	100
	"Moors Lott"	50
John Moor s/o William	"Gordens Delight"	100
45:1759:81 ...		
Stacey Miles	"Boyces Banks"	100
Elihu Messick	"Ellingsworths Hope"	50
	"Pasturage"	22½
	"Nantz"	50
John Maddux	"Rowley Ridge"	100
Samuel Miles	"White Oake"	125
	"Security"	172
Thomas Maddux	"Tilghmans Care"	76
	"New Town"	50
David Matthews	"Golden Lyon"	150
	"Cow Quarter"	100
Joseph Melson	"Partners Choice"	60
Solomon MackCreddy	"Matthews Adventure"	35
	"First Choice"	100
	"MackCreddys First Choice"	17¾
45:1759:82 ...		

John Morriss	"Bettys Choice"	100
	"Mealys Begginning"	87
Isaac MackCreddy	"Matthews Adventure"	50
John Mears	"Moorfields"	130
Covington Mezeck	"Covingtons Habitation"	100
Dannis Morriss	"Morriss Adventure"	50
Isaac Mitchell	"Middlesex"	180
	"Williams Hope"	62½
Neal MacClester	"White Chapple"	300
	"Oake Grove"	200
William McClemmey	"Coalbrook"	200
Joshua Moor	"Moors Advantage"	75
45:1759:83 ...		
Samuell Miles	"Miles's Lott"	150½
William Miles	"Pleasure"	49½
	"Exchange"	150
Matthew Mangarife	"Mangarife's Choice"	82½
Thomas Moor	pt. "Conveniency"	96
	"Moore's Priviledge"	100
George Miles	"Davids Adventure"	99
~~Fran. Martin~~	~~"Cherry Hinton"~~	~~21~~
Henry Miles, Jr.	"Good Luck"	50
Edward McDaniel	pt. "Bedford"	134
William Matthews, Jr.	pt. "Nights Success"	93
45:1759:84 ...		
Lodowick Milbourn	pt. "Prices Grove"	47
William Merrell	"Merrills Folly"	21
45:1759:85 ...		
Purnall Newbald	"Acquintaca"	200
	"Acquintace" (300 a.) pt. "Role"	200
	"Friendship"	100
	"Content"	77
Roger Nicholson	"Ellingsworth Hope"	100
Robert Nairn	"Georges Marsh"	50
	"Tarsey"	150
	"Hogg Quarter"	250

Henry Newman	"Marys Adventure"	40
	"Owens' Choice"	17
	"Newmans Conclusion"	280
	"Newmans Chance"	100
James Nairn	"Tersey"	150
	"Nairns Addition"	57
	"Pimino"	30
	"Northfield"	195
45:1759:86 ...		
James Nicholson	"Late at Night"	50
John North	"Cascoway"	300
John Nicholson	"Dudley"	80
	"Collins Good Success"	320
	"Bills's Priviledge"	50
William Nelson	"Wrights Choice"	50
	"Wrights Venture"	52½
	"Noble Quarter"	100
	"End of Strife"	9
	"Handys Discovery"	33
	pt. "Shiles's Folly"	25
William Nutter	"Delight"	194
	"Marsh Ground"	100
	"Nutters Adventure"	232
	"Dormans Delight"	50
	"Midle Tract"	50
Thomas Noble	pt. "Middle Neck"	100
George North	1 lot in Princess Ann Town – No. 24	<n/g>
45:1759:87 ...		
Abraham Outten	"Webbley"	130
	"Discovery"	116¾
	"Outtens Addition"	125
	"Wair Point Enlarged"	134
	"Irish Grove"	27½
	"Discovery"	58⅓
William Outterbridge	"Mothers Care" & "Brothers Goodwill" pt. "Double Purchase"	200

Matthew Oliphant	"Coxes Fork"	150
Purnall Outten	"Candoque"	50
	"Outtens Addition"	25
	"Wair Point Inlarged"	34
45:1759:88 ...		
Moses Owens	"Addams Purchase"	50
	"Turkey Trap"	100
	"Chance"	50
	"Addams Garden"	50
~~Michael Owens~~	~~pt. "Board Tree Ridge"~~	~~16⅓~~
	~~pt. "Golden Quarter"~~	~~75¼~~
	~~pt. "Golden Quarter"~~	~~108¾~~
Moses Owens	"Moses's Lott"	100
Margaret Olipher	"Rich Ridge"	30
45:1759:89 ...		
John Polk	"Good Luck"	100
Christopher Piper	"Barbers Rest"	150
	"Barbers Addition"	50
	"What You Please"	58
James Polk	"Dunagall"	100
	"Williams Adventure"	64
	"Smiths Resolves"	250
	"Smiths Hope"	100
	"Double Purchase"	163
	"Addition to Smiths Hope"	190
	"Moanan"	100
John Perkins	"New Town"	265
	"Winter Harbour"	150
	"Chesnutt Ridge"	50
John Paden	"Hackhilla"	80
	"Cherry Garden"	63
	"Timber Grove"	37½
	"Chance"	20
Thomas Prior	"Coney Warren"	125
45:1759:90 ...		

h/o William Piper	"Sallisbury Plains"	200
	"Wilson"	100
	"Marsh Hook"	75
	"Once Again"	75
	"Needless Cost"	150
Levin Powell	"Hickory Ridge" pt. "Greindfield"	19
	"Green Swamp Neck" pt. "Greindfield"	70
Samuell Phebus	"Nicholsons Adventure"	41
	"Addition to Littleworth"	242
Benjamin Piper	"Timber Ridge"	50
John Porter	"Longs Chance"	100
	pt. "Kings Glade"	57
	"Benjamins Advice"	50
George Pollit	"Smithfield"	100
	"Tom Roons Ridge"	100
	"Comby Chance"	10
	"Choice"	42
Henry Potter	"Mitchells Choice"	138½
	"Sunkin Ground"	100
	"Cow Quarter"	10
	"Daniels Denn"	50
45:1759:91 ...		
Thomas Pryor	"Mates Enjoyment"	100
Levin Polson	"Troblesome"	100
Arthur Parks	"Pitchcroft"	75
Thomas Parremore	"Good Luck at Last"	50
Thomas Phillips	"Greens Recantation"	80
David Polk	"Roxborough"	210
	"Comby Chance"	10
	"Fortune"	245
	"Hoggs Down"	55
	"Fathers Care"	283½
John Parker	"Davis's Choice"	184
Adam Price	"High Suffolk"	90
45:1759:92 ...		

Thomas Pollitt	"Daintery"	150
	"Trouble"	20
	"Recovery"	14
Richard Phillips	"Woodfield"	100
William Phillips	"Beverly"	107¼
Jonathan Pollitt	"Long Ridge"	125
	"Tomroons Ridge"	50
John Phillips	"Dudley"	50
	"Rowley Hill"	100
	"Greys Purchase"	100
	"Security"	51
	"Priviledge"	50
John Parsons	"Swanns Luck"	50
	"Plumton Salt Ash"	10
John Phebus	"Nicholsons Adventure"	97
	"Brothers Agreement"	79
45:1759:93 ...		
Isaac Parremore	"Purchase"	50
	"Weatherlys Purchase" pt. "Weatherlys Reserve"	18
Jabis Pitts	"Entrance"	145
	"Owens Gandore"	15
	pt. "Dales Adventure"	1¼
	"Milbourns Mistake"	1⅛
	"Entrance"	255
William Pollitt	"Wilsons Finding"	68
	"Wansborough"	50
	"Pollitts Victory"	198
Samuell Pryor	"Pryors Adventure"	24
	"Kings Glade"	100
William Polk	pt. "Illchester"	150
	"Conclusion"	85
Ann Pryor	"Conclusion"	47
John Parremore	"Crooked Ridge"	50
45:1759:94 ...		
Benjamin Parremore	"Parremores Misfortune"	50

George Phebus	"Nicholsons Adventure"	12
	"Addition to Littleworth"	98
h/o Richard Phillips	"Ægypt"	64½
Thomas Potter	"Owens Lott"	100
	"Mitchells Choice"	41½
Hugh Porter	pt. "Wallaces Venture"	352½
Michael Purkins	"New Town"	225
Stephen Parremore	"Ackworths Delight"	92
45:1759:95 ...		
James Quitturmas	"Meedfield"	50
	"Popler Neck"	200
Peter Quinton	"Wilsons Discovery"	175
Paterick Quitturmas	"Hogg Quarter"	100
45:1759:96 ...		
Randall Revill	"Double Purchase"	330
Edward Roberts	"Ellits Choice"	50
	"Edwards Lott" & "Jeshimon"	270
	"Greens Pasture"	200
	"Polks Meadow"	200
	"Robert Recovery"	100
	"Davids Distiny"	50
	"Venture Priviledge"	100
	"Edwards Chance"	100
	"Newfoundland"	125
Nicholas Rowe	"Purgatory"	37½
John Rigsby	"St. Peters Neck"	620
Mary Riggan	"Prices Conclusion"	50
	"Edwin"	10
~~Charles Riggan~~	~~"Golden Lyon"~~	~~235~~
45:1759:97 ...		
Thomas Rensher	"Renshers Security"	63
	"Covingtons Meadow"	50
	"Errondly"	88
William Rensher (cnp)	"Errondly"	230
	"Covingtons Meadow"	145
	"Renshers Security"	37

	"Comforts Adventure" & pt. "Covingtons Meadow"	205
Hezekiah Read for h/o William Langsdale	"Woodstock"	100
h/o John Read	"Hogg Quarter"	175
	"Waston"	200
Archibald Richey	"Mount Hope"	40
	"Turnstile"	10
h/o Thomas Row	"Purgatory"	37½
	"Graves End"	300
	"Winsors Prevention"	60
Daniel Rhodes	"Shantavanah"	200
	"Warrington" now called "Rhoads Choice"	10
45:1759:98 ...		
Joseph Reggan	"What You Will"	100
	"Reggans Content"	100
	"Harmsworth"	150
Benjamin Richardson	"Cascoway"	250
Hiron Redish	"Castle Haven"	40
	"Coxes Advice"	200
h/o John Robertson	"Irelands Edge"	150
h/o John Ricords	"Whetstone"	100
	"Good Luck"	40
	~~"Ricords Delight"~~	~~100~~
	"Shepherds Crook"	10
	~~"Givans Lott"~~	~~150~~
William Relph	"Good Luck at Last"	100
h/o John Robertson	"Robertsons Lott"	147½
	"Cow Pasture"	25
William Robertson	"Robertsons Lott"	147½
	"Cow Pasture"	25
	"Parremores Double Purchase"	100
45:1759:99 ...		
Jonathan Riggan	"Cork"	25
h/o Charles Roach (cnp)	"Make Peace"	150
	"Exchange"	50

	"Meadland"	32
	"Force Putt"	168
John Riggan	"Golden Lyon"	100
	pt. "Golden Lyon"	50
John Roach	"Meadland"	32
	"Lott"	36
	"Long Town"	150
	"Johnstons Lott"	68
Wilson Rider	"Westlocks Adventure or Venture"	200
	"Meadfield"	9½
	pt. "Warrick"	100
John Roberts	pt. "Edwards Lott"	50
	pt. "Jeshemon"	50
Zachariah Read	"Weatherlys Contrivance"	150
	"Ackworths Delight"	100
	"Sons Choice"	50
45:1759:100 ...		
Alexander Thomas Russell	"Trulocks Grange"	75
	"Good Success"	50
	"Russells Liberty"	78
Thomas Riccords	"Shepherds Crook"	70
	"Morriss Lott"	300
	"Partners Choice"	100
	"Whetstone"	50
	"Morriss Lott"	100
h/o Obediah Read	"Newberry"	300
h/o John Read	"Hogg Quarter"	350
	"Green Meadow"	75
Thomas Roberts	"Flowerfield"	165
	"Pharsalia"	50
	"Morriss Lott"	170
John Reddish for h/o Samuell Johnstone	"Friends Choice"	87½
Teague Reggan	"Meadow Ground"	100
	"Riggans Amendment"	285
45:1759:101 ...		

Thomas Relph	"Ralphs Delight"	20
Michael Raglin	"Comby Chance"	100
	"Raglins Chance"	50
James Read	"End of Strife"	272
James Robertson	"Irelands Eye"	150
Jo. Read	"Addition to Littleworth"	200
John Robertson	"Long Delay"	100
William Robertson	"Readbourn"	140
Teague Riggan	"Middle Plantation"	175
	"Riggans Chance"	45
	"Last Chance"	18
John Richardson	"Norths Situation"	481
45:1759:102 ...		
John Robertson	"Benjamins Adventure"	133
	"Ignoble Quarter"	182
	"Robertsons Addition"	37
	pt. "Shiles Folly"	25
Alexander Robertson	"Ahham"	1514
Francis Roberts	pt. "Ellis's Choice"	100
William Roberts	pt. "Davids Distiny"	250
	"Williams Begining"	50
Thomas Robertson	"Moore & Casit"	12
	"Bozmans Addition"	52
	"Moore & Casit"	420
Jo. Rawles	"Gladstones Choice"	150
	pt. "Hardship"	58
	"Gladstones Adventure"	42
Obid. Reggan	"Calf Pasture"	212
William Revill	pt. "Double Purchase"	100
45:1759:103 ...		
Alexander Riccords	"Jones Venture"	50
	"Jones Choice"	50
Ann Riccords	"Riccords Delight"	561
45:1759:104 ...		
John Summers	"Emessex"	108
	"Musketo Creek"	200

Day Scott	"Ahham"	392
	"Last Choice"	6
	"Munmoth"	300
Magdalane Smith	"Addition"	74
	"Hortlebury"	100
William Stevens, Jr.	"Blakes Hope"	200
	"Wooten Underidge"	50
	"Cowley"	100
	pt. "Piney Point"	150
William Smith for h/o James Traine	"Weatherlys Purchase"	225
	"Addition"	30
	"Slipe"	25
	"Weatherlys Purchase"	190
	"Compleat"	25
	"Marsh Hook"	25
	"Once Again"	25
45:1759:105 ...		
John Shiles	"Might Have Had More"	400
	"Adventure"	44
	"Noble Quarter"	33
	"Point Marsh"	6
	"Sidney"	50
	"Finish"	58
	pt. "Noble Quarter"	85
Henry Smith	"Bauld Ridge"	100
Henry Schofield	"Rehoboth"	200
Joseph Standford	"What You Please"	69
	"Dennis Addition"	50
	"Standfords Finding"	50
Henry Spear	"Dunagall"	70
	"Betty Shanney"	100
Isaac Surman	"Wrington"	88
	"Æygpt"	12
h/o Thomas Smith	"Mile End"	75
45:1759:106 ...		

h/o Robert Scott	"Bears Neck"	52
	"Bears Neck" & "Horse Hammock"	68
William Sauser	"Roodey"	200
	"New Point Pagnall"	50
	"Hanslop"	50
	"Woolf Harbour" pt. "Ignoble Quarter"	50
	"Something Worth"	150
	"Sausers Folly"	100
	"Addition"	50
	"Sausers Lott"	50
William Staughton	"Chance"	50
	"Saint Peters Neck"	100
	"Success"	300
	"Bloyces Hope"	125
	"Penny Wise"	95
	"Rainsbury"	345
	"Malbury"	
	"Chance"	
Nathaniell Smullen	"Goshen"	150
Archibald Stutt	"Dear Lott"	160
	"Smiths Polacy"	75
45:1759:107 ...		
Jobe Shurman	"Moore's 2nd Choice"	50
	"Kinneys Ridge"	50
William Steuart	"Panters Denn"	100
	"Kendall"	60
Margaret Smith	"Patricks Folly"	118
Isaac Shurman	"Bettys Choice"	100
h/o Alexander Steuart	"Long Hill"	150
Benjamin Sharpe	"Cannada Island"	50
	"Desart"	71
Archibald Smith	"Plumton Salt Ash"	200
	"Murtle Grove"	50
William Swilavan	"Winsor Castle"	100
45:1759:108 ...		
John Scott	"Bears Neck"	52

Jonathan Summers	"Annemessex"	54
	"Littleworth"	50
	"Jonathons Adventure"	30
	"Summers's Hard Fortune"	25
Henry Sterling	"Apes Hole"	192
Aaron Sterling	"Johnstons Lott"	6
	"Barnett"	35
	"Marsh"	25
	"Haphazard"	64
	"Frustration"	40
	"Industery"	5
	"Choice"	20
	"Comicle Joke"	26
	pt. "Cherry Hinton"	25
John Sterling	"Standards Abby"	50
	"Sterlings Choice"	50
	"Marsh"	25
	"Sterlings Chance"	38
~~Joseph Sterling~~	~~"Comicle Joke"~~	~~26~~
45:1759:109 ...		
William Stevens	"Whittingtons Choice"	150
William Shores	"Balahack"	200
	"Forlorn Hope"	100
	"Polks Folly"	100
	"Clemerill"	100
	"Fornlorn Hopes Addition"	90
	"Whittys Lott"	50
	"Come at Last"	10
William Smullen	"Goshen"	150
Jo. Scrogine	"Fairfield"	142
Jane Strawbridge	"Addition"	82
	"Conveniency"	100
	1 lot in Princess Ann Town – No. 2	<n/g>
	"Widows Chance"	1059
William Skerving (cnp)	"Owens Choice"	283
	"Browns Lott"	182

	"No Name"	57
45:1759:110 ...		
James Spicer	"White Oake Swamp"	100
George Sharpe	"Hogg Neck"	100
James Smith	pt. "Laytons Recovery"	100
George Summers	"Ennemessix"	54
	"Littleworth"	50
	"Summers Hard Fortune"	25
John Stilley	"Stilleys Cost"	66¼
	~~"Glasgow"~~	~~100~~
	"Priviledge"	50
	"Kinkins Folly"	49
Thomas Stevens	pt. "Dudley"	20
	"Late Discovery" now called "Thomas Inheritance"	50
	"Shadwell"	50
Thomas Sloss	"Conclusion"	138
	1 lot in Princess Ann Town – No. 22	<n/g>
	"Belfast"	75½
45:1759:111 ...		
Jacob Spear	pt. "Dumgall"	130
Jonathan Stoll	"What You Please"	225
	"Black Water"	25
	"Supply"	25
	"Dear Lott"	96
	"Worst is Past"	132½
William Standford	pt. "Standfords Finding"	50
John Shockley	"Shockleys Chance"	95
~~Stephen Stevens~~	~~"Ackworths Delight"~~	~~92~~
Thomas Seon (cnp)	"New Invention"	212½
	"Barnabys Lott"	100
	"Sallisburry"	110
	pt. "Invy"	94½
	"Canes Chance"	100
	"Trouble"	50
	"Littleworth"	6
	pt. "Barnabys Lott"	3¾

	~~"Londens Adventure"~~	~~25~~
	~~"Jericho"~~	~~100~~
	~~"Handys Choice"~~	~~175~~
	~~"Stephens Meadow"~~	~~188~~
	pt. "Wilsons Lott"	30
	"Salsbury"	90
	"Recovery"	48
	pt. "Cow Quarter"	322½
45:1759:112 ...		
Thomas Savage	"Baley Buggin"	190
45:1759:113 ...		
Thomas Tull	"Boston"	89
	"Goshen"	100
	"Troublesome"	24
Joshua Tull	"Desart" a/s "Tulls Purchase"	154
	"Winter Range"	200
	"Meadow"	50
	"Hopewell"	37½
	"Addition"	100
	"Harrissons Adventure"	50
Sarah Thompson	"Wellcome" pt. "Double Purchase"	51⅓
William Taylor	"Haphazard"	125
Whittey Turpin	"Barnabys Lott"	10
	"Poyk"	60
	"Furnis's Choice"	314
	"Good Luck"	22
	"Flints Situate"	50
45:1759:114 ...		
John Taylor	"Weatherlys Contrivance"	150
	"First Choice"	100
	"Commons" now called "Taylors Addition"	50
Gideon Tilghman	"Gideons Luck"	50
	"Williams Hope"	60
	"Tilghmans Care"	62
	"Plague Without Proffitt"	143½
John Tull	"Bear Point"	175

William Turpin s/o John	"Tottness"	250
	"Grays Improvement"	10
	"Long Lookt for" pt. "Davis's Choice"	175
	"Adventure"	100
	"Horse Hammock"	100
	"Fathers Care"	40
	"Loss & Gain"	44¼
	"First Choice"	39¾
	"Boyers Banks"	67½
Edm. Tabb	"Nutters Adventure"	50
	pt. "Shiles Choice"	220
James Trahairn	"Dixons Lott"	55
	"Trahairns Lott"	55
45:1759:115 ...		
Aaron Tilghman	"Pools Hope"	60
	"Tilghmans Adventure"	180
	"Davis's Choice" pt. "Pools Hope"	100
	"Hogg Yard"	50
h/o Samuell Taylor	'Laytons Recovery"	100
William Taylor	~~"Round Pond"~~	~~100~~
	"Taylors Addition"	527
William Turpin for h/o Thomas Williams	"Winter Refuge" pt. "Dixons Lott"	50
	"Williamstone"	230
	"Seccond Choice"	90
	"Williams Conquest"	72
	"Third Choice"	20
	"Vacancy"	19
John Tatum	"Tatums Habitation"	40
Solomon Tull	"Pearch & Pine"	50
	"Waterton"	100
	"Willsons Lott"	24
45:1759:116 ...		
William Turpin, Jr. (cnp)	"Poyk"	10
	"Normondy"	25
	"Fountains Lott"	150
	"Haw Tree Point"	100

	"Fathers Care"	90
	"Neighbours Agreement"	46
	"Turpins Choice"	100
Jo. Tilghman	"Pools Hope"	50
	"Amity"	196
	"Beans Hall" pt. "Amity"	100
	"Matthews Ridge"	60
	"Josephs Folly"	66
	"Sapling Ridge"	19
h/o Thomas Tyler	"Pitchroft"	200
Richard Tully	"Fairham"	78
	"Ægypt"	90½
	"Chelsey"	150
	"Commons"	83
Robert Twilley	"Woodstock"	100
h/o Benjamin Townsend	"Townsends Situation"	153
45:1759:117 ...		
William Thompson	"Welcome" pt. "Double Purchase"	100
Stephen Tilghman	pt. "Lott"	50
	pt. "Timber Lott"	15
Elias Taylor	"Dublin"	75
Joshua Turpin	"Doe Better"	150
Noble Tull	"Colemans Adventure"	250
	"Bickles"	93
Stephen Tull	"Providence"	36
	"Chance"	111
Jonathan Tull	"Coalmans Advent"	250
	"Beackles"	100
	"Chance"	50
William Tully	"Tulleys Choice"	50
45:1759:118 ...		
William Taylor	"Knights Loss"	39
Gideon Tilghman, Jr.	pt. "Lott"	50
	pt. "Timber Lott"	15
Isaiah Tilghman	"Beverdam Branch"	52

James Tull	"Accident"	37
	"Poor Swamp"	40
	"Buck Ridge"	40
	"Scotland"	5
Walter Taylor	"Carllisle"	100
	"Chadwicks Adventure"	50
Abraham Taylor	pt. "Hardship"	56
	"Gladstones Adventure"	44
45:1759:119 **<blank>**		
45:1759:120 ...		
Benjamin Vennables	~~"Bells First Choice"~~	~~200~~
	~~"Little Massaley"~~	~~200~~
	"Wilsons Lott"	100
	"Mile End"	150
	"Western Fields"	1400
	"Horse Island"	16½
Perkins Vennables	"Little Belean"	220
William Vennables	"Mill Security"	70
	"Friends Good Will"	50
Jethro Voughan	"Coxes Discovery"	250
Jacob Vinson	"Vinsons Choice"	125
Visitors of the Public School	"Smiths Recovery"	99
45:1759:121 ...		
Mathias Vincent	"Cockland"	100
Vestry of Stepney Parish	"Spring Hill"	2
Vestry of Somerset Parish	"Somerset"	50
George Vincent	"New Carey"	50
	"Charlstown"	50
Vestry of Coventry Parish	"Mitchells Lott"	150
Ephraim Vaughan	"Coxes Discovery"	150
Isaac Vincent	"Cockland"	100
45:1759:122 ...		
h/o Daniel Vance	"Cockmore"	100
45:1759:123 ...		
Capt. Thomas Williams (cnp)	"South Lott"	200
	"Williams Adventure"	83

	"Williams Conquest"	228
	"Cheap Price"	725
	"Double Purchase"	150
	"Winter Harbour" pt. "Dixons Lott"	150
	"Eastern Bounds"	100
	"Chance"	36
	"Security"	150
	"Woodstock"	50
	pt. "Dixons Lott"	50
	"Sunken Ground" pt. "Ackham"	256
	"Last Choice"	344
	"Williams Adventure" (more)	17
Capt. John Watters	"New Rumney"	43
	"Salem"	490
Richard Waters	"Waters River"	525
	"Flatt Land"	840
	"Friends Kindness"	116
	"Conveniency"	80
	"Londons Gift"	50
	"Partners Desire"	125
	"Security"	53
	"Miles's Choice"	77
45:1759:124 ...		
William Waters	"Waters's River"	452½
	"Peace & Pine"	50
	"Wilsons Lott"	20
	"Bear Ridge"	49
George Wilson	"Security"	243
John Wilson	"Hogg Ridge"	100
Thomas White	"Addams Garden"	100
	"Littleworth"	53
John White	"Dam Quarter"	110
	"Oxford"	100
	"Friends Content"	135
	"Father & Sons Desire"	33½

h/o John Waller	"Wallers Adventure"	300
	"Friends Advice"	45
	"Locust Ridge"	50
	"Marvells Chance"	27
	"Front of Locust Hammock"	75
	"Wallers Inlett"	64
45:1759:125 ...		
h/o John Williams	"Charles's Adventure"	140
	"Roberts's Lott"	100
h/o Thomas Walker	"Cascoway"	50
	"Last Purchase"	548
h/o Thomas Winder	"Whitteys Latter Invention"	200
	"Debtford"	110
	"Kickatons Choice"	300
	"Lime House"	40
Daniel Wailes	"Tossator"	150
	"Fortune"	100
	"Might Have Had More"	50
	"Josephs Lott"	58
	"Georges Priviledge"	50
Thomas Willen	"Hogg Quarter"	25
	"Whitteys Contrivance"	50
	"Handys Pasture" pt. "Shiles Folly"	175
	"Turnstile"	70
	"Hickory Ridge"	76
	"End of Strife"	5
45:1759:126 ...		
Grace Wallis	"Friends Acceptance"	95
	"Father & Sons Desire"	51½
	"Dam Quarter"	40
Barnaby Willis	pt. "Barnabys Lott"	40¼
	"Good Luck"	15
	"Littleworth"	6
Capt. John Williams	"Little Bolton"	810
	"Flat Cap"	50
	"Mistake"	400

Capt. John Williams for c/o William White	"Caldecutt"	438
	"Springfield"	486
	"Fair Meadow"	438
	"Reboboth"	600
	"Entrance"	400
	"Entrance" (another)	150
Maj. Sampson Wheatly	"Greenfield"	125
	"Irish Grove"	100
	"Merchants Treasure"	100
	"Wheatlys 2nd Addition"	45
45:1759:127 ...		
William Warwick	"Harpers Discovery"	100
	"Harpers Increase"	50
~~Martha Wallis~~	~~"Ware"~~	~~143~~
James Weatherly	"Ackworths Contrivance"	50
	"Snakey Island"	25
	"Addition"	200
	"Ackworths Folly"	27
	"Prevention"	70
	"Weatherlys Marshes"	33⅔
John Winsor	"Coxes Performance"	250
~~John Wallis~~	~~"Wallis's Venture"~~	~~700~~
Elijah Weatherly	"Ackworths Folly"	115
	"Snakey Island"	26
	"Addition"	128
h/o Thomas Wright	"Long Lott"	50
	"Worst is Past"	150
	"Friends Agreement"	28
	"Friends Advice"	40
45:1759:128 ...		
Southey Whittington (cnp)	"Goshen"	340
	"Scotland"	91
	"Scotts Folly"	50
	"Recovery"	200
	"Puzle"	170
	"Bridgetts Lott"	100

	"Gillead"	285
	"Chance"	164
	"Baltimores Gift"	250
William Wood	"Dublin"	186
	"Woods Contest"	161
James Winright	"Pasturage"	130
	"Clear of Cannon Shot"	100
Boaz Walston	"Double Purchase"	100
Jo. Ward	"Comby Chance"	100
	"Long Acre"	100
	"Paxon Hill"	100
Thomas Waller	"Parish"	29
	~~"Cockland"~~	~~50~~
	"Worlds End Swamp"	25
	"Stepney"	59
	"Swamp Ridge"	50
	"Round Sevannah"	153
45:1759:129 ...		
Nathaniell Waller, Sr.	"Swamp"	100
Archibald White	"Prices Conclusion"	12½
	"Tully Brisk" pt. "Manloves Lott"	118
	"Long Acre"	12½
	"Addition to Tully Brisk"	76
	"Whites Desire"	11
Capt. John Williams	"Williams Lott"	200
	"Hardford Broad Oake"	110
	"Middle Strand"	85
	"Capes Mouth"	12½
	pt. "First Choice"	21
	"North Border"	100
Isaac Williams	"Priviledge"	53
Levin Woolford	"Woolford"	600
	"Woolfords Venture"	33⅔
	"Happy Addition"	66⅔
	"Meadow"	53½
James Winsor	"Comby Chance"	40

45:1759:130 ...		
John Walter	"Shadwells Chance"	281
William Wright	"Chance"	66⅔
Francis White	"Davids Distiney"	50
	"Ellits Choice"	50
	"Out Lett"	100
Stephen Ward, Sr.	"Long Acre"	100
Cornelius Ward	"Cork"	50
	"Long Acre"	75
	"Folly"	19
	"Prices Conclusion"	275
	"White Oake Swamp"	150
Stephen Ward, Jr.	"Cork"	25
	"Littleworth"	50
h/o John White (PO)	"Prices Conclusion"	12½
	"Sons Choice"	133
	"Long Acre"	12½
	"Addition" pt. "Primico"	150
45:1759:131 ...		
h/o Capt. Samuell Wilson	"Kilglain"	500
	"Security"	150
	"Wilsons Discovery"	50
	"Tilbury"	50
	"Mount Ephraim"	375
	"Happy Addition"	100
	"Bozmans Addition"	148
	"Glasgow"	150
	"Gillead" pt. "Double Purchase"	26
	"Mothers Care"	795
	"Prospect"	449
Solomon Wright	"Solomons Delight"	100
James Ward (cnp)	"James Town"	100
	"Agreement"	25
	"Muckel Meadow"	75
	"Apes Hole"	8
	"Prices Vineyard" pt. "James Town"	50

	"Prices Conclusion"	150
	"Comby Chance"	17
	"Long Acre"	100
	"Wards Folly"	16½
	"Mickle Meadow"	150
45:1759:132 ...		
Jacob Ward	"Prices Vineyard" pt. "James Town"	150
	"Agreement"	50
	"Mickle Meadow"	75
	"Wards Folly"	52
h/o Thomas Ward	"Agreement"	25
Thomas Walston	"Winter Harbour"	40
	"London" pt. "Desart"	50
John Ward	"Cork"	75
	"Littleworth"	72
Mathew Wallice	"Contention"	36
	"Gunners Range"	64
	"Golden Quarter"	53
	"Long Delay"	53
	"Meadow"	25
	"Friends Content"	67½
Stephen Winright	"Noble Quarter"	100
	"Whitteys Contrivance"	50
	"Ignoble Quarter"	32
45:1759:133 ...		
Maj. Henry Waggaman	"Adventure"	200
	"Adventures Amendment"	37
	"Long Meadow"	78
	"Waggamans Lott"	384
	"Waggamans Purchase"	947½
	"Calcutta"	599½
	1 lot in Princess Ann Town – No. 14	<n/g>
	"Carneys Chance"	100
	"Abbington"	100
William Waltum	pt. "Waltums Improvement"	238½

Samuell Ward	"Cork"	250
	"Long Acre"	125
	pt. "Little Bolton"	40
George Wailes	"Golds Delight"	200
Daniel Walter & Jonathan Hickman	"Townsends Situation" formerly "Hartford"	50
James Wallis	"Meadow"	25
	"Friends Content"	67½
John Willin	"Mount Hope"	65
	"Turnstile"	70
45:1759:134 ...		
Henry Wright	"Contention"	50
	"Intent"	162
	<n/g> from (N) Robertson	100
	<n/g> from (N) Stoughton	50
Robert Waltor	"Waltors Chance"	50
	"Roberts Lott"	25
	"Poor Choice"	40
Capt. William Winder	"Commons"	117
	"Lyons Lott"	86
	"Twilleys Ridge"	134
	"Hongary Quarter"	71
	"Pembertons Good Will"	350
	"Maidenhead"	300
	"Golden Quarter"	50
	"Pembertons Good Will"	76
Richard Wallis	"Caldwells Lott"	200
William Williams	"Bay Bush Hall"	100
John Williams	~~"Puzel"~~	~~100~~
	"Hogg Island"	50
John White	"Andersons Adventure"	140
	1 lot in Princess Ann Town	<n/g>
	"Whites Adventure"	58½
	pt. "Andersons Adventure"	7
	1 lot in Princess Ann Town – No. 9	<n/g>
45:1759:135 ...		

Robert Willin	“Hogg Quarter”	25
	“Safety”	27
	“Daniels Choice”	39½
	“Daniels Priviledge”	23
Jo. Ward, Jr.	“Little Swamp”	29½
	“Crooked Ridge”	25
	“Winsor Swamp”	70½
John Wailes	“Golds Delight”	200
~~Thomas Waller, Jr.~~	~~“Ludgate Hill”~~	~~100~~
	~~“Sharpes Chance”~~	~~50~~
	~~“Hogg Pallace”~~	~~50~~
Mary Whittingham	“Moores Barrow”	323
Edward Walters	pt. “Whartons Folly”	66½
	pt. “Timber Tract”	312
	“Tilghmans Lott”	50
	“Bad Luck”	162
Joseph Ward (AN)	pt. “Cork”	25
45:1759:136 ...		
William Wheatley	“Cabbin Swamp”	150
	“Roaches Folly”	74
	“Wheatlys Pleasure”	16½
Ephraim Wilson	pt. “Samuels”	64
	“Wilsons Lott”	658
	“Wilsons Conclusion”	318
	“Conveniency”	299½
	“Cow Quarter”	350
Samuell Wilson	“Great Hope” pt. “Double Purchase”	165
	“Wilsons Lott” pt. “Double Purchase”	100
	pt. “Double Purchase”	94⅔
	“Kilglain”	250
	“Security”	75
	“Tilbury”	25
	“Wilsons Discovery”	25
	“Glasgow”	75
	“Cloverfield”	200
	2 lots in Princess Ann Town – No. 5 & No. 6	2

Stephen Ward, Jr.	"Harmsworth"	150
Richard Waller	"Williams Green"	50
	"Conlett"	380
	pt. "Stepney"	41
	pt. "Parrish"	41
	"Cockland"	50
	pt. "Parish"	30
45:1759:137 ...		
Mary Woolford	"Thornton"	400
	"Jeshemon"	33⅔
	"Hachilla"	200
	"Woolford"	300
	"Woolfords Venture"	16½
	"Happy Addition"	33⅓
	"Meadow"	26½
Levin Woolford for Charles Woolford	"Thornton"	200
	"Jeshemon"	16⅔
	"Hachilla"	100
Thomas Ward	"Coulbourns Ridge"	100
	pt. "Scotland"	17
	pt. "Bears Neck"	3
Thomas Whitney	"Woolfs Denn"	53½
Joshua Whittington	"Givens Security"	300
William White	pt. "Priviledge"	15½
45:1759:138 ...		
William Walston	"Winter Harbour"	40
	"London" pt. "Desart"	50
	"Loss & Gain"	14
	"First Choice"	16
James Wilson	pt. "Darby"	175
David Wilson	pt. "Darby"	175
John Waters, Jr.	~~"Salisbury"~~	~~90~~
	"Envy"	478
~~John Waller~~	~~pt. "Parish"~~	~~58~~
Thomas Wright (cnp)	pt. "Contention"	50
	pt. "Intent"	155

	"Discovery"	44
Joseph Weatherly	"Ackworths Folly"	50
	"Prevention"	20
	"Snakey Island"	24
	"Weatherlys Ridge"	100
45:1759:139 ...		
Cannon Winright	"Woolf Hope"	75
	pt. "Pastureadge"	130
John Willen	"Ignoble Quarter"	50
Thomas Willen, Jr.	"Ignoble Quarter"	50
Levin Willen	"Shiles Meadow"	60
James Williss	"Good Luck"	53
	pt. "Envy"	9½
Isaac Winsor	"Woolwidge"	150
	"Long Delay"	90
William Waller	"Hogg Pallace"	50
45:1759:140 ...		
John Weatherly	"Ackworths Contrivance"	50
	~~"Fathers Delight"~~	~~100~~
	"Addition"	122
	"Queoxuson Neck"	86
	"Snakey Island"	25
	"Weatherlys Marshes"	33¾
	"Weatherlys Conveniency"	200
	"Weatherlys Purchase"	110
James & William Weatherly	"Weatherlys Marshes"	102⅔
~~John Watson, Jr.~~	~~"Recovery"~~	~~48~~
Spencer Waters	"Teagues Addition"	78
	"Teagues Down" & "Last Choice"	26
Cornelius Ward, Jr.	"Littleworth"	25
George Wilson	"High Suffolk"	200
Benjamin Wills	"Lott"	36
45:1759:141 ...		
Edward Wooten	"Woottens Fancy"	2
George Wetherly	"Matthews Adventure"	50
John Wilson	"Batchellors Choice"	100

Planer Williams	"Winter Refuge" pt. "Dixons Lott"	100
45:1759:<unnumbered> <blank>		
45:1759:<unnumbered> Certification		

54E:1		**Acres**
Charles Ackworth	"Manloves Delight"	100
George Addams	"Adventure"	34
Phillip Askue	"Turkey Hall"	116
Cornelius Anderson	"Bilboa"	50
William Aylford	"First Lott"	600
William Aylward	"Aylwards Addition"	100
	"Aylwards First Lott"	425
Samuel Allexander	"Monmouth"	100
Isaac Boston	"Bostons Purchase"	355⅓
George Boston	"Nag Hill"	100
	"Leatherland"	150
	"Winter Quarter"	40
Thomas Brereton (BA)	"High Meadow"	250
h/o Richard Brereton	"Cock More"	100
~~h/o Sarah Bannester~~	~~"Double Purchase"~~	~~43~~
~~Sarah Blair~~	~~"Wood Hall"~~	~~50~~
William Bounds	"Barron Lott"	100
David Brown	"Browns Chance"	55
Pearce Bray	"Clonmell"	40
Dockith Beauchamp	"Contention"	65
54E:2 ...		
Jeremiah Barrinclue	"Pearce"	200
James Bradey	"Wallis's Adventure"	200
William Beauchamp	"First Choice"	59
Jarret Bashaw	"Hoggs Down"	125
Henrietta & Ann Bondloe	"Prestons Addition"	125
John Boyce (WO)	"Hickory Hill"	100
Daniel Boyce (WO)	"Poor Choice"	50
h/o Benjamin Cottman	"Berks"	150
Adam Carlisle	"Hopewell"	300
	"Addition"	100
	"Force Putt"	50
Daniel Clifton	"Daniels Hazard"	50
h/o William Cox	"Rook Prevented"	144

~~Hill Cox~~	~~"Alderbury"~~	~~72~~
	~~"Plumton Salt Ash"~~	~~28~~
Jacob Carter	"Mount Charles"	50
Francis Crowder	"Cow Quarter"	100
Nehemiah Covington	"White Marsh"	100
	"Suffolk Neck"	150
	"Snow Hill"	200
54E:3 ...		
Thomas Carrey	"Careys Delight"	300
Allexander Carlisle	"Friends Advice"	30
James Conner	"Coalrain"	200
	"Stooping Pine"	50
John Cheasman	"Coopers Hall"	200
Thomas Chappel	"Kingston"	100
Peter Callaway	"Harlington"	200
	"Little Brittain"	200
Daniel Curtis	"Curtis's Improvement"	150
Andrew Callaway	"Recovery"	288
Thomas Cottingham	"Contention"	65
Joseph Cottman	"Nobles Lott"	75
h/o Thomas Caldwell	"Island Glade"	50
~~Moses Calloway~~	~~"Chance"~~	~~50~~
John Davis	"Cow Quarter" sayd Unk:	1150
Michael Dorman	"Elliards Choice"	200
h/o Daniel Dulany	"Uniacks Choice"	50
h/o William Dorman	"Nelsons Choice"	175
Thomas Davis	"Enlargement"	100
George Downes	"Chance"	150
Thomas Dasheill	"Chance"	150
54E:4 ...		
John Davis	"Sallop"	100
	"Battlefield"	50
	"Marsh Ground"	40
Peter Doutty	"St. Jermon"	50
	"Douttys Priviledge"	50
Edward Dixon	"Contention" a/s "Dixten"	300

Robert Dorman	"Josephs Choice"	50
John Ellis	"Barshaba"	100
	"Bethsaida"	100
Mary Evans	"Pitchcroft"	100
h/o William Evans	"Island Glade"	50
Col. Joseph Ennalls	"Desart"	100
	"Caldwells Lott"	15
	"Inclosed" now called "Willeys Frollick"	40
	"Givans Lott"	100
Henry Ellitt	"Wassawomack"	250
Margaret Fenton	pt. "Wood Hall"	50
54E:5 ...		
~~Margaret Fenton~~	~~pt. "Wood Hall"~~	~~100~~
William Figgs	"Glasgow"	50
	"Figgs Chance"	180
Massey Fountain	"Neighbours Agreement"	16
John Frizell	"Island Marsh"	50
John Peter Franks	"Lozange"	100
h/o Robert Givens	"Addition"	100
	"Begging" pt. "Pasturage"	7
	"Inclosed"	22
	"Denn Pasture"	100
	"Lyons Lott"	14
John Godart	"Bears Denn"	50
~~h/o Ezekiel Gilliss~~	~~"Gilliss Addition"~~	~~100~~
Michael Gray	"Grays Improvement"	140
Mary Games	"Lonnom Devoreys"	300
h/o James Givens	"Largey"	100
John Gladston	"Glads Town"	100
	"Gladstones Delight"	100
	"John Gladstons Land"	300
Stephen Horsey, Sr.	"Waterskewant"	600
	"No Name"	500
Michael Holland	"Increase"	50
	"Pomfrit"	77

h/o Absolam Hobbs	"White Oake Swamp"	100
	~~"Thomas Chance"~~	~~50~~
	~~"Chance"~~	~~100~~
h/o John Handy	"Orphans Lott"	136⅓
Tunstall Hack (VA)	"Long Meadow"	248
	"Bluff Hammock"	50
	"Spring Island"	25
	"Pembertons Good Will"	250
54E:6 ...		
~~h/o Solomon Hitch~~	~~"Weatherlys Ridge"~~	~~100~~
Samuell Hall	"Point Patience"	143
Outerbridge Horsey	"Coulbourn"	195
h/o Noble Hobbs	"Abbington"	100
	~~"Carney Chance"~~	~~58~~
~~William Haine~~	~~"Lawsons Adventure"~~	~~52~~
	~~"Joas Ridge"~~	~~10~~
	~~"Beards Ballem"~~	~~3½~~
	~~"Long Acre"~~	~~8~~
Peter Spencer Hack	"Bluff Hammock"	50
	"Spring Island"	25
Col. Robert Jenkins Henry	"Providence"	200
Jonathan Heath	"Hogg Ridge"	100
George Hutchens	"Manloves Grove"	250
h/o Daniel Hill (VA)	"Hold Fast"	400
Adam Hitch	"Fortune"	50
John Hall	"Something Worth"	200
David Harriss	"Hearts Content"	300
Thomas Holster	"Leverpool"	500
John Holder	"Chance"	32
Thomas Huggitt	"Carpenters Folly"	190
Jo. & Benjamin Hardy	"Orphans Lott"	333⅔
~~Ebenezar Handy~~	~~"Coxes Fork"~~	~~75~~
Henry Hayman	"Shapleys Neglect"	50
	"Haymans Hill"	200
	"Bagg Shott"	200
	"Twillingham"	200

Smith Horsey	pt. "Smiths Island", "Yorksare Island", "Prices Conclusion", "Persimon Hammock"	150
54E:7 ...		
Arthur Hickman	"Poor Choice"	10
~~Abraham Heath~~	~~"Worth"~~	~~13~~
	~~"End of Strife"~~	~~37~~
Capt. John Jones	"Accompson"	150
William Jones	"Jones's Delight"	65
John Jurdin	"Turkey Cock Hill"	40
John Johnson	"Angola"	44
James Johnston	"Long Guila"	50
James Jolly	"Cobham"	100
	"Jollys Delight"	700
Ezekiel Jackson	"Now or Never"	4½
John Knight	"Hap Hazard" pt. "Wilsons Discovery"	100
Zoro. King	"Gullets Advisement"	100
~~Isaac Kinney~~	~~pt. "Desart"~~	~~50~~
Mary King	"Hogg Ridge"	100
William Keen	"Partners Choice"	50
	"Washwater"	36
54E:8 ...		
Peter Kersley	"Townsends Neck"	150
Stephen Kinney	"Kenneys Luck"	50
h/o John Lecat	"New Haven"	209
Levin Larremore	"Cold Quarter"	125
Capt. Aaron Lynn	"Coxes Performance"	100
	"John Folly"	55
	"Addition"	250
	"Carlisle"	300
~~Thomas Langford~~	~~"Chance"~~	~~33⅓~~
~~Daniel Long~~	~~"Benjamin Advice"~~	~~50~~
	~~"Coney Warren"~~	~~125~~
	~~pt. "Kings Glade"~~	~~1~~
Thomas Langake	"Francis Solomon"	50
John Long	"Longs Lott"	200

John Lawrence	"Lawrence"	200
John Lamee	"Pastureage"	50
Richard Lewis	"Stepney"	150
Daniel Lingoe	"Pembertons Good Will"	100
	"Plumton Salt Ash"	100
54E:9 ...		
h/o Jonathan Mills	"Winter Quarter"	100
Mat. Magloughlin	"Magloughlins Chance"	50
Thomas Maddux	"Conveniancy"	52
Ralph Milbourn	"Cork"	200
~~David Marvell~~	~~"Hardshift"~~	~~100~~
John Mears	"Durham"	150
John Manlove	"Manloves Improvement"	300
John Marvell	"Lyons Denn"	200
	"Ferry Hall"	100
h/o Joshua Morriss	pt. "Partners Choice"	150
Robert Nairn	"Neighbourhood"	250
James Nairn	"Nairns Adventure"	30
	"Entrance"	155
Charles Nutter	"No Name"	50
	"Nutters Rest"	450
	"Rich Ridge"	239
Benjamin Nesham	"Benjamin Good Success"	16
54E:10 ...		
h/o James Otley	"Morriss's Hope"	206
	"Boyards Security"	34
~~Margaret Oliphon~~	~~"Rich Ridge"~~	~~30~~
~~Moses Poors~~	~~"Moses's Lott"~~	~~100~~
Michael Owens	pt. "Beard Tree Ridge"	16¾
James Polk	"Raccane"	100
h/o William Piper	"Toswandock"	130
	"Attawattaquaes"	800
William & Benjamin Polk	"Kilmanum"	150
	"Derry"	77
George Pollit	"Preston"	30

Thomas Pryor	"Dixons Kindness"	100
	"Bear Neck"	50
h/o Col. Peter Presley	"Janes Island"	100
	"Two Brothers"	100
	"Buck Ridge"	1
	"Ceader Hammock"	4
Benjamin Parremore	"Addition"	31
Mary Price	"Mackee Meadow"	150
Ephraim Polk	"Locust Hammock"	50
John Panter	"Ignoble Quarter"	50
Robert Polk	"Polks Lott"	50
54E:11 ...		
Magdaline Polk	"Richens Addition"	100
Henry Peasley	"Thornbury"	1000
Timothy Pead	"West Ridge"	150
John Parker	"Cambridge"	300
Rebecca Price	"Prices Purchase"	100
William Phillipson	"What You Will"	200
Edward Price	"Prices Hope"	200
James Quittermas	"Wilsons Discovery"	150
h/o John Riccords	"Turtle Ridge"	50
William Rodulphas	"Chance"	200
John Richardson	"Would Have Had More"	50
Richard Russell	"New Ireland"	500
John Rutter	"Tower Hill"	150
h/o Col. John Rider	"Three Brothers"	136
54E:12 ...		
Day Scott	"Cypress"	18
Magdaline Smith	"Stevenson"	150
	"Bringingham"	500
	"Barkin"	300
~~h/o Thomas Smith~~	~~"Mile End"~~	~~75~~
Mary Shehon	"Malborough"	150
Joseph Sterling	"Marsh"	25
John Seon	"Balain"	280

Robert Swann	"Walbrook" & "Aarons Folly"	260
	"Aarons Folly"	150
	"Carters Lott"	100
William Scott	"Bigland"	150
	"Jones's Caution"	200
	"Scottlands Addition"	65
Thomas Shaw	"Masons Adventure"	100
Arthur Smith	"Suffolk"	150
	"Fluders"	50
William Stevens	"Meant More"	400
Oliver Smith	"Mounmouth"	40
Raymond Stapleford	"Staplefords Neck"	250
54E:13 ...		
Henry Smith	"Davis's Choice"	140
	"Smiths Hope"	1002
Samuel Taylor (ACC)	"Discovery" pt. "Laytons Recovery"	100
John Tilghman	"Beauchamps Priviledge"	79
William Twyford	"Hickory Levell"	40
Alexander Thomas	"Happy Enjoyment"	144
Samuel Taylor (ACC)	"Harrissons Adventure"	50
George Tull	"James's Choice"	150
John Twyford	"Prickle Pair Island"	5
	"Cow Quarter"	5
John Trahairn	"Holders Chance"	65
Joshua Tull	"Harrissons Adventure"	50
Saward Tomlinson	"Manloves Lott"	44
	"Venture"	100
54E:14 ...		
Benjamin Vennables	"Goslins Lott"	50
	"Mile End"	75
Vestry of Somerset Parish	"Davis's Choice" called "Turners Purchase"	130
George Wilson	"Wilsons Folly"	50
Daniel Wailes	"Beaverdam"	100
	"Good Luck"	180
~~John Winsor~~	~~"Coxes Performance"~~	~~200~~

h/o Littleton Waters	"Halls Adventure"	1
Ann West	"Trible Purchase" pt. "Double Purchase"	50
~~John Willen~~	~~"Mount Harper"~~	~~65~~
	~~Turnstile"~~	~~78~~
Thomas Wallis	pt. "Camp"	150
54E:15 ...		
~~George Weatherly~~	~~"Matthews Adventure"~~	~~50~~
Samuel West	"North Wailes"	200
Benjamin Wailes	pt. "Quackison Neck"	100
Wrixham White	"Batchellors Delight"	50
Elijah Weatherly	"Ackworths Folly"	115
	"Snakey Island"	26
	"Addition"	128
William White	"Kings Norton"	100
Richard Whitemarsh	"Whitemarshes Choice"	200
Michael Williams	"Farmingham"	300
~~James Weatherly~~	~~"Weatherlys Pasture"~~	~~<n/g>~~
William Winright	"Doughtys Lott"	50
James Wyth & Marmaduke Masters	"Batchellors Delight"	250
	"Batchellors Invention"	250
	"Batchellors Contrivance"	150
James Warrington	"Chance"	300
Andrew Whittington	"Monmouth"	50
~~John Wilson~~	~~"Batchellors Choice"~~	~~100~~
Cornelius Ward	"Bear Point"	200
William Waters	"Afriends Choice"	600
John Williams	"Puzle" – lies in WO & conveyed to William Todvine	100
54E:16 ...		
Robert Wair	"Increase"	182
Richard Wallis	"Folly"	50
Isaac Williams	"Williamstone"	70
	"Third Choice"	44
Thomas Waller, Jr.	"Pleasent Grove" – in WO	50

John Weatherly	"Weatherlys Conveniency"	200
	"Fathers Delight"	100
Thomas West	"Beverly" – in WO	100
Samuell Young	"Coventry"	300
William Yaulding	"Hansloe"	50
54E:17 ... [This page is unnumbered.]		
h/o Sarah Bannester	pt. "Double Purchase"	43
Sarah Blair	pt. "Wood Hall"	50
Francis Crowder	"Cow Quarter"	100
Thomas Caldwell	"Island Glade"	50
h/o Daniell Dulany	"Uniacks Chance"	50
h/o William Dorman	"Nelsons Choice"	175
h/o Ezekiel Gilliss	"Gilliss's Addition"	100
John Hoffington	<n/g> – land not charged	<n/g>
Col. George Gale	<n/g> – land not charged	<n/g>
Ebenezar Handy	"Coxes Fork"	75
Ezekiel Jackson	"Now Or Never"	4½
William Kinney	<n/g> – land not charged	<n/g>
Isaac Kinney	"Desart"	50
Thomas Langford	"Chance"	33⅓
Margaret Olipher	"Rich Ridge"	30
h/o Col. John Rider	"Three Brothers"	136
Outterbridge Horsey	"Bauld Ridge"	91
	"Dixons Choice Enlarged"	4½
Seward Tomlinson	"Manloves Lott"	44
	"Venture"	100
54E:18 ... [This page is unnumbered.]		
h/o Daniell Vance	"Cockmore"	100
John Winsor	"Coxes Performance"	200
Thomas Wallis	pt. "Camp"	150
John Williams	"Puzle"	100

Atkinson
(N) 39, 99
Angell 99
Angelo 99
James 34, 99
John 54, 94
Joshua 6
Samuell 34
Timothy 24
Atkinsons Adventure 99
Attawattaquaco 121
Attawattaquaes 274
Attawattaquaquo 50, 191
Auskaukin 54
Austin
Jos. 13
Robert 13, 14, 48, 99, 203
William 167, 203
Avery
John 20, 181
Averys Choice 20, 67
Averys Policey 181
Averys Pollicy 20, 22
Aydelot
Benjamin 68
John 54, 68
William 94
Aydelott
Benjamin 68
John 54
William 94
Aylford
William 178, 192, 269
Aylward
William 178, 186, 187, 269
Aylwards Addition 71, 178, 186, 269
Aylwards First Choice 71
Aylwards First Lott 178, 187, 269
Aylworth
John 177, 203
widow 177
Ayres
Comfort 94
Jacob 203
John 94

Bable 74, 79
Bacbus Rest 228
Back Lodge 36
Bacnar 194
Bacon
Dudson 144, 205
Bacon Hill 81
Bacon Quarter 53, 66, 72
Bacors Folly 134, 172, 207, 225
Bad Luck 265
Badors Folly 228
Bagg Shott 192, 272
Bagshot 179
Bailey
Benjamin 205
Elias 205
George 205
Jonathan 204
William 205
Baileys Lott 204
Baileys Purchase 205
Baileys' Chance 205
Baily Began 23
Baker
(N) 91, 97
Bakers Folly 97
Balahack 152, 252
Balain 275
Bald Beach 76
Baley
(N) 189
Benjamin 133
Elias 132
George 87, 132
Jonathan 26, 114
Sarah 23, 87
William 132
Baley Buggin 254
Baleys Chance 132
Baleys Lott 114
Baleys Purchase 133
Ball
Samuell 101
Thomas 70, 191
Balla Magerrey 228
Balla Magorrey 127
Ballard
(N) 87
Arnald 170
Arnold 207
Charles 19, 112, 204
Henry 19, 28, 140, 205
Jarvice 171
Jervice 29

233, 235
Boston Towne 2, 108
Bostons Adventure 4, 141, 142
Bostons Chance 204
Bostons Green 204
Bostons Lott 140, 205
Bostons Pasture 201
Bostons Purchase 39, 99, 119, 239, 269
Bottle Ridge 106
Bottom 167, 228
Bottom of the Neck 135, 145, 167, 217, 231, 235
Boucher
James 80
Bouger
James 80
Bougher
(N) 26
Frances 80
Francis 80
John 46
Bound
Jonathan 142, 205
William 69
Bounds
James 194
Jessee 124, 204
John 185
Jonathan 18
Jos. 105
William 124, 171, 175, 207, 269
Bounds Lott 142, 205
Bowdwick
Robert 92
Bowen
(N) 95
Edward 94
Elizabeth 94
John 65
Littleton 65, 105
William 65, 94
Bowens Choice 65
Bower 52
BowLand
William 105
Bowler
William 31, 105
Boyard
Robert 38, 39
Boyards Security 126, 274
Boyce
Daniel 269
John 47, 269
Boyces Bancks 3
Boyces Banks 108, 110, 116, 156, 234, 240
Boyer
(N) 24
Boyers Banks 208, 255
Bozeman
John 28
Bozemans Choice 5
Bozman
(N) 86, 89
Ballard 132, 205
George 16, 89, 132, 181, 182, 205
John 28, 89, 182, 187
John 89
William 9, 82, 89, 132, 180, 181, 205
Bozmans Addition 28, 142, 171, 187, 249, 262
Bozmans Advent 218
Bozmans Choice 180
Bozworth 142, 235
Bradey
James 178, 269
Bradford
John 79, 91
Bradley
James 159, 206
John 151, 206
Samuel 151
Samuell 206
Bradshaw
Ann 42
William 42
Bradshaws Purchase 42, 92
Bradys Chance 225
Brambles 203
Bramford 4
Brandford 208
Branford 109, 186
Brasier
Ann 39
Bratten
Brough 206
John 206

Bratton
Brough 153
James 56
John 56, 161
Samuell 56
William 153, 206
Bray
Pearce 35, 176, 269
Pierce 194
Breadys Chance 132
Bredall
Isaiah 21, 67, 103
Breedell
Isaiah 95
Breeding 100
Breedy
James 72
John 101
Bremelow 165
Brents Marsh 62, 65, 66
Brereton
(N) 78, 98
Ann 26
Richard 21, 141, 269
Thomas 21, 140, 183, 188, 197, 269
William 22, 113, 192, 195, 197, 204
Breretons Chance 78, 113, 204
Bretherd
Richard 96
Brick Hill Hoe 65
Brickle How 129, 214
Brickles 119, 201
Brickleshoe 10
Bridgers
Jos. 182
Bridgers Lott 182, 230
Bridges Lottery 30
Bridgets Lott 128
Bridgetts Lott 81, 260
Bridgwater 54
Brigers Lott 149
Brimilaw 17
Bringingham 31, 191, 275
Brisco
Arthur 75, 185
Briscoe Lott 75
Briscoes Lott 185
Brittain 72, 125, 224, 226
William 75
Brittaine 148
Brittingham 117
(N) 43, 79, 84, 88, 92, 98
Elizabeth 65
Isaac 95
John 10, 43, 91
Joseph 65
Macajah 42
Nathaniell 84
Rebecca 98
Samuell 91
widow 68
William 10, 36, 43
Broad Ridge 91
Broadwater
William 71
Brooks
Richard 35
Broomley
Christian 88
Broomly
Timothy 88
Brotherhood 96
Brothers Agreement 9, 66, 219, 245
Brothers Agrement 110, 160
Brothers Conveniency 101
Brothers Gift 59, 100
Brothers Good Will 100
Brothers Goodwill 135, 242
Brothers Love 52, 54
Brotherwood 67
Broughton
(N) 92
Brough 33, 38
John 38
Broughtons Choice 39
Brown
(N) 2, 22
David 29, 70, 176, 182, 184, 197, 269
George 172, 207
James 172, 207
John 172, 192, 207
Robert 151, 206
Thomas 27, 70, 182
William 65, 124, 172, 205, 207
Brown Stone 213
Browne

211
Robert 23, 192, 193, 197
Crouches Choice 74, 172, 184, 189, 231
Crouches Desart 23, 197
Crouches Desire 23
Croutch
John 26
Crowder
Francis 169, 212, 270, 278
Crowland 55
Crowley 10, 43
Cubeys Choice 164
Cubys Chance 236
Cuckolds Delight 69, 192
Cullen
Jacob 109, 208
Cullens
Jacob 4
John 4
Cullin
Henry 141
Cullins
Henry 3
Culver
John 161, 211
Cumberland 21, 63, 65, 67, 99, 101, 115, 224
Cunney Warrin 150
Cunningham
Arthur 105
Curle
(N) 97
Curry
William 72
Curtis
Charles 5, 109, 208
Daniel 75, 178, 270
James 5, 173, 212
Martin 70
Curtis Improvement 75, 178
Curtis Lott 5
Curtis's Improvement 270
Curtis's Improvment 193
Curtis's Lott 109, 208
Cutherwood
Robert 30
Cypress 47, 275
Cypress Swamp 227
Cypriss 112
Cyprus Swamp 45, 54, 162
Dahaughty
James 85
Daintery 149, 245
Dakes
James 151, 215
Dale
(N) 80
Archibald 55, 59
David 186
John 81
Dales Adventure 36, 90, 133, 137, 142, 160, 186, 218, 238, 245
Daley
Patrick 84
DalSerfe 77
Dam Quarter 169, 218, 226, 233, 236, 258, 259
Damm Quarter 1, 11
Damquarter 111, 114, 159
Danbury 75, 189
Dane
(N) 92
Daniells Adventure 20
Daniells Denn 8
Daniells First Choice 98
Daniells Luck 77
Daniels Advent 218
Daniels Adventure 136, 169, 187, 228
Daniels Chance 148, 239
Daniels Choice 160, 265
Daniels Denn 125, 127, 238, 244
Daniels Hazard 150, 269
Daniels Hope 239
Daniels Previledge 148, 160
Daniels Priviledge 239, 265
Dantary 202
Dantery 127, 181
Dany Neck 129
Darby 50, 169, 192, 266
Daniell 106
Walter 102, 137
Darmas Improvement 136
Darsey
Thomas 102
Dasentry 24
Dasheild
(N) 72
Christopher 71
Dasheill

Flints Situate 254
Flodders 33
Flowerfield 92, 154, 236, 248
Fludders 176, 191
Fluders 276
Fluelin
(N) 93
Fluellin
Samuell 25, 49
Fluelling
Samuel 184
Foard
Absolam 219
Absolom 70
Fogg
Aaron 89
Folly 38, 42, 52, 77, 78, 141, 179, 194, 262, 277
Foolks Choice 39
Force Put 141, 143, 147, 215
Force Putt 20, 49, 248, 269
Ford
Absolem 133
Forked Neck 72, 76, 89, 140, 205
Forlorn Hope 152, 252
Forlorn Hopes Addition 152
Forlorne Hope 17, 67
Fornlorn Hopes Addition 252
Forr
John 194
Forrest 68
Forrest Chance 106
Forrest of Dean 68
Forsith
Thomas 71
Fortune 20, 24, 113, 116, 148, 176, 201, 244, 259, 272
Forwell
Richard 188
Foscull 238
Foscutt 32, 129, 198
Fosken
(N) 96
Foskin
John 66
Simon 66
Foster
Martha 64
Mary 64
Fouler
(N) 48, 99
Foulks
Benjamin 4
Fountain
Mary 115, 219
Massey 271
Nicholas 28, 29, 90
William 220
Fountaine
Mary 29, 90
Nicholas 28
Fountains Lott 28, 219, 255
Fountin
Massey 115
Nicholas 182, 190
Samuel 185
Fountins Lott 115, 140, 185
Fowle
Edward 93
Fowler
Edward 26, 99
John 84, 135, 219
Fox Hall 136, 218
Fox Island 173, 231
Foxcroft
Isaac 183, 197
Foxen
(N) 79
William 9
Foxhall 17
Francis Solomon 104, 160, 273
Francklyn
Charles 74
Frank
John Peter 178, 192
Franklin
John 59
Franklyn
Ebenezar 61
Edward 59
Franks
John Peter 271
Freeman
(N) 91
John 67, 74, 186, 191
Robert 24
William 79
Freemans Choice 79
Freemans Contentment 59
Freemans Discovery 69

William 82
Hackorths Choice 47
Hackworth
Richard 193
Hackworths Charety 74
Hackworths Charity 193
Hacworth
Richard 74
Hadder
Richard 64
Warren 65
Hailes
Jeremiah 102
John 90
Hails
Hannah 102
John 40
Haine
William 229, 272
Haines
David 229
Haines Grave 229
Hains 227
Francis 154
Hains Grove 104
Hains's Grave 154
Hairn
Ebenezar 229
Edward 137, 225
Elijah 225
George 155, 227
Isaac 229
Nehemiah 155, 227
Thomas 132, 225, 229
William 132
Hale
David 167, 228
Half Quarter 240
Hall
(N) 94
Alexander 99
Alice 3
Charles 3, 19
Ezekiel 154, 226
Henry 53
Jo. 69
John 35, 53, 97, 142, 168, 177, 226, 272
Joshua 108, 175, 229
Phenix 18, 66
Richard 3, 108, 223
Robert 95
Samuel 134
Samuell 97, 272
William 69
Zorobabel 171
Zorobable 228
Halls Adventure 3, 108, 149, 160, 206, 223, 277
Halls Choice 3, 108, 223
Halls Hammock 108, 154, 223, 226
Halls Humock 3
Halls Kindness 226
Halls Pasture 3, 108, 154, 226
Halls Posture 223
Hamans Chance 112
Hamblin
(N) 94
Francis 62
Hamblyn
John 51
Hameltons Fortune 207
Hamilton
John 162, 227
Hamm 36, 118
Hammond
(N) 77, 92
Hamon 209
Hamons Chance 223
Hampton
John 94
Mary 36, 40, 77, 81, 88, 94
Handy
Eben 67
Ebenezar 6, 21, 22, 96, 99, 229, 272, 278
Ebinezar 179
Elioner 99
Elizabeth 40, 42
George 168, 228
Isaac 89, 132, 162, 181, 183, 185, 225, 227
John 86, 143, 166, 185, 221, 228, 272
Samuel 109, 120, 169, 224, 228
Samuell 6, 229
Sewell 174, 229
Stephen 98, 164, 228
William 6, 42

John 195
Harrisson Venture 227
Harrissons Advent 225
Harrissons Adventure 133, 166, 170, 179, 195, 254, 276
Harrissons Venture 119, 163, 220, 224
Harry Gate 65
Hartford 6, 155, 183, 207, 264
Meckley 169
Hartford Broad Oak 109
Hartford Broad Oake 208
Harthbury 32
Hartington 10
Hartlebury 117, 182
Harts Comfort 239
Harts Contract 1, 147
Harts Ease 84, 129, 238
Harvey
John 101
Timothy 73
Hasely
Jane 93
Hast
Daniell 20
Hastford
George 184
Hastford Purchase 75
Hastfords Purchase 184
Hastin
John 228
Robert 127
Hasting
Robert 82
Hath
Abraham 115, 182, 224
Jonathan 171
William 135
Haths Chance 135, 225
Haw Tree Point 255
Hawtree Point 30, 140
Hayman
(N) 75
Charles 143, 226
Henry 14, 179, 180, 190, 192, 272
Isaac 131, 225
James 97, 134, 225
William 72
Haymans Chance 14
Haymans Exchange 72, 75
Haymans Hill 14, 179, 190, 272
Haymans Purchase 131, 134, 225
Haymon
(N) 190
Haymond
James 97
John 97
William 67
Haynes
Francis 104
Haynie
William 156
Hayward
Thomas 85, 98, 101, 130, 171, 182-184, 224, 228
William 229
Haywards Dear Purchase 85
Haywards Lott 130, 224
Hazard 19, 68, 112, 123, 129, 162, 203, 204, 213, 238
David 61, 68, 82
Hazard I 30
Head of St. Laurences Neck 95
Head of Tyaskin 139, 215
Head of Tyaskin Creek 12
Headly Hill 53
Health
William 99
Heap
Francis 71
Hearafter 146
Heard Quarter 41
Hearn
(N) 1
Thomas 88
William 88
Hearn Quarter 27, 29
Hearne
William 88
Heart
Robert 180
Hearts Content 65, 177, 186, 272
Hearts Ease 180
Heath
(N) 21, 84, 86, 88
Abraham 29, 76, 105, 273
Adam 24
James 47
John 2
Jonathan 272

James Groom 104
James Meadow 76
James Town 262, 263
Jameses Town 143
James's Choice 179, 276
James's Lott 125, 238
James's Town 143
Janes Island 157, 275
Jarman
(N) 27, 94
Job 102
Jobe 102
William 66
Jarratt
(N) 87
Jarrett
(N) 79, 87
Graves 22
Jefferson
(N) 98
Richard 76
Jenkins
(N) 56, 88, 90
David 163, 231
Francis 36, 77
Jarvice 156
Jervice 23, 231
John 172, 231
Jonathan 173, 231
Joseph 172, 231
Mary 88
William 91
Jenkins Mistake 229
Jenkins Mistaken 111
Jericho 6, 109, 254
Jerman
Henry 67, 70
Jermons Lott 47
Jersey 25, 41, 150, 202
Jeshemon 205, 248, 266
Jeshimon 13, 22, 27, 36, 89, 111, 144, 167, 168, 184, 246
Joanes Hole 6
Joas Ridge 156, 272
Jobs Lott 106
John Boqueto Norton Hundred 56
John Folly 273
John Gladsteans Land 51
John Gladstons Land 177, 192, 271
Johns Chance 134, 225
Johns Desire 165, 203
Johns Folly 80, 102
Johns Lott 79
Johns Town 180
Johns Towne 79
Johnson
(N) 2, 24, 57, 62, 79, 84, 93, 94, 96
Afradosie 53
Benjamin 78
Cornelius 71
David 54, 96
George 75
James 31
John 24, 161, 176, 190, 231, 273
Leonard 66
Peater 54
Purnal 230
Robert 54
Thomas 106
Johnsons Addition 144, 215
Johnsons Delight 106
Johnsons First Choice 1
Johnsons Folly 101
Johnsons Hope 54
Johnsons Lott 4, 19, 42, 78, 84, 181
Johnston 7, 193
Cornelius 180
George 7, 180, 181, 188, 193
James 176, 273
John 66
Leonard 66
Purnaell 112
Purnall 17
Samuel 155
Johnstone
Samuell 248
Johnstons First Choice 190
Johnstons Lot 151
Johnstons Lott 109, 141, 208, 248, 252
John's Folly 137
Jolley
James 176, 191
Jolleys Delight 176
Jolly
James 34, 273
Jollys Delight 273
Jonathans Addition 150
Jonathons Adventure 252

Panter
John 51, 176, 180, 188, 275
Panters Denn 90, 140, 152, 180, 236, 251
Panther Swamp 77
Panthers Denn 15
Paradice
John 39
Paramore
(N) 77
Paramores Double Purchase 23
Paris 49
Parish 82, 170, 261, 266
Parker
(N) 8, 70, 96
Charles 67, 70
Dorothy 96
George 70, 71
John 70, 148, 178, 192, 207, 244, 275
Mathew 75
Peter 66
Phill. 67
Phillip 39, 70
Parkers Adventure 67, 70
Parkers Choice 35
Parkers Denyall 62
Parkers Peace 10, 192
Parkes
Arthur 89
John 162
Parks
Arthur 89, 132, 244
Parramore
(N) 50, 96
James 82
John 70
Jos. 103
Mathew 50
Thomas 57, 106
Parramores Double Purchase 55, 57, 70
Parramores Folley 82
Parramours Double Purchase 57
Parramours First Choice 46
Parremore
Benjamin 169, 245, 275
Isaac 160, 245
John 169, 191, 245
Stephen 246
Thomas 138, 244
Parremores Double Purchase 140, 247
Parremores First Choice 121, 220
Parremores Misfortune 169, 245
Parris 122, 153, 209, 211
Parrish 135, 167, 266
Parsons
(N) 72
John 18, 22, 68, 159, 181, 245
Partner Choice 75
Partners Agreement 202
Partners Agrement 85, 130
Partners Choice 47, 51, 56, 60, 79, 87, 91, 93, 101, 103, 105, 128, 136, 145, 149, 150, 158, 165, 174, 177, 182, 189, 195, 205, 212, 222, 226, 232, 238, 240, 248, 273, 274
Partners Contention 66
Partners Desire 1, 4, 67, 107, 184, 258
Pasteridge 92
Pasturadge 125, 134, 224
Pasturage 20, 65, 131, 134, 177, 238, 240, 261, 271
Pastureadge 219, 267
Pastureage 274
Pastureidge 197
Pasturidge 47, 82, 121, 156, 172, 194
Paswater
Thomas 21
Patrick
(N) 95
Daniell 64
John 65
Mathew 94
Patricks Folly 29, 142, 147, 239, 251
Patricks Lott 65
Patten
William 95
Paxon Hill 43, 135, 261
Peace 71, 178, 192
Peace & Pine 258
Peacemaker 208
Peach & Pine 37, 108, 140
Pead
Timothy 177, 191, 275
Peal
Thomas 38
Peale

Puzell 236
Puzels Injoyment 216
Puzle 6, 120, 127, 158, 204, 260, 277, 278
Puzzle 85

Quackison Neck 277
Quaturmus
(N) 49
Isaiah 103
James 11, 44
Queoxuson Neck 267
Quiakeson Neck 44, 45
Quiankeson Neck 197
Quiaukason Neck 125
Quiaukeson Neck 164, 170, 175, 195, 211
Quiet Entrance 174, 218
Quiett Entrance 97
Quillen
Thomas 39
Quillin
widow 38
Quinton
(N) 85
Peter 150, 246
Philip 38
Phillip 79, 85, 183
William 38
Quittermas
James 137, 147, 275
Quittermus
Patrick 174
Quitturmas
James 246
Paterick 246
Quoackeson Neck 209

Racans 117
Raccane 274
Rachells Lott 80, 98
Racnax 32
Radburne 50
Raglin
Michael 164, 249
Raglins Chance 164, 249
Rain
Mathew 80
Raine
Mathew 82
Rainsbury 14, 131, 251
Ralph
(N) 53, 86
Thomas 26, 46, 161
William 106, 138
Ralphs Delight 161, 249
Ralphs Prevention 86
Ralphs Purchase 26, 46, 152
Ralphs Venture 46, 114, 204
Rambling Point 72, 97
Ramsey
Charles 43
Rapha 24
Ratclief
Charles 58, 0
Elias 58
Ratcliefs Quantity 62
Ratcliff
Elias 62
Ratcliffe 60
Charles 62
Nathaniell 60
Ratcliffs Adventure 64
Ratcliffs Late Discovery 64
Ravenstone 92
Raw
Joseph 132
Rawles
Jo. 249
Rawley
(N) 86
Rawls
Joseph 173
Rawly
(N) 13
Raymon
Jonathan 187
Raymond
(N) 24
Jonathan 78
Raymonds Chance 78
Raymons Chance 187
Read
Hezekiah 123, 247
James 165, 183, 249
Jo. 249
John 50, 125, 149, 194, 247, 248
Joseph 167
Obadiah 149

Rhodey 190
Riccords
  Alexander 249
  Ann 249
  John 275
  Phillip 51
  Thomas 248
Riccords Delight 249
Rice
  Nicholas 181, 195
Rice Land 136, 181, 218
Rich
  Henry 61
Rich Island 77
Rich Land 33
Rich Ridge 45, 73, 114, 154, 159, 177, 204, 240, 243, 274, 278
Rich Swamp 18, 24, 87, 123, 161, 163, 187, 209, 213, 231
Richard Ridge 79
Richards
  (N) 56, 80, 87
  Charles 38
  John 87
  Phill. 93
  William 58
Richardson
  (N) 64, 96
  Benjamin 132, 247
  Charles 56
  John 25, 27, 64, 170, 176, 189, 249, 275
  Robert 75
  William 48, 64
Richardsons Land 56
Richardsons Ridge 52
Richens
  John 188
Richens Addition 31, 275
Richey
  Archibald 125, 247
Richins
  John 192
Richins Addition 176, 190
Ricketts
  Benjamin 51
  John 57, 58
  William 58
Ricketts Chance 57, 58
Ricords
  John 247
Ricords Delight 247
Rider
  (N) 189
  Heathley 133
  Heathly 93, 230
  John 81, 179, 189, 275, 278
  Wilson 93, 144, 248
Ridge 32
Ridge Glade 165, 233
Ridgely
  Lawrence 40
Ridger 223
Ridges 122, 151, 157, 201, 202
Ridgley
  Robert 181, 185, 198
Riely
  Laurance 56
Rigen
  Ambros 91
Riggan
  Charles 246
  John 34, 72, 248
  Jonathan 247
  Mary 246
  Teage 34
  Teague 34, 199, 249
Riggans Amendment 199, 248
Riggans Chance 249
Riggans Mine 76, 213
Riggen
  Ambros 43, 76
  Darby 98
  John 7
  Joseph 86
  Samuell 6
Riggin
  (N) 40
  Teague 183
Riggin Content 40
Rigin
  (N) 90
Rigland 186
Rigsby
  John 115, 246
  Lewis 29, 182
Riley
  Thomas 56
Riple 43, 61

Selbye
Thomas 57
Selbys Purchase 56
Self Preservation 232, 234
Selfe Preservation 116, 128
Seon
John 275
Thomas 253
Seward
Josias 194
Sewards Purchase 39, 119, 204
Sewell
(N) 62
Henry 74
Shackly
Richard 76
Shadewell 214
Shadwell 2, 48, 93, 134, 153, 164, 183, 211, 253
Shadwells Chance 138, 262
Shafsbury 92
Shaftsbury 55
Shahe
(N) 50
Shanks
(N) 32
Thomas 182
Shantavanah 45, 129, 247
Shapleighs Neglect 14
Shapleys Neglect 179, 272
Sharp
Benjamin 5, 145
George 89, 160
Sharpe
Benjamin 251
George 89, 253
John 103
Sharpes Chance 226, 265
Sharps Chance 164
Sharps Grove 103
Sharrett
widow 37
Shaw
Thomas 14, 175, 276
Shearbourne 92
Shearman
(N) 76
Sheep 104
Sheha
(N) 23
Shehan
John 97
Shehane
John 97
Shehe
Potter 101
Shehon
Mary 134, 275
Sheilds Choice 45, 46, 92
Sheldon
John 80
Shellitor
Thomas 8
Shepherds Crook 247, 248
Sheppard
Rowland 55
Sheppards Crook 137, 149
Sherburn 77
Sheridon
Daniel 179, 195
Sheridons Desire 179, 195, 213
Sherly
John 102
Sherman
Job 106
Peter 25
Thomas 24
Sherridon
Daniell 102
Sherridons Desire 102
Shewell
(N) 62
Shewells Addition 62, 71
Shields Choice 123
Shields Folly 197
Shiels
(N) 87
Shiels Folly 12
Shiels's Ridge 196
Shiles
(N) 41
John 21, 50, 123, 181, 250
Thomas 87, 181, 200
Shiles Choice 46, 255
Shiles Folly 132, 135, 148, 162, 203, 214-216, 225, 239, 249, 259
Shiles Meadow 21, 267
Shiles's Folley 163
Shiles's Folly 123, 139, 144, 152, 209,

Spring Banck 65
Spring Garden 104
Spring Hill 36, 138, 257
Spring Island 119, 160, 272
Spring Quarter 58, 94
Springfield 36, 118, 260
Srewsbury 192
St. Albans 48, 81, 207
St. Albins 169, 177, 195
St. Giles 3, 14, 116, 209
St. Gyles 125, 185
St. Gyles Lott 222, 223
St. Jermans 49
St. Jermon 177, 270
St. Jermons 194
St. Lawrances Neck 69
St. Lawrences Neck 59
St. Leonards 55
St. Martins Desart 91
St. Martins Rige 9
St. Patricks Hill 64
St. Peters Neck 29, 115, 131, 182, 246
Staines 225, 229
Stains 88, 132, 155
Stake Ridge 6, 109
Stanaway 207, 226
Stand Reads Abby 8
Standards Abby 252
Standford
  Joseph 250
  William 253
Standfords Finding 250, 253
Standreds Abby 151
Stanford
  Jos. 25, 72, 125
  William 171
Stanfords Finding 125, 171
Stanidge 181
Stanleys 43
Stanlys 91
Stannaway 93, 155, 169
Stannaways 81
Stannett
  (N) 35
Stapleford
  Raymon 178
  Raymond 75, 193, 276
Staplefords Neck 75, 178, 193, 276
Staughton
  (N) 156
  William 131, 251
Steavens
  John 18, 22, 33
  Richard 18
  William 33
Steavenson
  James 97
  John 66
  Joseph 39
Stephens Conquest 18
Stephens Freehold 132
Stephens Frehold 234
Stephens Meadow 6, 109, 254
Stepney 75, 135, 167, 179, 261, 266, 274
Sterling
  Aaron 151, 198, 252
  Henry 151, 252
  John 8, 30, 151, 252
  Joseph 151, 252, 275
Sterlings Chance 151, 252
Sterlings Choice 8, 151, 252
Steuart
  Alexander 251
  William 251
Stevens
  (N) 84, 89, 100, 101
  Edward 33
  John 33, 194
  Richard 18, 186
  Stephen 253
  Thomas 106, 164, 253
  William 33, 117, 153, 176, 180-187, 190, 191, 193-197, 199, 200, 250, 252, 276
Stevens Inheritance 33, 164
Stevens Lott 239
Stevenson 31, 93, 117, 150, 226, 275
  (N) 70
  James 97
Stevens's Conquest 151, 211
Stevens's Lott 142
Stewart
  Alexander 145
  Sarah 34, 35
  William 70, 140
Still
  Archibald 98
Stilley

Swain
William 98
Swamp 135, 261
Swamp in Fellowship 96
Swamp Ridge 135, 261
Swan
Robert 173
Swann
Robert 276
Swanns Luck 245
Swans Luck 159
Sweet Wood 111, 174, 212, 229
Sweet Wood Hall 122, 237
Sweetwood 15, 212
Sweetwood Hall 48
Swilavan
William 251
Swine Harbour 81
Swulavan
William 149
Sylus's Chance 76

Tabb
Edm. 123, 255
Tar Kill 219
Tarikil Hammock 122
Tarkill Humock 48
Tarr
John 73
Michaell 73
Michall 106
Tarr Kill 173
Tarr Kill Ridge 170, 222
Tarsay 129
Tarsey 241
Tatmans Folly 50, 144, 205
Tatum
John 103, 255
Tatums Habitation 103, 255
Tauntin Dean 208
Tauntin Deane 114
Taunton 39, 55, 60, 192
Taunton Dean 18, 24, 211
Taunton Deane 153
Tayler
Elias 153
John 134, 181, 192
Robert 183
Samuel 133, 149, 179
Walter 187, 193
William 110, 135, 171
Taylers Addition 134
Taylers Chance 151
Taylers Choice 193, 194
Taylers Hill 154
Taylor
(N) 38, 73, 91, 95, 96
Abraham 93, 257
Ann 10
Charles 67, 96
Elias 256
George 61, 95
Hope 99
James 83
John 10, 254
Robert 36, 96
Roger 105
Samuel 276
Samuell 91, 102, 255
Thomas 87, 103
Walter 37, 257
widow 36
William 99, 254-256
Taylors Addition 254, 255
Taylors Adventure 103
Taylors Chance 206
Taylors Choice 10, 37
Taylors Hill 51, 236
Taylors Lott 37, 38
Taytom
John 137
Taytoms Habitation 137
Teage
John 65
Teags Content 67
Teags Down 6
Teague
John 65
Teague Down 200
Teagues Addition 65, 107, 267
Teagues Down 107, 267
Tearse 42
Teauges Folly 102
Teauxbury 88, 94
Teaxbury 59
Temple Comb 55, 105
Temple Hall 81
Templin
John 92
Terrey

James 69
Willen
John 267, 277
Levin 267
Thomas 259, 267
Willet
Ambrose 54
Willett
Ambros 82
Willetts Discovery 82
Willeys Frollick 271
William Ston 186
Williams
(N) 6
Charles 16, 50
Edward 67
Isaac 2, 138, 187, 261, 277
John 1, 4, 16, 101, 112, 118, 137, 158, 259-261, 264, 277, 278
Michael 177, 187, 277
Michaell 47
Planer 268
Thomas 1, 2, 29, 107, 136, 186, 255, 257
William 157, 180, 264
Williams Adventure 2, 33, 82, 107, 117, 187, 243, 257, 258
Williams Begining 249
Williams Chance 80
Williams Conquest 2, 107, 136, 255, 258
Williams Desire 43
Williams Green 167, 266
Williams Hope 26, 37, 98, 116, 153, 161, 172, 183, 184, 199, 206, 217, 241, 254
Williams Lott 74, 101, 261
Williamson
(N) 100
John 100
William 42
Williamston 1
Williamstone 136, 138, 255, 277
Williamstons 2
Williams's Lott 137
Willin
John 154, 172, 264
Levin 172
Robert 160, 265
Thomas 17, 21, 113, 172
Willis
Barnaby 259
James 28
Williss
Barnaby 13, 115
James 173, 267
Wills
(N) 79
Benjamin 267
Willson
(N) 29
Ephraime 16
Francis 103
John 74
Robert 32
Thomas 50
Willsons Discovery 16, 44
Willsons Finding 32
Willsons Folly 3
Willsons Lott 50, 255
Willsons Mistake 65
Wilson 244
(N) 18, 84
David 16, 17, 27, 29, 32, 90, 166, 169, 181, 182, 184, 185, 233, 266
Ephraim 166, 265
Francis 14, 32, 181
George 3, 108, 180, 258, 267, 276
James 169, 266
John 3, 50, 108, 178, 193, 197, 258, 267, 277
Levin 182, 184
Margaret 50
Martha 180
Robert 9
Samuel 142, 166
Samuell 16, 17, 30, 101, 262, 265
Thomas 188
Wilsons Conclusion 131, 166, 221, 265
Wilsons Discovery 142, 145, 147, 150, 166, 197, 232, 233, 246, 262, 265, 273, 275
Wilsons Finding 164, 245
Wilsons First 229
Wilsons Folly 108, 127, 202, 276

www.ingramcontent.com/pod-product-compliance
Lightning Source LLC
Chambersburg PA
CBHW070545270326
41926CB00013B/2203